Books of Merit

Arctic Front

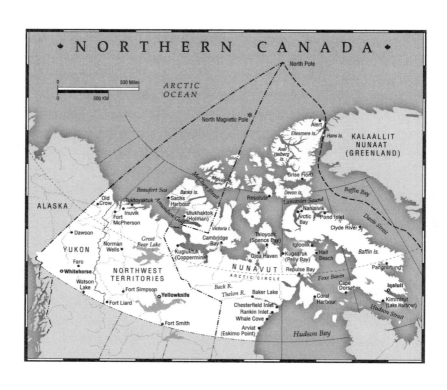

NORTHERN CANADA

ARCTIC FRONT

DEFENDING CANADA
IN THE FAR NORTH

Ken S. Coates
P. Whitney Lackenbauer
William Morrison
Greg Poelzer

Thomas Allen Publishers
Toronto

Library and Archives Canada Cataloguing in Publication

Arctic front : defending Canada in the far north / Ken S. Coates . . . [et al.].

Includes bibliographical references and index.
ISBN 978-0-88762-355-4

1. Canada, Northern. 2. Canada, Northern—History. 3. Jurisdiction, Territorial—Canada. 4. Canada—Boundaries—Arctic regions. 5. Canada, Northern—Economic conditions. 6. Canada, Northern—Politics and government. 7. Arctic regions—International cooperation. I. Coates, Kenneth, 1956–

FC3956.A724 2008   971.9   C2008-903340-X

Editor: Janice Zawerbny
Maps: Lightfoot Art and Design
Jacket images: Norbert Wu/Getty (ship); iStockphoto (bear)

Published by Thomas Allen Publishers,
a division of Thomas Allen & Son Limited,
145 Front Street East, Suite 209,
Toronto, Ontario M5A 1E3 Canada

www.thomas-allen.com

ONTARIO ARTS COUNCIL
CONSEIL DES ARTS DE L'ONTARIO

Canada Council
for the Arts

The publisher gratefully acknowledges the support of the Ontario Arts Council for its publishing program.

We acknowledge the support of the Canada Council for the Arts, which last year invested $20.1 million in writing and publishing throughout Canada.

We acknowledge the Government of Ontario through the Ontario Media Development Corporation's Ontario Book Initiative.

We acknowledge the financial support of the Government of Canada through the Book Publishing Industry Development Program (BPIDP) for our publishing activities.

12 11 10 09 08   1 2 3 4 5

Printed and bound in Canada

"The Arctic Sea is not at the end of the earth,
but must . . . become in time a polar Mediterranean."

— VILHJALMUR STEFANSSON, explorer

CONTENTS

Arctic Front arises out of our collective frustration. Recently, debate about Arctic sovereignty has filled the nation's newspapers. It's an old, old story, dating back many decades. This time around, the challenge of global warming, the retreat of the polar ice cap, and the race for Arctic oil and gas have given the discussion a twenty-first-century twist. But the underlying issue—does and can Canada exercise effective control over its High Arctic islands and the Northwest Passage—has changed little since the nineteenth century.

Canada has had this debate before, notably during the Klondike gold rush, the Second World War, the Cold War, and the voyage of the *Manhattan*. Our motivation in joining it was a desire to change the national debate on Arctic sovereignty. Questions about Canadian control of the Arctic—and national responsibilities in the Far North—have bedevilled this country since the 1880s. Canadians have yet to get it right, and, equally important, our nation continues to forget the history of early episodes when Canadian sovereignty in the North came into question. We see the issue as a classic example of the truism that those who do not know their history are doomed to repeat it. *Arctic Front* is our attempt to explain the origins of the contemporary debate and to challenge long-standing Canadian assumptions about its northern role and commitments.

It is unusual to have four people collaborate on a book, but our individual backgrounds and experiences all proved pivotal to the development of the project. Greg Poelzer is a political scientist and a specialist on circumpolar Arctic affairs. He made sure that we understood the global context of the current debate. Whitney Lackenbauer is a historian specializing in post–Second World War sovereignty and security issues in the Arctic. His field research has taken him from the Labrador Sea to the wilds of the Yukon to Ellesmere Island—and it doesn't get any farther north than that! Bill Morrison has been writing on Arctic sovereignty issues for many years, focusing initially on the role of the North West Mounted Police in establishing Canada's presence in the North. Ken Coates, raised in Whitehorse, Yukon, has had a long-standing professional interest in the American military projects in the Canadian North during World War II and in contemporary northern politics. What we share is a powerful belief that historical understanding matters—on this issue and others—and that Canada needs to think seriously about its commitment to the Far North, though in ways different than that typically argued in the current sovereignty debate.

That this book has come together in a timely and professional fashion is due, in large measure, to the wonderful assistance provided by others. Our agent, Denise Bukowski, provided superb guidance and timely interventions that kept us on track and on time. Several professional associates read the manuscript very carefully and saved us from some crucial errors; their timely advice was greatly appreciated. Jim Allen and Patrick Crean of Thomas Allen Publishers saw the merit in what we proposed and agreed to publish our thoughts. Janice Zawerbny provided excellent editorial assistance and advice, for which we are truly grateful. And, as always, our families and professional colleagues at the University of Waterloo, St. Jerome's University, the University of Northern British

Columbia, and the University of Saskatchewan offered both support and encouragement.

Ken S. Coates
P. Whitney Lackenbauer
William Morrison
Greg Poelzer

Arctic Front

Arctic sovereignty seems to be the zombie—the dead issue that refuses to stay dead—of Canadian public affairs. You think it's settled, killed and buried, and then every decade or so it rises from the grave and totters into view again. In one decade the issue is the DEW Line, then it's the American oil tanker *Manhattan*, steaming brazenly through the Northwest Passage, then the *Polar Sea* doing the same thing. In August 2007, a Russian submarine planted a flag at the North Pole. Or perhaps it was under the North Pole, as the UK *Daily Telegraph*[1] reported, raising an image of a striped pole floating in the ocean, with the devious Russians diving underneath it. Perhaps the flag did land on the pole, though good luck with that, since the pole is a point with no size at all, so the Russians likely missed it. However it was, they are up there, and the zombie has come to life once more.

And the Russians aren't the only ones who make us nervous. The United States, one of the countries that does not agree that the Northwest Passage lies within Canada's internal waters, is running cruise ships in the Arctic, and somewhere in the boardrooms of America plans are being drawn up for more northern voyages by oil tankers. We've even had issues with Denmark, usually the most inoffensive of countries, over an island in the High Arctic that very few Canadians had ever heard of a few years ago. Everyone knows that the main reason for all this activity and concern is global warming. Recent satellite images have shown that the ice is melting faster than even the most pessimistic doomsters predicted, and that quite soon the Northwest Passage will be open for navigation for much of the year. A hundred and fifty years ago, the passage was difficult or impossible to get through, a death trap for many, including the Franklin expedition. It was conquered early in the twentieth century by Roald Amundsen, but he had to spend two winters in the North to get through. When the passage was locked fast in ice for ten or eleven months of the year, no one much cared who owned it or the waters around it, or who went through it, and under what authority. Even today, no state disputes that Canada owns the waters, but the U.S. contends that a strait runs through them. When these waters become freely navigable, pessimists suggest, Canada may face new challenges to its control over this part of the country.

The Canadian High Arctic is very much in the news, front and centre, in a heady and ominous mixture of money, science, and politics. The United States disagrees that the Northwest Passage is Canadian internal waters, believing instead that it is an international strait. The Russians, on the other hand, have no problem with our assertion that the Passage is internal waters, but their claims to a huge area of the polar seabed may compete with Canada's. Continental shelves, of which the Grand Banks off Newfoundland is a good example, belong to the country to which they are attached. But you have to prove that the shelf is continuously attached. That is basically what those Russian submarines are doing at the North Pole—trying to establish as big a limit as possible for that country's continental shelf. No one knows how much oil and gas lies under the ocean, but with Russia's return to the international stage funded by petroleum dollars, exclusive jurisdiction to exploit the Arctic seabed is of more than simply scientific importance.

Speaking of science, the Arctic is also at the centre of the global warming controversy. It has been reported that the summer Arctic sea ice, measured at its summer minimum, was smaller in September 2007 than at any time since satellites began measuring it in 1979. On the sixteenth of that month it was measured at 4.13 million square kilometres (1.59 million square miles); the previous low, two years earlier, was 5.32. The difference, 1.19 square kilometres, or 436,000 square miles, is the size of Texas and California combined. It's a fifth smaller than it was in 1979. The effects of this change are political, economic, social, and environmental, a potent brew that one stirs and tastes at one's peril. We will taste it in later chapters, but for now will note only the dramatic effect of a possible opening of the Northwest Passage—not the one that Amundsen took a century ago, twisting around the Boothia Peninsula and across the shallow waters off the Arctic mainland, but the broad passage leading west from Lancaster Strait. Cruise ships, warships, oil tankers, all steaming through what Canada considers its internal waters, perhaps six months of the year, perhaps ten. What is Canada doing about this? What *can* we do?

It's hard to believe how recent this situation is. Twenty years ago, global warming was only a theory proposed by a few scientists, and most of the public had never heard of it. Now it is Holy Writ, at least among the political left, and schoolchildren run campaigns to Save the Planet.

What a difference two decades make! Claims now circulate that one-quarter of the undiscovered reserves of oil and gas lie in the North. Into the increasingly ice-free waters race government scientists, capitalists, and the military, as the industrial world seeks the additional supplies of oil and gas necessary to maintain western styles of living. Indigenous leaders, whose claims and accomplishments grabbed headlines a few years back, have been reduced to bit players—and there is an unstated recognition in government and development circles that one of the key attractions of the High Arctic is that there are virtually no indigenous people living there, and thus no one to consult before development takes place. For developers now used to adapting to the realities of indigenous autonomy and expectations for local control, the prospect of working in a largely indigenous-free zone is a dream come true.

The issues that dominate this debate in northern Canada are not new; it's just that energy needs and global warming have now made them urgent. Given the parent-child military relationship between Canada and the United States and Canada's historic unwill-ingness to take a strong public stand against its prime ally, the question of the Northwest Passage seemed merely theoretical. The Russians have traditionally pushed against the boundaries, maintaining floating scientific stations on the Arctic ice, to the alarm of several generations of North American military leaders. During the Cold War, from the mid-1940s to the early 1990s, the boundary testing caused both irritation and concern, but the massive American military presence in Alaska stared down any substantial Russian intrusions. The collapse of the Soviet Union in 1991 and the apparent chaos within the new Russian Federation appeared to remove Russia from the Arctic equation. If they could not control terrorists in the southwest, they hardly seemed capable of or interested in expanding their sovereignty claims in the northeast. With the emergence of a stronger Russia, this seems likely to change. Although Russia repeatedly stated that the submarine at the North Pole was part of its scientific research and that they were not laying claim to anything, the planting of a flag was clearly provocative. North Americans are not off base feeling insecure about the real intentions of their neighbour across the melting ice cap.

The uncertainty begins with ice. For decades, the government of Canada has argued that the frozen waters of the High Arctic constitute a formal part of national territory in the North. The Inuit certainly see it this way, for winter living typically involved many weeks spent on the ice; for northern indigenous peoples, the standard European division between water and land made no sense at all. But Arctic ice is more than a thin, seasonal covering over northern seas and waterways. For hundreds of years, it has been a thick, almost impenetrable barrier to any regular or reliable use of Arctic waters. Climatic circumstances—warm summer weather, favourable winds, and quirks of nature—could occasionally permit ships to make headway through the Arctic islands. Some explorers were lucky and got through, while others were unlucky, and died, but on the whole the region was impenetrable.

Now the ice is receding. Al Gore's documentary, *An Inconvenient Truth*, was the first to popularize images of the retreating polar ice cap, drawing on scattered bits of Arctic science that pointed to disturbing trends in the regional climate. More scientific investigations followed, predicting a time in the near future when the polar seas would be open for navigation and when massive environmental changes would hit the Arctic. Increasingly dramatic images from the North showed more and more open water in the Arctic. The ice cap seemed to be melting like an ice cube on a Toronto sidewalk in August. Scientists became increasingly alarmed, as did northern indigenous leaders and environmental activists. The North seemed to be proving that all the worst fears of Gore, David Suzuki, and other doomsayers were coming true. Only the small number of people directly affected and the complexity of the scientific debate about the meaning and extent of global warming prevented wide-scale panic.

One person's crisis is another's opportunity, however. The receding ice cap seemed a boon to shipping companies and resource developers. The same open water that signalled ecological melt-down created possible new shipping lanes through formerly ice-locked passageways. Asian companies, in particular, salivated at the prospect of the time-saving opportunities that accompanied a secure Arctic route to Europe and the eastern United States—a Great Circle route for ships to match the long-use air lanes that have accelerated intercontinental travel in earlier decades. Resource exploration in the region had also been stalled for years because of the dangers and challenges of working in High Arctic waters. The ice sheets that look so serene and placid on maps and aerial photographs are actually twisting and crushing masses of ice, many metres thick, with the power to snap oil rigs and smash drilling platforms. The costs of exploring and developing resources in the North seemed so astronomical that few companies and governments were prepared to venture into the region. That scenario looked to be melting away as well. With the possibility of large stretches of open water, and with ready access to the Arctic seabed, huge fields lay open for oil and gas exploration.

The High Arctic may well be the last true empty space on the planet. Even the upper reaches of the Amazon basin and the most remote corners of the Sahara Desert exist within well-defined national boundaries. Antarctica, which belongs to no one nation, has worked under a collaboratively managed and supervised jurisdiction for decades. While some countries, mostly in Africa, have trouble defending and enforcing their national borders, and while there are still disputed borders—Kashmir is a good example—the world's boundaries seem generally stable. The exception is the Arctic, where tiny islands, the shape of the continental shelf, and longitudinal projections have suddenly become the stuff of international politics. There may be a lot at stake, if there truly are large deposits of oil and gas in the North. On the other hand it may turn out to be, as in the past, much ado about a lot of ice and cold water. The Russians, though, are deadly serious—and the West continues to misunderstand and underestimate both that nation and its leadership. The Americans are intractably stubborn on both military issues and questions of international straits, and—if we believe journalists and academics—the pesky Danes and others (including the Russians and Chinese) cast covetous looks at Canadian areas of interest.

That there is still a void speaks volumes about Canada's approach to and neglect of the High Arctic. For reasons that will become clear in subsequent chapters, Canadians have never strayed far, either physically or spiritually, from the Canada–U.S. boundary. We are northern nation in fantasy and imagery only. Our galleries are full of Inuit sculptures and Group of Seven paintings and our libraries are stocked with books by authors from Rudy Wiebe to Margaret Atwood and Mordecai Richler extolling the mysteries and haunting beauty of the Arctic and northern regions generally. But for every canoe-paddling celebrity, like Pierre Elliott Trudeau, who routinely ventured north, there are hundreds of thousands of Canadians who rarely venture out of southern cities—a trip to Muskoka or the Laurentians being a northern adventure, and a vacation in Algonquin Park providing the complete frontier experience. Canada has never embraced the North beyond symbolism and mythology. Now, "purveyors of polar peril" suggest that the country is paying for its neglect and lack of interest in the High Arctic and the North in general. Some observers, to be sure, would argue that Canada has not been neglectful in terms of "sovereignty," given that we have successfully controlled navigation in the Northwest Passage and everyone—even the U.S.—respects our laws. Either way, though, it is clear that Canada certainly faces public embarrassment over its lack of Arctic capabilities and presence.

In the chapters that follow, we lay out the history of Canada's relationship with the North and its episodic and tentative approach to sovereignty in the region. Although Canada managed to expand and entrench its sovereignty in a cautious and reactive manner through the twentieth century, we write with a fair degree of frustration for our northern predicament is, as Yogi Berra once said, "déjà vu all over again." Canadians have been down the current path of panic and sweeping promises many times in the past, and there are familiar echoes in the latest Canadian response to northern challenges. But this is not simply a replay of nineteenth- or twentieth-century contests. There is much more at play—oil, gas, northern passageways, and a painful illustration of how ill prepared we are for Arctic disputes in the twenty-first. The issues are global, in the form of the climate change debate; local, through indigenous claims and self-government initiatives; and circumpolar, in terms of military issues and competition for northern resources. If Canada faces a twenty-first-century challenge to its northern future, it is entering the battle with twentieth-century perspectives and nineteenth-century credibility. Global warming and the race for resources have opened an Arctic front. Canada's northern flank is ill defended. Moreover, our country is distressingly complacent about the North, its role in the country, and its place on the world scene. Rousing Canadians from the southern perspective that defines and directs this country will not be easy, but there is potentially a great deal at stake, not the least being our self-respect as a nation and our belief in the sustainability of Canada as a northern country.

PLANTING THE FLAG

ESTABLISHING BRITISH/CANADIAN
SOVEREIGNTY IN THE NORTH

"The authorities . . . were carrying more important bur-
dens than the remote and useless Arctic."
— DIAMOND JENNESS, anthropologist, 1964

Sir Martin Frobisher
(c. 1539–1594) *Library and Archives*
Canada (LAC) C11413

Canada's Arctic sovereignty ought to
be rock solid and unchallengeable,
and yet commentators in the political,
media, and academic worlds assert that
it isn't. This is just a jaw-dropping fact,
for the British, our predecessors in the
region from whom our sovereignty
descends, first claimed northern lands
half a millennium ago. It's been more
than five hundred years since John
Cabot came to Labrador (1497), and
more than four hundred since the
first Englishman came to the Arctic
(Martin Frobisher's three expeditions
to Baffin Island in the 1570s), so you would think that there would
be not the slightest question about Britain and then Canada's sovereignty in the North. Despite this, Canadians remain concerned,
rightly or wrongly, that foreign powers such as Russia, the United
States, and Denmark are still trying to gnaw at Canada's claims.

A sensible person would wonder how this could possibly be, but the reason is fairly straightforward. It was summed up fifty years ago by Prime Minister Louis St. Laurent: the region has been "governed in a fit of absence of mind." In other words, most of Canadians' anxieties about sovereignty are our fault, caused by indifference and neglect. Readers who expect this book to be a diatribe against the United States and others are going to be disappointed. First, the main historical challenge to Canadian sovereignty in the North came not from the U.S.A. but from traditionally inoffensive Norway. Second, as the history of the Klondike gold rush, the building of the Alaska Highway, and similar episodes show, when the Americans wanted something in our North, they didn't have to invade us or throw their weight around:[1] all they had to do was ask, and we usually said "sure, take what you need." In the current dispute, which concerns Arctic waters rather than the land area, the Americans have an arguably good case that an international strait runs through the Northwest Passage, and have no need to be threatening.

Besides Canadian neglect, the issue has to do with some of the most basic requirements for the establishment of sovereignty. Territorial sovereignty under international law is established by several means, among them cession (someone gives it to us), purchase, and discovery. All of these have figured in the Canadian North: Britain ceded or transferred its northern territories to Canada; there was a kind of quasi purchase of claims to certain Arctic islands from Norway; discoveries were made; some of Canada's claim to northern sovereignty is based on the fact that some territories are attached to or lie near others. Of the above factors, however, the most important has been discovery.

One way to acquire sovereignty over territory is to discover it, but an ongoing claim must be established as well. The most important way to do this is by control, often demonstrated through administration, especially of the law. In a nutshell, the historical difficulties Canada has encountered in regards to sovereignty have been connected to the two factors of discovery and control: much of the

North, particularly the Arctic islands, was discovered by men who were not British or Canadian. As well, through indifference and neglect, Canada's control over the region was virtually nonexistent in the nineteenth century and spotty for much of the twentieth, though it became stronger over time. Indeed, it still comes under question, as far as the Arctic waters are concerned, in the twenty-first. This chapter traces the process from the early days of Canada's northern history until the Second World War.

When ordinary Canadians think about territorial sovereignty nowadays it is usually in connection with First Nations land claims. This brings up a question that First Nations people often raise, though government lawyers and scholars take the answer for granted: what right do Europeans have to declare sovereignty in any case? When England,[2] for example, granted a charter to the Hudson's Bay Company in 1660, it did so on the assumption that it had sovereignty over Rupert's Land (the watershed of Hudson Bay). But Rupert's Land was not unoccupied, nor was it *terra nullius* (no man's land). It had been occupied by people, mostly Cree and Dene, for thousands of years. Britain claimed ownership of this territory through the exploring activities of Martin Frobisher, who sailed into Hudson Strait in 1578, John Davis and Martin Weymouth, who ventured into it in 1587 and 1602, respectively, and especially Henry Hudson, who explored much of the bay from 1610 to 1611, and was left to die there. These episodes are where most accounts of the British claim begin. The question of what right England had to claim sovereignty over occupied land is not often raised, probably because an honest answer contains a harsh truth: that English and British sovereignty over the northern regions, like that of other European nations over the rest of the western hemisphere and other parts of the world, whether benign (as we would like to think ours is) or brutal, is based in its essence on force, the threat of force, or the possibility of force. In 1660, no Englishman lived in Rupert's Land, and only a few had even seen it; no towns or trading posts had been built, no farms cultivated. It was English because a few English explorers had seen it and claimed it, and because the English said it was and had the army and navy to enforce the claim against the indigenous inhabitants and against the French.

Because it suggests warfare and death by sword and gun, we don't use the word "conquest" here in speaking of Britain or of France in northern North America, though of course it fully applies to the history of Spain in the new world. The workings of force in the process were more subtle. Essentially what happened was that English settlers appeared on the eastern seaboard of what is now the United States early in the seventeenth century, and signed treaties or agreements of various sorts with the Indians, the purpose of which was mostly to permit the English to settle and farm. The Indians were much more powerful than the English in the early years, and the newcomers bargained from weakness rather than strength. The English trade goods were attractive, they exploited tribal rivalries when they could, and the introduction of diseases from Europe took a terrible toll of the native population. In the second period, from the later seventeenth century until the end of the War of 1812, the indigenous people were sought as allies in the wars between England and France, and then between Britain and the United States. The treaties of this period were often like alliances between military equals. The third period, which took up the rest of the nineteenth century, was one in which the two parties were increasingly unequal, and in which treaties were designed to extinguish aboriginal rights to permit settlement over the whole of the United States and Canada. Although force was used often enough in the United States, it was only at the very beginning of contact that it would have been possible for the Indians to throw the Europeans off the continent. Even then, had they slaughtered the colonists at Plymouth and Jamestown, colonization would probably have been delayed, not thwarted.

In Canada, naked force was very rarely used, but the power of law, which is a form of veiled force, was the lever by which First Nations were pried off their land and into reserves. As one commentator put it, the great symbol of Canadian Indian policy in the nineteenth century was the figure of the lone Mounted Policeman riding bravely into the Indian camp to inform the Queen's new subjects of their lack of civil rights. And if they failed to get the message, as in 1885, the Queen's Own Rifles could be sent out to make it clear.

Labrador was the first part of what is now considered to be the Canadian North to come under British sovereignty, by virtue of the voyages of the late fifteenth century. Next was Rupert's Land, thanks to Henry Hudson. Rupert's Land is a huge area, about 7.77 million square kilometres (3.00 million square miles), comprising much of northern and western Canada. Not all of Rupert's Land is northern, of course, however one defines north in Canadian terms, for it includes all of Manitoba, Saskatchewan, and southern Alberta. Except during time of war with France, the Hudson's Bay Company was secure for the first century of its operations. For a hundred years it operated out of posts on the shores of Hudson and James Bays, avoiding the interior, and compelling the Indians to travel to the river mouths to trade. Eventually, when after the British conquest of Quebec, Montreal-based fur traders began to invade the Company's territory, it was forced to awaken from its "sleep by the frozen sea," as critics put it, and move inland to counter its rivals. But in this rivalry both parties were British, so there was no threat to sovereignty. In fact, it was strengthened because the trade war between the Hudson's Bay Company and the Northwest Company, based in Montreal, led to a vigorous period of northern exploration and discovery. The period between 1770 and 1821, when the two companies merged, saw Samuel Hearne, Alexander Mackenzie, and John Franklin explore the Mackenzie Valley and reach the Arctic coast.

It was in this period that British sovereignty over the mainland area of the northern territories and northern Quebec was established. Before that time it had been claimed by Britain, but little actual occupation or control had existed inland from the coast of Hudson Bay. The expeditions of Samuel Hearne (1745–92) took the British presence to the Arctic coast. Hearne joined the Hudson's Bay Company as a young man, and in 1766 was stationed at Fort Prince of Wales, just outside modern Churchill, Manitoba. The

Sir Alexander Mackenzie (1764–1820) *Photo © National Gallery of Canada*

Hudson's Bay Company, facing increasing competition from the Montreal traders, was looking for new sources of trade and revenue. Rumours had come from the North that there were deposits of native copper (copper that did not need to be refined) in the region, and Hearne was sent out to investigate. The episode that followed is one of the classics of Canadian exploration. Beginning in 1769 it took Hearne three tries to reach his goal, and it was not until he secured the help of a First Nations man, Matonabbee, that he was able to reach the mouth of the Coppermine River in the summer of 1771, the first European to reach the Arctic coast by land. Although his expedition was the kind of episode that reinforced British sovereignty, its success was due almost entirely to Matonabbee, who insisted that the expedition follow the game to supply food instead of heading straight north, which is why the expedition took eighteen months. Hearne was impatient, but he got there and back alive. It was a lesson that future explorers had to learn again, to their cost.

Alexander Mackenzie made two great discoveries, the first one by accident, and both of them important to sovereignty, since in both cases he was the first European to travel over significant stretches of Canada. The first was the accidental discovery in 1789 of the river that bears his name; it led him to the Beaufort Sea instead of the Pacific, but it opened the Mackenzie Valley to the fur trade and established a British presence down the length of the river. By 1840, the Hudson's Bay Company had built a post at Fort McPherson near the Mackenzie Delta, and a string of posts dotted the river. In the second trip of 1792 Mackenzie achieved his objective and reached the Pacific Ocean, but an even more important achievement was to open northern British Columbia to the fur trade.

Sir John Franklin
(1786–1847) *Photo © National
Maritime Museum, Greenwich, UK*

John Franklin also played an important early role in establishing the British presence in the western Arctic. Although he is mostly now known for his disastrous last expedition of 1846, in which he and all his crew perished, he commanded two earlier expeditions, in 1819–21 and 1825–27, that put much of the western Arctic coast on the map, and led the way for later Hudson's Bay posts along the coast.

The importance of the fur trade activities of the Hudson's Bay Company to sovereignty is shown by the history of the Canadian-American boundary in northwestern British Columbia—the so-called Alaska Panhandle. The first Europeans to exploit that area were the Russians, who began trading with indigenous people for sea otter pelts in the mid-eighteenth century, and who established permanent settlements beginning in 1784. Russia claimed sovereignty over all of what is now the state of Alaska, but when the Hudson's Bay Company began to operate in British Columbia early in the nineteenth century, the border between the British and Russian territories was not delineated. Except for the Hudson's Bay Company, there was no presence on the west coast to counter the influence of the Russians.

Fortunately, and this is a major theme of this chapter, there was no essential conflict of interest in this situation. As was to happen elsewhere in the North, British sovereignty prevailed partly because the British were on the ground, but equally because the foreign power had no reason to challenge British assertions. As it happened, British and Russian interests did not clash at all. The Russian trade was based on the sea otters of the north Pacific coast and the Aleutians, while the Hudson's Bay Company traded inland. The Anglo-Russian treaty of 1825 set the border between British and Russian America, giving the Russians a strip of coastline, which

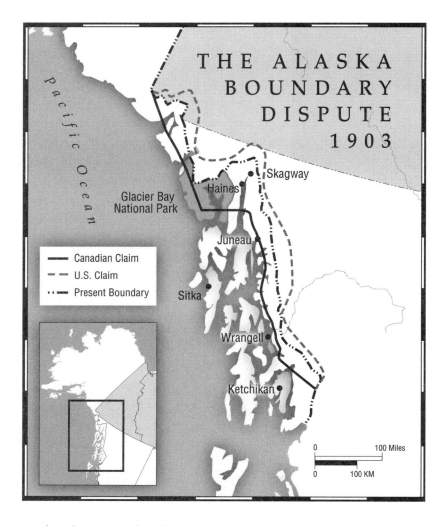

THE ALASKA
BOUNDARY
DISPUTE
1903

Pacific Ocean

Skagway
Haines
Glacier Bay
National Park

Juneau

Canadian Claim
U.S. Claim
Present Boundary

Sitka

Wrangell

Ketchikan

0   100 Miles
0   100 KM

is what they wanted, with the British confirmed in their rights to the
interior. In the North, the boundary ran up the 141st meridian to the
Arctic Ocean, and in the south it ended at the 54°40' line. The contrast with what happened in southern British Columbia and south
of that—the so-called Oregon Country—is instructive, for there
the British and Americans had overlapping claims and interests,
and resolving them was not so easy. An even better comparison is
what happened when the boundary of the panhandle was delin-

eated. In 1825, neither the British nor the Russians cared about the exact location of the boundary; so long as the Russians were on the coast and the British in the interior, the location didn't matter. But in 1867 the Russians sold Alaska to the Americans, and the new owners did care, especially when gold was found in the Yukon in 1896, because the quickest route to the goldfields lay across the panhandle. In this case, interests clashed strongly, and the result was the Alaska Boundary Dispute, in which Canada did not win its case.

The Alaska Boundary Dispute of 1903 (the year the issue was settled) concerned the boundary between the Alaska Panhandle and British Columbia, and is worth mentioning here as an example of what happened on a rare occasion when Canadian sovereignty in the North was actually challenged by another power. There was little interest in the region for decades after the Anglo-Russian Treaty of 1825; when the province of British Columbia requested soon after it entered Confederation in 1871 that a joint boundary survey be made, the Americans rejected the idea as not being worth the money, since there was very little non-Native settlement outside the old Russian villages. What brought the issue to the boil was the discovery of gold in the Klondike in 1896. The cheapest route to the goldfields involved a voyage up the Pacific coast to Skagway, at the head of the Lynn Canal, a climb over the coastal mountains of the Panhandle across what is now the international border into British Columbia, to the headwaters of the Yukon River, then a downriver trip into the Yukon. Skagway was in Alaska, and thus the Americans controlled access to the Klondike.[3]

Although the general intent of the 1825 treaty was clear enough—the Russians got the coast and the British got the interior, the actual wording of the treaty made a variety of other interpretations possible. The crucial passages were

> . . . the said line shall ascend to the north along the channel called Portland Channel as far as the point of the continent where it strikes the 56th degree of north latitude; from this last-mentioned point, the line of demarcation shall follow the

summit of the mountains situated parallel to the coast as far as the point of intersection of the 141st degree of west longitude. . . . Whenever the summit of the mountains shall be at a distance of more than ten marine leagues from the ocean, the limit shall be formed by a line parallel to the winding of the coast, and which shall never exceed the distance of ten marine leagues therefrom.

These were words drawn up by negotiators who had never seen the region in question and who understandably had only a shaky grasp of its geography. Using them, Canada claimed a line much closer to the open sea than the present boundary, a line that cut through the deep coastal inlets, putting Skagway well into British Columbia, and leaving the Americans a line of truncated peninsulas. The United States used the same words to draw a line well into British Columbia. The issue was whether the "ten marine leagues" (30 nautical miles, 34.5 miles or 55.5 kilometres) was to be measured from the heads of the long inlets or from some sort of baseline. The two countries reached a compromise in 1898, but the government of British Columbia rejected it. Finally, under the terms of the Hay-Herbert Treaty of 1903, the matter was put to binding arbitration; each side was to appoint "three impartial jurists[4] of repute."

At this point the episode entered Canadian mythology. In that era, Canadian foreign affairs were still handled by Britain, so the British appointed three of the arbitrators. Two, as a courtesy to Canada, were Canadians (Louis-Amable Jetté, the Lieutenant-Governor of Quebec[5] and Allen Aylesworth, a prominent lawyer from Ontario[6]), and the third, Lord Alverstone, was Lord Chief Justice of England. President Theodore Roosevelt appointed Elihu Root, secretary of war, Senator Henry Cabot Lodge, and George Turner, a former senator from Washington State. The arbitrators voted four to two, with Lord Alverstone siding with the Americans, to draw a line that supported neither claim, but was considerably closer to the American position than to the Canadian. There was a firestorm of criticism in Canada, which had loyally supported Britain during the Boer War (1899–1902), and nationalists ever after have believed that Alverstone had supported the Americans because Britain, worried about the growing military power of Germany, had sacrificed Canadian interests to curry favour with the United States. The Alaska Boundary Dispute is generally considered to have stimulated Canada's desire to conduct her own foreign affairs, though concrete steps in this direction were not taken until after the First World War.

One of the iconic scenes of Canadian history: gold miners climbing the final stage of the Chilkoot Pass during the winter of 1897–98. *Author's collection*

Several comments can be made about this result. It is true that President Roosevelt spoke of sending troops to Alaska if the decision went the wrong way. It is also true that the three American commissioners were Republican supporters of the president, who might be expected to favour the American position. What is less often stated, though, was that the two Canadian commissioners were both Liberal politicians. Jetté had been a Liberal member of the House of Commons, and Aylesworth would serve in Wilfrid Laurier's cabinet and later as a Liberal senator. It is not clear how these men were less partisan than the Americans. Finally, though it is perhaps true that the British were anxious to secure American friendship, the essential point about the dispute was that the Canadian case was fraudulent. It was absurd to think that in 1825 the Russians would have agreed to a treaty that relegated them to a series of peninsula tips and islands; the whole point of the treaty was to give them an unbroken coastal strip. The dispute still echoes in another way as well, for the southern end of the boundary, where the line comes out of Portland Canal into the Pacific, is still in dispute.[7]

From the point of view of northern sovereignty, however, the episode had the important result of spurring Canadian interest in the North. During the buildup to the dispute, the Klondike gold rush took place. What is now the Yukon was not part of Rupert's

Land, but was added to the Hudson's Bay Company's territory along with the rest of the mainland part of the territories after the merger of 1821. In 1831, the first tentative exploration was made of the southern Yukon on behalf of the company, and in 1842 the first post was built. However, until 1870 there was only a handful of Europeans in the region—the staff of two fur trade posts and the occasional missionary. After 1870, miners began to trickle in, and by the 1890s there were about a thousand men and women, the majority of them Americans, living and mining around Fortymile on the Yukon River near the 141st meridian. Not from any sense of purpose or plan, but simply out of necessity, the miners had established de facto control over the region in the form of the "miners' meeting." This was a kind of citizens' assembly, based on the mining laws of the western United States, that acted as both criminal and civil court.[8] Someone with a grievance or knowledge of a crime—usually theft—could call a meeting of the whole community, which would render a verdict and a sentence. The existence of this institution on Canadian soil at the very end of the nineteenth century is explained by the fact that there was no Canadian official presence anywhere in the Yukon, despite the size of the mining community. The nearest official resided in Edmonton, and might as well have been on the moon. Almost incredibly, no one in Ottawa showed concern even when the situation was brought to their attention by William Carpenter Bompas (1834–1906), Bishop of the Yukon, who was worried about the moral effect of the miners on the First Nations people of the region. In the years before 1894 he wrote several letters to government officials talking about the "debauchery" that resulted from the miners abusing First Nations women. As a result, the government reluctantly sent two members of the North West Mounted Police (NWMP) to the region in 1894, and in 1895 a detachment of twenty was sent north, luckily, the year before the great discovery of 1896.

This episode is an early example of something that is not often noted in writing about the North, or about Canada in general. We call it the "embarrassment factor." Cynics have said of government

Superintendent Charles Constantine (1846–1912), second row, fourth from the left, with his detachment of Mounted Police at Fort Constantine, their post at Fortymile, on the Yukon River west of what is now Dawson. It is the winter of 1895–96, and the police have come north in some strength to show the flag on the eve of the gold rush. *Glenbow Archives, NA-919-15*

that it is wrong to attribute to malice actions that could be better attributed to stupidity, but they rarely consider the possibility that government policy may have been influenced by the embarrassment factor, in which actions are dictated by fear of criticism and public shame for doing the wrong thing, or (particularly in the North) fear of not taking action when action is warranted. This is currently evident in events that take place in First Nations communities across Canada—Davis Inlet and Kashechewan are painful recent examples—and has been an important motivation to government in the history of sovereignty in the North.

When the first Mounted Police detachment arrived at Fortymile in 1895, it represented the first real extension of government presence into northern Canada. Despite the fact that most of the miners were not Canadian, the police encountered almost no difficulty in establishing their authority over them. They were quick to move against the miners' meetings, the only organized institution that might have resisted them. In that year, a miners' meeting was called—the last of its kind, as it turned out—to listen to a complaint of some men who had been hired to work on a mining claim but had not been paid. The meeting ruled they had a case, and ordered the claim seized and sold to a third party, with the money going to the unpaid workers. Although this was the kind of decision that miners' meetings regularly made, it was of course contradictory to Canadian law. When the police learned of it they sent twelve of their number, armed with rifles, to the claim, and told the workers to leave, and that no more meetings of this sort should be held. None were. This was a dramatic and forceful assertion of official control, one of the hallmarks of sovereignty.

During the height of the gold rush, from the fall of 1897 to 1899, the newcomer population of the Yukon (which was made a separate territory in 1898) rose to nearly 40,000, though there are no accurate figures. Again, Canadians were a minority of the population, yet despite a good deal of grumbling, there was never any serious challenge to Canadian control in the region. This fact speaks to a recurrent theme in Canadian sovereignty over the North—the virtual lack of challenge to Canadian authority. There were several reasons why this was the case in the Yukon. In the first place, the Klondike was an exception to the general rule of government indifference to the North. Unlike the mining towns of the American West, which were often virtually lawless in their early days, the Yukon was very heavily policed. At the height of the rush there were over 300 members of the force in the Yukon, assisted by the Yukon Field Force, a 200-man contingent of the regular Canadian army. More than 500 law enforcement officers for a community of less than 40,000 is a far higher percentage than in a modern Canadian community.[9] Secondly, the population was highly concentrated, and thus easier to control. Although the Yukon covered a large area, the miners occupied only a very small part of it—just the Yukon and Klondike river valleys, so it was not difficult for the police to keep track of them.

Moreover, the geography of the Yukon worked in favour of the authorities. There were only a few ways to get in and out of the territory, and the police guarded them closely. When the newcomers

Members of the Yukon Detachment of the North West Mounted Police pose at the international boundary at the summit of the White Pass, August 8, 1899. The boundary was in dispute, but the police simply put their posts at the heads of the Chilkoot and White Passes, and these locations were accepted as part of the Alaska Boundary settlement in 1903. *Yukon Archives, 82/390 H-179*

reached the tops of the mountain passes inland from Skagway (the route the vast majority used) they found the police waiting for them, taking names and inspecting gear. The police gave the boats that floated down the Yukon numbers and recorded the names of passengers. It was almost impossible to get out of the country overland without the bush skills that most miners lacked. If a wrongdoer fled Dawson and went upriver to Whitehorse, intending to escape, the police simply telegraphed the Whitehorse detachment and had the person arrested. Thus geography, which in other regions hindered Canadian sovereignty by making it difficult or unpleasant for Canadians to stay in the North, in this instance strengthened it by helping to enforce the authority of Canadian officials there.

Another reason why Canadian control over the Yukon was never challenged from within is that it was not really in the interest of the miners to subvert it. Despite all the talk from the police about the average miner being the scum of U.S. coastal cities, the miners on the whole seem to have been a fairly orderly lot, at least as compared with western U.S. cities such as Bodie, Wyoming, which had far more murders per capita than Dawson did. The Yukon was not easy to get to, and those who made the trip were highly motivated. The majority wanted to find gold, get it out, and return home, not to die in a gunfight or serve a long sentence at hard labour in the Dawson jail.

Finally, as in other places in the North, Canadian sovereignty in the Yukon was secure because no other country was interested in making claims to the place. The logical claimant would have been the United States, of course, and in some of the more paranoid Canadian quarters it has been suggested that the United States had evil designs on the Klondike. Farley Mowat, for one, suggested that the Ottawa bureaucracy was preparing to turn the Yukon over to the rapacious Americans until a few brave souls intervened and sent the police north.[10] This is a fantasy. The Americans were not interested in owning the Yukon. So long as the rights of their citizens were protected there, they were content to let Canada bear the costs of administration. In any case, it would have been difficult for them to press a claim, since the treaty of 1825, whose provisions they had bought along with Alaska, made the northern boundary perfectly clear. They would have had to do what they did with Mexico, which was to provoke a war, and that was out of the question, given Canada's position in the British Empire. The price to be paid for the Yukon would have been unthinkably high, had the Americans wanted it, which they did not.

Another example of the embarrassment factor in this process is the initial expansion of a Canadian presence into the Arctic early in the twentieth century. This was at first focused on the northwest coast of Hudson Bay and on Herschel Island in the western Arctic. Both places became important in this era because of their use by foreigners as whaling stations. Herschel Island (named by Franklin after the Astronomer Royal, Sir John Herschel) lies in the Beaufort Sea, just 5 kilometres (3.1 miles) off the Yukon coast, and has the only safe harbour for hundreds of kilometres along the coast. By the end of the nineteenth century, the whaling industry had almost wiped out the whales in the Pacific Ocean. In 1888–89 an American whaler named Joe Tuckfield ventured east of Point Barrow and spent a season hunting whales with the Inuit in the Mackenzie Delta. He reported back that the bowhead whales were "thick as bees" in the region, and other captains seized the chance to make money, flocking to Canadian waters to hunt. The whaling ships were based in San Francisco, and because the voyage north and around Alaska was so long, they had to overwinter in the North, and Herschel Island was the logical place to do so. The Inuit of the region naturally gravitated to the island in the winter, where they could work and trade with the whalers, and within a year or two the island became the centre of human activity in the western Arctic. By 1895 there were fifteen ships wintering at the island. The trade was immensely profitable, since the market for whale oil and baleen[11] was still strong. Whales were worth as much as $15,000, and one ship, the *Mary D. Hume*, returned to San Francisco in 1892 with a cargo worth $400,000, one of the richest catches in the history of whaling. By the end of the whaling era, around 1910, $15 million worth of whales had been killed, and another $1.5 million worth of goods traded with the Inuit.

This activity had a considerable effect on the Inuit. The ships' crews were a rough lot; it was hard, filthy work, and the pay was low, so many of the crew members were desperate, fleeing the law, or had been shanghaied on board while drunk. The ships' officers sometimes kept Inuit women as servants and sex partners, but the crews were not permitted to do this, a situation that sometimes led to violence. By the mid 1890s tales of debauchery and orgies were making their way south, especially after the first missionary arrived on the island in 1893.[12] How much damage was being done is open to question, for debauchery is very much in the eye of the beholder, and at least one Inuit who witnessed it lived to write in his memoirs that he found the experience a great deal of fun.[13] More importantly from the point of view of sovereignty, however, as Bishop Bompas took pains to point out to the government, large sums were being made by foreigners on which no customs duties were being paid (there was a lively market in trade goods as well as whales), crimes of various sorts were being committed far from any police officer, the Inuit were being given alcohol, and so on. Whether the Inuit were being debauched or not, they were certainly suffering from disease, particularly measles and influenza, which they caught at Herschel Island and carried to the remote camps. So many had died by the middle 1890s that the whalers had to import Inuit from Alaska to work for them. It is estimated that by 1930 only a handful of the original 2,500 or so Inuit indigenous to the region were left; the Inuvialuit of the region are more recent arrivals.

For several years, however, the government did nothing about the situation. The reason for this has little to do with the North per se, and a great deal to do with the way government operated in those days, so a short digression is necessary by way of explanation. The Second World War was a pivotal point in Canadian history in a number of ways, one of the most important being that it marked the dividing line between small-government and big-government Canada. Before the war there were hardly any government welfare programs except for workmen's compensation at the provincial level and a rudimentary old age pension. During the war, unemployment insurance and the mothers' allowance were introduced, and the principle of equalization payments to the provinces was planned. In the decades after the war a blizzard of programs was launched, along with new taxes to support them. Before the war, the government's attitude towards expenditure was to ask, "What are we forced to do, and where do we find the money to do it?" After the war, it became "What could we do if we had the money?" and eventually, "What are we going to do with all this money we have?" Before the war, a balanced budget was sacred, and the government spent as little and kept taxes as low as possible; after the war, the sky was the limit. In short, the government's attitude towards the North was ruled by parsimony, especially because the region was politically unimportant. Ottawa ignored Herschel Island simply because it did not want to spend the money to establish its authority there.

What changed this was the embarrassment factor. The year that Canada asserted its sovereignty in the western Arctic and Hudson Bay (where American whalers were also operating, though apparently doing less harm) was, significantly, 1903, the year of the unsatisfactory settlement of the Alaska Boundary Dispute. The government of Sir Wilfrid Laurier, stung by its perceived defeat in this dispute, was anxious to avoid responsibility for further losses of face and power. As an official in the Department of the Interior wrote: "It is feared that if American citizens are permitted to land and pursue the industries of whaling, fishing, and trading with the Indians [sic] without complying with the revenue laws of Canada, unfounded and troublesome claims may hereafter be set up."14 In the summer of that year the government sent parties of Mounted Police to Hudson Bay and to the western Arctic, and posts were set up at Cape Fullerton on Hudson Bay, Fort McPherson in the Mackenzie Delta, and on Herschel Island.

The operation of the Mounted Police post at Herschel Island is an early example of yet another theme in the history of Canada's sovereignty in the North: the distinction between developmental or concrete sovereignty and symbolic sovereignty. Developmental or concrete sovereignty consists of those acts of control and administration that make sovereignty real and unquestioned, whereas symbolic sovereignty involves, as the name suggests, the symbols rather than the practical realities of sovereignty. Geologist Albert Peter Low and five Mounties spent the winter of 1903–4 in Hudson Bay on the sealing ship *Neptune*, trying to track down an American whaling ship to enforce Canadian regulations. They followed this up by sailing north into Smith Sound between Ellesmere Island and Greenland, raising the Union Jack on Ellesmere, proclaiming Canada's claim and customs laws, and erecting a cairn of stones to show the dominion's occupation. But all this was essentially

J.-E. Bernier (1852–1934), the Québécois sea captain and Arctic enthusiast who showed the flag in the North for Canada, doing "more than any other person to solidify Canada's claim to the Arctic islands."

LAC, PA102292

symbolic. When the government of Canada sent Joseph-Elzéar Bernier on voyages to the eastern Arctic between 1904 and 1911, he was "showing the flag,"[15] rather than doing anything concrete. Nationalists might think, as one article has it, that in setting a cairn and a plaque on Melville Island in 1909, Bernier "did more than any other person to solidify Canada's claim to the Arctic islands,"[16] but what he did was totally symbolic, though, admittedly, it was more than Canada had done up to that point, which was nothing.

In 1907, Canadian senator Pascal Poirier articulated a "sector theory" upon which Canada's claims might be based. According to this principle, countries exercise sovereignty between their mainland territory and the North Pole in an area bounded by the lines of longitude running from their east and west coasts. So, in a nutshell, this theory simply drew lines on a map and created pie-shaped wedges extending to the North Pole. Everything within the wedge belonged to Canada. This was a convenient way, it seemed, for Canada to declare sovereignty over all the islands in the archipelago. But no one in the Senate seconded his motion, so it never became official government policy. Bernier, however, decided to proclaim it on the ground. In 1908, the *Arctic* headed north to collect customs duties and to claim every island in the Arctic Archipelago for Canada. At each island they visited, Bernier and his crew went ashore, climbed a high point or hill, and erected a stone cairn containing a metal box with a proclamation claiming the land for Canada. The next year, unable to reach Victoria Island as planned, Bernier delivered his master stroke. On July 1, 1908, he and his entire ship's company of thirty-three men, accompanied by a baby muskox, marched up to Parry's

Rock on Melville Island. The officers, in shirts and ties, the brass buttons on their peacoats glistening in the sun, unveiled a bronze plaque claiming for Canada the whole Arctic Archipelago between 141 and 60 degrees west longitude up to 90 degrees north latitude. This blanket declaration, which was little more than a restatement of the sector theory claiming everything from the Yukon to Baffin Island up to the Pole, freed Bernier of feeling that he needed to keep flying flags everywhere he visited in the Arctic from this point onward.[17] If his gesture "did more than any other person to solidify Canada's claim to the Arctic islands," as nationalists are prone to suggest,[18] it was still totally symbolic. But he had high hopes. "We have annexed them—we want the people to settle there now!" Bernier told the Empire Club of Canada that December. "I am glad that you approve of that because progress moves not only westward but northward too."[19] But if settlement was the measure of progress, then Canada had little to boast about in the North.

Only the lonely vigil mounted by the Royal North West Mounted Police (RNWMP) in its isolated posts represented effective occupation in the Arctic. Of the three posts established in the summer of 1903, the one on Herschel Island was the most important because that was where the threat to Canada's interests was felt to be most acute. A police post, of course, is a concrete example of sovereignty, but this is true only if it exercises its powers effectively. This was not the case with the Mounted Police detachment on Herschel Island during the whaling era. The detachment was staffed by two members of the force: Sergeant F.J. Fitzgerald and Constable F.D. Sutherland. When a steamer rented from the Hudson's Bay Company was wrecked, they were forced to go to the island from Fort McPherson that summer in an open boat, with very little in the way of supplies or equipment; nor did they have anywhere to live. As a result, they were compelled to buy food and rent living quarters from one of the whaling companies. More significantly, because they had no proper boat, they were unable to make patrols at sea, so that the only way they could figure out the amount of tax to charge on trade goods was to accept the sums the captains reported to them.

Outpost of Empire—buildings at Herschel Island, c. 1909. By this time the whaling industry was on its last legs, but the Canadian government maintained the Mounted Police detachment on the island as a demonstration of sovereignty over the western Arctic. *RCMP Photo, 4071-13*

This approach was not very effective, but it was highly symbolic. Once again success was achieved through lack of opposition. The whaling captains, who might have been expected to resent the presence of the police, in fact welcomed it. The police did not hinder their operations much; they had a relaxed attitude towards debauchery, and in fact Sergeant Fitzgerald had a child by an Inuit woman. Moreover, they were of assistance to the captains in preserving order by arresting violent crew members. Again, Canada's assertion of sovereignty on the cheap succeeded largely because it was unopposed. Although the whaling era was over by the outbreak of the First World War, the police maintained the detachment on Herschel Island until 1937, using it as a base from which to patrol the western Arctic.

The Yukon gold rush had alerted Canada to the fact that there was more wealth in the North than the profits from furs and whales, and in the twentieth century the idea of the region as a treasure house of mineral wealth gained currency. In order for this potential wealth to be exploited, however, government control over the region would need to be established. In the more southerly parts of the North this control was shown by treaties signed with the First Nations, notably Treaty 8, signed in the southern Mackenzie watershed in 1899 and designed to smooth the path for an all-Canadian route to the Yukon. In the more remote parts of the Northwest Territories, control was marked by a number of remarkable demonstrations of authority on the part of the police. In three criminal cases, the government made it clear, through the actions of the police, that it was determined to show and enforce its authority through application of the law.

The first case involved two explorers, H.V. Radford, an American, and George Street, a young man from Ottawa, out in the tundra in search of adventure. In June 1912, while travelling with Inuit guides near the southern end of Bathurst Inlet, they were murdered by one of their guides after Radford threatened and struck the man. To do such a thing was extremely foolhardy, as Radford, who had travelled in the North before, must have known, for it was important in Inuit culture for people to behave in a friendly fashion to one another. Anger was seen as a kind of madness, and people who fell into rages could be killed to protect the community. Radford, however, had a reputation for bad temper, and his temper got both men killed. In 1913, word of the incident reached the authorities, and a patrol was sent out to contact the Inuit, not to arrest and punish them, but to explain the law to them and to establish friendly relations with them. The authorities believed that the Inuit were friendly and that the explorers had brought their fate on themselves, and that once the Inuit were told that this was not the way to behave, they would conform to Canadian law. Unfortunately, unlike most police patrols, this one was something of a disaster, mostly due to hesitant leadership, and it was not until the winter of 1917–18 that the police found the men responsible and passed along the official message. No further action was taken. This was not a very convincing demonstration of authority—in fact, it made the government look rather weak. It is interesting to note that as early as 1912 the

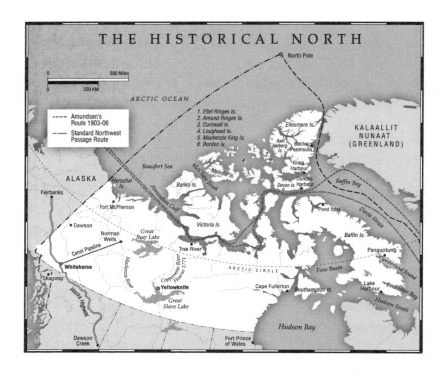

authorities would take such a tolerant view of indigenous culture. But they always had a soft spot for Inuit, though not for Indians.[20]

The next case was similar, but ended differently. This one involved two Oblate missionary priests, Fathers Rouvière and Le Roux, who had been working among the Inuit of the Coppermine region. Late in 1913 they were killed by their two guides near Bloody Falls, at the mouth of the Coppermine River. The motive for the killings was the same as with the two explorers: Father Le Roux had become impatient, and had struck one of the Inuit. The confession of Sinnisiak, one of the killers, showed what had happened:

> Ilogoak [Le Roux] was carrying a rifle. He was mad with us when we started back from their camp and I could not under- stand his talk. I asked Ilogoak if he was going to kill me and he nodded his head . . . he pushed me again and wanted me to put

on the harness and then he took his rifle out on top of the sled. I was very scared and started to pull. We went a little way and Uluksuk and I started to talk and Ilogoak put his hand over my mouth. Ilogoak was very mad and was pushing me. I was thinking hard and crying and very scared and the frost was in my boots and I was cold. I wanted to go back. I was afraid. Ilogoak would not let us. Every time the sled stuck Ilogoak would pull out the rifle. I got hot inside my body . . . I was very much afraid . . . he looked away from me and I stabbed him in the back with a knife.[21]

Sinnisiak and Uluksuk, the killers of Fathers Rouvière and Le Roux, on trial for murder in Alberta in the summer of 1917. *RCMP Photo, 302-2*

Although the circumstances of the killings were almost exactly the same as in the case of the two explorers, the case worked out differently. The news got out when a trader saw an Inuit man wearing a priest's cassock, and the police patrol found the killers quickly. As usually happened, the Inuit cheerfully confessed. The dynamics were different too: it was one thing to kill a bad-tempered American and his unfortunate companion, but it was another to kill two priests; the hierarchy of the Church was determined, not on an un-Christian vengeance, but certainly to ensure that the loss of their priests' lives was taken seriously. Four killings of Europeans in a year made the Canadian authority look weak in the region, so this time the government decided that an example needed to be made. Thus, Sinnisiak and Uluksuk were taken to Edmonton in the summer of 1917 and tried for the murder of Father Rouvière. To the amazement and chagrin of the authorities, the verdict was "not guilty"; the jury, reflecting the anti-Catholic bias of the times, apparently felt that the priests had got what they deserved. The two Inuit were then taken to Calgary and tried for the murder of Father Le Roux, and this time they were convicted. The judge told them, however, that the "great white Chief" had decided to be merciful, and they were sentenced to life imprisonment at the Fort Resolution police detachment, where they spent two relatively pleasant years before being released back to their people. The government did not want to make them suffer, but simply to make it possible for whites to travel safely in the region. Again, the episode shows a remarkable tolerance of the Inuit and their customs, but then as has been noted, the authorities took a very benign view of the "Eskimos" in those days. If the killers had been Cree or Dene, they would have been tried and hanged in short order.

This tolerance had its limits, as the third case showed, and when yet another murder occurred, and when the victim was a member of the Mounted Police, official attitudes hardened. For a third time two white men had been killed, one of them a police corporal, an act that struck directly at Ottawa's authority in the North. In April 1922, a young man named Alikomiak, while being held under arrest at the Tree River detachment (on the Arctic coast east of the mouth of the Coppermine River) for the murder of a man named Pugnana, shot and killed Corporal W.A. Doak while the officer was sleeping, then shot Otto Binder, the local Hudson's Bay Company trader, when he arrived for morning coffee. Alikomiak later claimed that Doak had behaved in a threatening manner towards him, and had forced him to do "women's work," though he had not been struck, and he had killed the policeman for that reason. The police tracked him down, and in the summer of 1923 he and Tatamigana, another Inuk, were taken to Herschel Island for trial. Tatamigana was also charged with the murder of Pugnana and of another man named Hanak.

In this case the government felt that an example had to be made to keep the North safe for non-Natives, and that the two Inuit would have to be punished to the full extent of the law, something that some southern newspapers were demanding. The trial of Alikomiak and Tatamigana was thus something of a show trial.

Lawyers working for the government were appointed as attorneys for the Crown and for the defence. T.L. Cory, the defence lawyer, had written that since "kindness has failed in the past I strongly recommend that the law should take its course and those Eskimos [*sic*] found guilty of murder should be hanged in a place where the natives will see and recognize the outcome of taking another's life." A judicial party consisting of a presiding judge from Edmonton, the lawyers, other officials, and the hangman, who brought along a portable gallows, was sent down the Mackenzie River, picking up a jury from the white population of the posts along the river.

The two men were first tried for killing the other Inuit; these trials were completed in a single day. Alikomiak's trial for killing Doak and Binder took place the next day. Since he had made a full confession, the result was not in doubt. The importance of the trial lay in its theatrical aspect, particularly Judge Dubuc's address to the jury at the end of it. Dubuc made it clear that the real purposes of the trial were not only to impress on the Inuit that the government would not tolerate further killings, but also to reassure the Mounted Police and Canadians in general that the government's policy was to make the North safe for outsiders. He first gave a dramatic definition of the role of the police in the North; Doak was "one of those lonely and fearless sentinels for Law and Order, posted somewhere on some barren and desolate point in the Polar Sea. A man whose duty was to prevent if possible, and if not, to detect and help in punishment of crime . . . always on guard for us."

He warned the jury against excessive sympathy for the accused:

> I am further satisfied that you shall not fail to bring a correct verdict because you have not forgotten I am sure those undying principles of British fair play which go with British justice, for although you may feel that you should have some consideration for the simple mentality of these primitive people, yet you also feel that you owe a duty to your country, who extends to them its generous protection in every way.

He then spoke to the main point, and warned the jury that if they did not do their duty it would send a dangerous message to the Inuit:

> It is your duty as Jurymen who have taken the oath as such to decide according to the evidence, and make these tribes understand that the stern but at the same time just hand of British justice extends also to these northern shores. We want it plainly understood in the minds of these people that one of our most important laws is for the protection of human life which flows from the Divine command "Thou shalt not kill." . . . Our Government has not undertaken this expensive Judicial Expedition to have exhibited here a mockery and travesty of Justice before these primitive people. You have a duty to perform as Jurymen, a duty to your Country and to our Laws, and a duty to yourselves. We are leaving this Island very shortly after these Trials and the result of your verdict shall fall on you who are to remain here, and it is you who shall have to bear the consequences.[22]

The jury duly brought in a verdict of guilty, and after a debate in the press over whether mercy should be shown, the two men were hanged at Herschel Island on February 1, 1924. Whatever comfort the episode may have brought to the general public, it does not seem to have had much immediate effect on the Inuit of the region. The explorer Knud Rasmussen, for example, who spoke to Alikomiak's people after the execution, was scornful of the government's policy and its impact on the Inuit. What was not to be scorned, however, was the demonstration of sovereignty that this episode implied. Its purpose was to make the region "safe for white men," as a contemporary official put it, and although it did not necessarily do that, it certainly was a strong demonstration of the application of authority.

Things did not go as smoothly in the Arctic islands, however, where in some places Canadian sovereignty was questionable at best. Officially, the islands had belonged to Canada since 1880,[23] but Britain's right to the islands, and thus Canada's, was not totally secure. In the first place, a number of the islands had been explored by men who were not British. In the second, in 1880 a large part of the Arctic island archipelago was still completely unknown when Britain transferred its nebulous rights to the young dominion.[24] During the 1870s the British government, which was anxious to turn over responsibility for the Arctic to Canada, wrestled with the difficulty of finding a legal definition for a territory, part of which was yet to be discovered. There was some urgency because Britain had received requests for permission to fish and mine in the Arctic. Particularly concerning was an 1874 request from a Lieutenant W.A. Mintzer of the U.S. Army Corps of Engineers for permission to mine in the Cumberland Gulf region.[25] One Colonial Office official noted of this request, in the sneering tone British officials often used in referring to Americans in the days when the United Kingdom was still great and powerful,

> It would be desirable to ascertain the views of the Dominion Govt I think before the F[oreign] O[ffice] give [sic] any answer. We must remember that if this Yankee adventurer is informed by the British FO that the place indicated is not a portion of H.M. dominions he would no doubt think himself entitled to hoist the "Stars and Stripes" which might produce no end of complications.[26]

Between 1875 and 1880 there was a flurry of correspondence between the British Foreign Office, the Governor General of Canada, and the Canadian government on the issue of sovereignty over the Arctic islands. Two issues complicated the proposed transfer: no one knew the boundaries or extent of the lands in question, and the Canadian government was not particularly keen to accept the transfer.

The matter of boundaries was solved by defining the northern limit of British possessions as "the utmost northerly limits of the

North American continent and the islands appertaining thereto."
Getting the Canadian government to accept the gift proved more
difficult. By 1877, Lord Carnarvon, the British foreign secretary,
was growing impatient, writing to Lord Dufferin, the Governor
General,[27] in elegant Victorian prose:

> From reports which have appeared in the Newspapers I have
> observed that the attention of the citizens of the United States
> has from time to time been drawn to these territories and that
> private expeditions have been sent out to explore certain por-
> tions of them, and I need hardly point out to you that should it
> be the wish of the Canadian people that they should be included
> in the Dominion great difficulty in effecting this may easily arise
> unless steps are speedily taken to place the title of Canada to
> these territories upon a clear and unmistakable footing.
>
> I have therefore to request that you will move your minis-
> ters to again take into their consideration the question of
> the inclusion of these territories within the boundaries of the
> Dominion, and that you will state to them that I shall be glad to
> be informed, with as little further delay as may be possible, of
> the steps which they propose to take in the matter.[28]

Or, as our contemporaries would say, "Use it or lose it."

Several more years elapsed, however, before the transfer was
finally made official, the delay being due mostly to ongoing uncer-
tainties about how to word the document when no one knew
exactly the limits of the territory involved. Finally in July 1880, by
Order in Council, the Arctic was transferred to Canada, the land
involved being described in the most general terms possible:

> . . . all British territories and possessions in North America,
> not already included within the Dominion of Canada, and all
> islands adjacent to any of such territories or possessions, shall
> (with the exception of the Colony of Newfoundland and its
> dependencies) become and be annexed to and form part of the

said Dominion of Canada; and become and be subject to the laws for the time being in force in the said Dominion, in so far as such laws may be applicable thereto.[29]

As documents of this sort go, this is vague in the extreme, reflecting the uncertainty of Britain's claim to some of the islands, and the feeling in official circles that attempts at being more precise might simply draw attention to this uncertainty. As one authority put it, "The British Government did not know what they were transferring, and on the other hand the Canadian Government had no idea what they were receiving."[30]

Fifteen years passed before, in 1895, Canada created four provisional districts in the northern territories, one of them the District of Franklin, including the Arctic islands, but other than a few exploratory summer voyages north, nothing else was done to demonstrate Canada's control over

Roald Amundsen (1872–1928) led the first party to traverse the Northwest Passage, 1903–6.
LAC,C14073

the region. In the meantime, explorations were carried out, mostly by citizens of other countries. Between 1903 and 1906, Roald Amundsen traversed the Northwest Passage from east to west, the first expedition to do so, but he made no claims to Canadian territory. More alarming from Canada's point of view was the remarkable expedition of Otto Sverdrup, like Amundsen a Norwegian, from 1899 to 1902. During those years, using Ellesmere Island as a base, he discovered and explored land that was totally unknown: the Sverdrup Islands (Axel Heiberg, Amund Ringnes, and Ellef Ringnes Islands, named after his sponsors, Norwegian brewers). Most alarming of all, he claimed the islands for Norway. Luckily for Canada, Norway had more urgent issues than solidifying its claim, chiefly establishing its independence from Sweden, a process that was completed in 1905. The issue was not dead, however, but merely sleeping, and Canada's title to the region was to remain cloudy for another quarter century.

The Amundsen and Sverdrup expeditions, along with the unsatisfactory conclusion to the Alaska Boundary Dispute, were all factors in the spread of Canadian authority via Mounted Police posts to the Arctic coast in 1903. They also ensured that when someone offered to mount a Canadian expedition to the Arctic, the government would welcome the offer, despite the expense involved, especially when the offer came from a man as persuasive as Vilhjalmur Stefansson.[31] Stefansson was nominally a Canadian, having been born in Gimli, Manitoba, in 1879 to Icelandic immigrant parents, though he spent most of his life in the United States. He was a highly controversial figure who inspired strong admiration and even stronger dislike. To be fair to the man, he depended on publicity to sell his books and finance his expeditions; this explains some of the more unfortunate episodes of his life. An example occurred after his 1910 Arctic expedition in which he met Inuit who had never met Europeans. He decided that they were lighter in complexion and hair than the norm, and when he talked to reporters about this, the press turned it into a story about "Blonde Eskimos," which exposed him to a good deal of ridicule.

Nonetheless, Stefansson was tough, resourceful, and determined, and when just before the First World War the Canadian government decided that it was well past time that it sent an exploratory expedition to the Arctic, Stefansson jumped at the chance to lead it. The result was the Canadian Arctic Expedition of 1913–16, during which the last islands of the western Arctic were discovered: Borden Island, Lougheed Island, Meighen Island, and Mackenzie King Island. At last, land had been discovered in northern Canada by a Canadian. The expedition was dogged with controversy; when its ship, the *Karluk*, became stuck in ice, Stefansson went off to hunt and explore. When he returned, a storm had blown the ship far to the east, where it was crushed and destroyed, with some loss of life. He was accused of abandoning it. Nevertheless, he was amazingly successful at using what he called, naturally, the "Stefansson method" of exploration, which was essentially to adopt indigenous techniques and live off the land—the exact opposite of what Sir John Franklin had done.

Stefansson was a tremendously important figure in the history of Canadian Arctic sovereignty, for both positive and negative reasons. There is no question that the Canadian Arctic Expedition was a huge success from the point of view of discovery and thus sovereignty, despite the loss of life and the cost overruns. Stefansson also was a great enthusiast for the future development of the region, and spent the rest of his life, mostly in the United States, as a kind of Arctic prophet. He talked of the Arctic Ocean as a "polar Mediterranean," at the centre rather than at the periphery of civilization, and was an early proponent of the idea of shipping through the Northwest Passage (though in those years, before global warming, he thought it would have to be done by submarine).

Vilhjalmur Stefansson (1879–1962), the Canadian-born Arctic explorer who discovered new islands in the High Arctic and spent much of his life lecturing about the "Polar Mediterranean" on Canada's northern coast. *LAC,C86406*

Some of Stefansson's schemes, however, were far-fetched, and one in particular concerned sovereignty and embarrassed the Canadian government. This was his Wrangel Island expedition of 1921. The island lies north of eastern Siberia, and Stefansson's plan was to send a party there to claim it for Canada. The island is large, about 7,200 square kilometres (2,772 square miles) in area. Among its claims to fame is that the world's last mammoth seems to have died there as recently as 1,700 years ago, but more importantly, it is strategically located from the point of view of controlling the Arctic basin. Stefansson sent a party of three Canadians, an American, and Ada Blackjack, an Inuit woman, though he did not go himself. The expedition was a disaster; everyone died but Ada Blackjack, and a later party was arrested by the Russians. More dangerously, Stefansson's enthusiasm so infected the Mackenzie King government that it made approving gestures towards asserting sovereignty over the island, though it soon backed off. Given the uncertain sovereignty over its own Arctic islands, the thought that the Canadian government would assert its sovereignty over someone else's island seems foolhardy if not insane, and probably the government realized it. The episode was embarrassing, and made Stefansson *persona non grata* in Ottawa for the rest of his long life.

In 1920, Canada had had title to the Arctic islands for forty years, and yet had no permanent presence on them. There had been a series of official voyages to the region, notably the ones mentioned above, made in the early years of the twentieth century by Joseph-Elzéar Bernier (1852–1934). Bernier was the son of a sea captain from Quebec, and was commanding his own ship at the age of seventeen. He was fascinated by the North, and in 1904 outfitted a ship for an attempt to reach the North Pole. The federal government learned of his plans, and hired him and his ship instead to patrol the eastern Arctic. He made several voyages north, wintering on Baffin Island and Melville Island, collecting fees from whalers and traders, and carrying scientists north. It was on Melville Island in 1909 that he unveiled a plaque claiming the Arctic islands for Canada.

Certainly the activities of Bernier in the east and Stefansson in the west in this era were important to Canada's claims of sovereignty, but still, on the outbreak of war in 1914 there was no permanent official presence anywhere in the Canadian territories except in the Yukon, and there the government was being downsized as the population shrank after the end of the gold rush.[32] In the Northwest Territories there was none at all; the Territory's capital remained in

Ottawa until the mid 1960s. At the end of the war, however, events occurred that forced Canada to take a more active approach to demonstrating sovereignty. As is the case now, the issue was environmental—specifically, the protection of the muskox.

Muskoxen were protected under the Northwest Game Act of 1917, and could not be shot except by special permission for scientific purposes. In 1919, government interest in the animals was further demonstrated by the Reindeer and Musk-ox Commission, which looked into their biological and economic potential as a source of food for the Inuit. The muskox herd on Ellesmere Island, however, could not be entirely protected, for the Inuit of northern Greenland regularly crossed Smith Sound to hunt them. In July 1919, as the commission was beginning its work, the Canadian government sent a request via Britain to Denmark asking the Danes to restrain the Inuit of the Thule region from killing Canadian muskoxen. Denmark, which did not officially proclaim its sovereignty over Greenland until 1921, asked the advice of Knud Rasmussen, the famous explorer who had opened a trading post at Thule in 1910. In his reply, he said, "As everyone knows, the land of the Polar Eskimos [Ellesmere Island] falls under what is called 'No Man's Land,' and there is, therefore, no authority in this country except that which I myself am able to exert through the Trading Station."[33] Ominously, the Danish government replied to Canada that it agreed with Rasmussen.

Canada hastened to reply that Ellesmere Island was not no man's land, but was part of Canada, but the officials in the Department of the Interior were privately worried. Much of Ellesmere Island had been discovered by non-Britons, and it was entirely unoccupied. The Greenland Eskimos and the occasional explorer, such as Robert Peary and Adolphus Greely (both Americans), were the only humans who had ever set foot on it in recorded times. An internal department memo suggested that Canada's sovereignty over this huge island (nearly four times the size of Nova Scotia), and in the rest of the High Arctic as well, was very tenuous:

The situation in the northern islands, therefore, appears to be that Britain has had an inchoate title which now probably through the lapse of time may be considered to have terminated; that the Low and Bernier expeditions may have established a "fictitious" title which also has probably lapsed; and therefore, that Denmark or any other country is in a position to acquire sovereignty by establishing effective occupation and administration.[34]

This was a startling admission. An "inchoate title" is one that is incomplete or imperfectly developed. International law contained the concept that discovery established title to land, but it was inchoate until some effective form of administration or occupation took place.[35] A "fictitious" title was a made-up or fabricated one. For an Ottawa bureaucrat to admit that Canada had no real claim to the High Arctic, and that the region was up for grabs, was of course something of a bombshell, and this memo was not publicly circulated.

It did, however, stimulate action, albeit grudging. J.B. Harkin, Canada's first commissioner of National Parks, who was interested in the muskox issue, wondered if Ellesmere and the other islands were worth bothering about. At a meeting of northern experts, including Stefansson (who was still in Ottawa's good graces), it was concluded that they were, for two reasons. First, the islands might be worth something. Second, and here the embarrassment factor surfaced again, there was a "sentimental" reason: "Ellesmere and the other northern islands have always been regarded in Canada as Canadian, and there doubtless would be a strong sentiment against their being taken possession of by any other flag."[36] More pointedly, Harkin wrote to his superior reminding him of the public uproar in 1903:

One has but to recall the outburst of public indignation and protest in Canada at the decision of the Alaskan arbitration to realize what public opinion would be if any neglect on the Government's part resulted in the loss of an area thousands of times larger and more important than was involved in the Alaskan case.[37]

So it seemed that something must be done to make Canadian sovereignty more real in the Arctic islands. But what? Harkin suggested, in a strange forecast of what actually happened thirty-five years later, that some Inuit[38] be sent to Ellesmere Island, where a police post could protect them and the muskox as well. Stefansson agreed, and said that two police posts should be set up on the island, because it would not do for Canadian authority to be established on the southern part of the island if the Danes claimed the north. The idea of sending the police to the High Arctic was accepted. They seemed the logical people to send because they had done such good work in the Yukon. Moreover, their pay was low and they represented Canadian authority in a manner that no other Canadian agency could. It might be noted, however, that there were other ways of establishing national sovereignty among and over the Inuit. The Danes, for instance, had not used police in Greenland, preferring to work through missionaries and other civilian agents of the government.

More than a year was taken up with preparation. This was carried out in secret, partly so as not to alert the Danes, and partly so that Stefansson could be kept out of the loop. He was anxious to command the expedition north, but his stock was falling fast in Ottawa, and when he gave an interview to the American press in which he spoke of "islands and country lying north of Canada," it fell even further, for of course the Canadian government's position was that there was nothing north of Canada. Finally, in the summer of 1922, an expedition was sent north on the *Arctic*, Captain Bernier's old ship which was refitted for the occasion, captained by Bernier himself. The expedition was led by J.D. Craig, the advisory engineer for the Northwest Territories Branch of the Department of the Interior. Two posts were to be set up, one at Pond Inlet on northern Baffin Island, where a trader named Robert Janes had

The Mounted Police detachment at Craig Harbour, on the southeast corner of Ellesmere Island, photographed in the summer of 1925. The post was staffed by two members of the RCMP, accompanied by a family of Inuit employees. Since no one lived anywhere near the detachment, its function was purely a symbolic demonstration of sovereignty. *LAC, PA100771*

been shot in 1920, for the same reason that the two explorers and the two priests had died in the west—he had behaved in a violent and irrational way.[39] Staff Sergeant A.H. Joy had visited the community in 1921 to investigate the incident, and it was a logical place for a detachment. The location of the other detachment was to be on Ellesmere Island, and since the island was unoccupied, the exact location was left to Craig. Eventually, ice conditions dictated a harbour at the extreme southeast corner, which he named after himself, and the detachment of Craig Harbour was established.

Each of the detachments was staffed with two members of the police, usually a fairly senior officer and a constable. Craig Harbour was commanded by Inspector C.E. Wilcox, and Pond Inlet (often called Pond's Inlet in this period) by Staff Sergeant Joy. An Inuit family or sometimes two was hired to live at the detachment and work for the police. When Bernier and the *Arctic* returned south in the fall, the press hailed the expedition as a demonstration of Canada's rights: "Canada's Northern Empire Within 850 Miles of North Pole, Making Our Sovereignty Certain," exulted the Ottawa *Journal*.[40] Although this was not altogether true, it was closer to the truth than it had been ten or twenty years earlier.

Landing supplies at Craig Harbour, summer 1925. *LAC, PA102444*

By 1927, six RCMP posts had been opened in the Arctic islands: Craig Harbour and Pond Inlet in 1922, Pangnirtung (on the east coast of Baffin Island) in 1923, Dundas Harbour (southeast Devon Island) in 1924, Bache Peninsula (halfway up the east coast of Ellesmere Island) in 1926, and Lake Harbour (south coast of Baffin Island) in 1927. Nor did the government go back to sleep once these posts had been established. In the spring of 1925 the Northern Advisory Board was set up to deal with sovereignty and other matters concerning the Arctic. Its members were senior officials of the various government departments with interests in the region: the Department of the Interior, the RCMP, External Affairs, Indian Affairs, and Fisheries. The impetus for the board's formation was another shock to Canada's assertion of Arctic sovereignty. It had been discovered that an American explorer named Donald B. MacMillan, a man with considerable Arctic experience, was planning a new expedition based at northern Greenland, with stations on Ellesmere and Axel Heiberg Islands, to carry out aerial exploration of the polar region under the command of Admiral Richard Byrd. When Ottawa heard of this, MacMillan was informed through the British embassy in Washington that licences were required if the expedition planned to collect plant or animal specimens. The deputy minister of the interior made a trip to Washington in May 1925 to tell the secretary of the navy that Canada's permission should be obtained before the expedition landed on Canadian terri-tory, and offered to assist the expedition in any way possible, including supplying the "necessary permits." In August, Inspector Wilcox travelled north on the *Arctic* and visited MacMillan at Etah, in northern Greenland. During the visit, which was apparently friendly, Commander Byrd asked if any Canadian had ever visited Axel Heiberg Island. The answer was no, and the implications of the question were worrying.

Because the American government had no interest in making claims to Ellesmere Island, nothing untoward came of this episode, but it did lead directly to the establishment of the most unusual Mounted Police post in the history of the force. In 1926, an expe-dition was sent to set up a detachment at Bache Peninsula, in the vicinity of where the MacMillan expedition had been operating. The detachment was located on the east coast of Ellesmere Island at about 79 degrees north latitude. It was the most northerly police post in the British Empire, and the most northerly in the history of the RCMP. What made it unusual, however, was that there was no one there to police, because no one lived there; in fact, except for the Greenland Inuit at Etah, there wasn't another human being within hundreds of kilometres of the place.

The Bache Peninsula detachment was in operation for only a few years. Because it was so far north, it was hard to supply. A ship came once a year with supplies; one year weather conditions were so bad that the supplies had to be left on the ice a considerable dis-tance to the south. Bache Peninsula was the quintessential example of symbolic sovereignty. The detachment, for instance, was a Cana-dian post office, supplied with stamps and a cancellation stamp, though the mail was collected and delivered once a year and could just as easily have been stamped when the ship docked in Halifax. The operation of a post office is a major proof of effective sover-eignty, and since there was no one around to arrest, the police ran a post office. They had customs declaration and other forms, though it's unclear if they were ever used.

There was more going on at Bache Peninsula than symbolic sovereignty, however, for in the late 1920s the Mounted Police made a number of remarkable patrols in the High Arctic. Of course, the police had nothing else to do. Two of these patrols are particularly worthy of mention. Between March and May 1929, Inspector A.H. Joy, the constable at the detachment, three Inuit and four dog teams made a patrol of over 2800 kilometres (1740 miles) from Dundas Harbour to Bache Peninsula via Melville, Lougheed, Ellef Ringnes, Cornwall, Axel Heiberg, and Ellesmere Islands. The police were not the first to travel in these regions, but at least for the first time it could be said that a Canadian had actually visited the Arctic regions claimed by Canada. In 1934–35 Corporal H.W. Stallworthy, on loan to the Oxford Arctic expedition, reached 82 degrees 25 minutes north, and was made a fellow of the Royal Geographic Society.

At the other detachments where there were people living— Pond Inlet, for example—the police carried out most of the functions of government, since there were still no other government officers anywhere in the Arctic. As well as performing law enforcement functions when necessary, they took the census, registered births, marriages (for Inuit who had accepted Christianity) and deaths, sometimes gave out rough-and-ready medical assistance, ran the post office, wrote reports for the Department of Indian Affairs, served as customs and tax officials, and did whatever else needed to be done along those lines, demonstrating actual rather than symbolic sovereignty. Until the 1940s, when Ottawa at last took a more active role in the North, the police were the entire face of government in the region. By 1930, Canada had

> exercised jurisdiction in and over the Arctic islands by establishing police, customs, and post offices at strategic and necessary points and by conducting patrols over the surrounding territory. . . . The title of Canada to the Arctic islands was recognized by Norway in 1930; and the claims of Denmark and

the United States have been nullified by Canadian occupation of the territory.[41]

Getting Norway to recognize Canada's title proved something of a sticky matter. Remember that Norway's claim was to the islands discovered by Otto Sverdrup at the turn of the twentieth century, a claim that, it could be argued, was better than Canada's, for Norway's rested on actual discovery, while Canada's rested merely on an assertion made by Britain.[42]

The settlement of Norway's claims, while peaceful, involved a good deal of diplomacy.[43] The usual interpretation of events is that in 1930, as Sverdrup lay dying, the Canadian and Norwegian governments agreed that Canada should pay $67,000 to Sverdrup, ostensibly for his maps and papers (which are now in the national archives in Ottawa), but in reality because Norway insisted that Sverdrup be compensated for his efforts as a condition of that country relinquishing its claims to the islands bearing his name. The reality, however, was a good deal more complicated. The question of the Sverdrup Islands became linked with several controversies that were ongoing between Britain and Norway over other territory in the Arctic and in the Antarctic as well. "The polar regions played an important role in the perception of the national destiny of Canada, Norway and Britain between 1920 and 1930," historian Thorlief T. Thorliefsson recently explained. "The final agreement over the Sverdrup Islands reflected these national and imperial aspirations."[44]

The sequence of events that led to Norway's formal recognition of Canada's sovereignty over the Sverdrup Islands is a complicated one, but it was essentially a triangular agreement among the three countries, ending amicably, with each party gaining its main objectives. Canada wanted a clear title to the Arctic islands, Norway wanted Jan Mayen in the Arctic,[45] and Britain wanted a free hand to pursue sovereignty over Antarctica. A scholar who has studied the agreement calls it "a fundamental illustration of Canada's growth as an independent nation in the years between the Imperial

Conference of 1926 and the passage of the Statute of Westminster in 1931."[46] O.D. Skelton, undersecretary of state for External Affairs and the most important Canadian civil servant of the inter-war years,[47] handled the delicate negotiations with supreme skill. Britain wanted to use the Sverdrup issue as a pawn in convincing Norway to drop its Antarctic claims, but Skelton made Canada's interests paramount. The difficulty with Norway was that public opinion in that country was proud of Sverdrup's achievement and reluctant to abandon his claim. The problem was solved when Canada not only paid the $67,000 to Sverdrup, who was in need and very ill, but also guaranteed Norway access to hunting and fishing rights on the Sverdrup Islands, rights that were meaningless in prac-tice, but which satisfied the Norwegian public. Canada also recog-nized Norway's sovereignty over Jan Mayen Island, as did Britain. It was a happy outcome, in which all three countries got what they wanted.

On the eve of the Second World War, Canada's sovereignty in the North was unchallenged, partly because on the mainland it was unchallengeable under international law, and partly because farther north no one wanted to challenge it. Canada's sovereignty still man-ifested itself largely in symbolic ways: the Mounted Police posts, the flags flown at them (Union Jacks in this era), the post offices and the other paraphernalia of bureaucracy used to show that the region was under formal Canadian control. The Northwest Territories had seen the development of the gold-mining town of Yellowknife, and other economic booms had taken place at Norman Wells (oil) and on the shores of Great Bear Lake (radium). Yet outside Yellowknife, the newcomer population of the Northwest Territories in the 1930s consisted of a handful of scattered traders, missionaries, and police. There were no civilian representatives of the Canadian government permanently stationed north of the mainland.

The government was aware of this vacuum, and pondered how to fill it at the lowest possible cost. One solution was to be perhaps the most symbolic of all the symbols of sovereignty. In 1928, the RCMP commissioned a schooner for Arctic service. The *St. Roch* was launched in April of that year, and in 1929 began a series of annual patrols of Arctic waters, for most of that period under the command of Inspector Henry Larsen (1899–1964), a Norwegian seaman who immigrated to Canada in 1927 and joined the RCMP the next year.[48] The *St. Roch* was able to visit remote Inuit camps and to operate in waters where there had never been a Canadian presence. Some years the ship wintered in the North, and in

Henry Larsen (1898–1964), the Norwegian-born RCMP officer who commanded the schooner *St.Roch* on Arctic patrols from 1928 to 1948.
LAC, C70771

1940–42 it traversed the Northwest Passage from west to east, the first ship to do so. In 1944, it achieved another first, when it made the passage from east to west in a single season, and yet another when in 1950 it sailed from Halifax to Vancouver in a single season, becoming the first vessel to circumnavigate North America.

The achievements of the *St. Roch* were well publicized in Canada and throughout the world, serving as powerful symbols of Canada's northern sovereignty. And symbols they were, for in 1940 there was still virtually no official Canadian presence north of the mainland except for the police. The Inuit were mostly left to their own devices, with no schools, no doctors (one might accompany a supply ship on its annual visit), no welfare or assistance of any kind, except perhaps handouts of food from a Hudson's Bay Company post in times of starvation. Almost all the Inuit of what is now Nunavut still lived on the land as their ancestors had done. For those who gravitated to settlements such as Pond Inlet, tuberculosis was becoming a scourge. Yet a real government presence had to wait until after the war.

ARCTIC   FRONTIERS

THE   CANADIAN   NORTH
AND   THE   COLD   WAR

*"Apparently we have administered these vast territories of
the north in an almost continuing state of absence of mind.
I think all honourable members now feel the territories are
vastly important to Canada."*

— LOUIS ST. LAURENT,
Prime Minister of Canada, 1953

Canada has always had two strong allies on its northern flank, what Canadian military historian C.P. Stacey called "those two famous servants of the Czar, Generals January and February mount[ing] guard for the Canadian people all year round." For decades, Canada relied on a simple geographic truth: the North was cold and ice-bound for most of the year, and no nation on earth had the capacity to move quickly across the land and frozen waters to pose any real threat to southern Canada. The RCMP provided the basics: the flag was flying in remote islands across the Arctic, Canadian law was nominally enforced, and the country's claims to northern sover-eignty seemed well protected from foreign challenges. Why spend money on a region that lacked economic importance, faced no strategic threats, and had a tiny and widely scattered population that was content to be left alone? Vilhjalmur Stefansson might raise fanciful ideas about the northward course of civilization, but few saw his speeches as more than parlour talk. Stacey understood the situation perfectly. The North, he wrote, was "clearly not particularly important, and this fact greatly narrows, for practical purposes, Canada's actual area of defence." What Canadians were concerned about in the 1930s was not the abstract question of sovereignty, but where their next meal was coming from. Stefansson's talk of an "Arctic Mediterranean" during the 1920s may have been prophetic, but it was nothing more than fodder for after-dinner speeches until the military significance of the Canadian North became clear during the Second World War and particularly the ensuing Cold War.

Between the two world wars, Canada was strongly isolationist and timid in its approach to international affairs. William Lyon Mackenzie King, arguably the most wily and thus the most successful of all our prime ministers, at least in terms of survival, had a single goal throughout his career: the preservation of national unity (his secondary goal, on which he believed the first depended, was staying prime minister forever). King, afraid that involvement in international affairs would harm national unity, as had happened in the First World War, shared Senator Raoul Dandurand's view that "Canada was a fireproof house, far from flammable materials." Canada would avoid committing itself to overseas conflicts, in hopes that this would prevent internal divisions. Mackenzie King's frequent refrain that "Parliament would decide" was a way of defusing controversies and avoiding commitments. In any case, geography insulated the country from European and Asian crises. As for the United States, Canadians had not been at war with their southern neighbour since 1815, and prided themselves on sharing the longest undefended border in the world. This was not a time for alarm. The North was not even on the national radar; in fact, radar hadn't been invented.

A shared continent meant that the defence of Canada was vital to American interests, and vice versa. The Monroe Doctrine of 1823, which pledged that the United States would respond to any external aggression in the western hemisphere, extended north as well as south. "We as good neighbors are true friends," American president

Franklin D. Roosevelt assured Canadians in 1938, going on to say that the United States would "not stand idly by" if any foreign power threatened Canadian soil. Nowadays such a statement would certainly raise hackles on the Canadian political left, but then it was received joyfully, especially because it suggested that Americans would do the heavy lifting of continental defence. Mackenzie King declared that Canada also had its obligations as a friendly neighbour to ensure that no enemy forces would ever be allowed to pass through Canada on their way to the United States, though how Canada would prevent such a thing with its tiny armed forces he did not say. In any case, these were easy promises to make while the likelihood of invasion remained remote.

The Second World War

The Second World War sent the "fireproof house" theory up in a puff of smoke. When war broke out, Canadian policy-makers assumed that the Arctic was a natural defensive barrier and that the threat of an Axis foothold in North America was impossible. Later on, when the Japanese captured territory in Alaska and German submarines popped up in the Gulf of St. Lawrence and sank American merchant ships within swimming distance of Miami, they found they were wrong. In 1940, fears that Nazi Germany might conquer Britain led to the Ogdensburg Agreement between Canada and the U.S. to provide for the shared defence of North America. The Americans were particularly concerned about the security of Alaska, whose far-western tip was uncomfortably close to Tokyo, and the overland and air routes to their northernmost territory. Any land route to Alaska, of course, would have to go through Canada.

As Vilhjalmur Stefansson and others had noted before the war, the shortest air route from the continental United States to the Far East went over western Canada. In wartime, such considerations assumed heightened significance, particularly after the Soviet Union

U.S. Army trucks somewhere on the Alaska Highway in the early primitive stage of its construction, summer 1942. The original caption is "Through the Wilderness."
U.S. National Archives, 111-SC-139950

entered the war in the summer of 1941. To help the Soviets fight the Germans on the Eastern Front, the allies promised aircraft as part of the Lend-Lease program. In the same year the Canadian government began to build the Northwest Staging Route, a series of airfields and radio ranging stations between Edmonton and Fairbanks, Alaska, for civil aviation and defence purposes. Warplanes built in the United States were flown over this route to Fairbanks, where they were handed over to Soviet pilots, many of whom (to the surprise of the Americans) were women. The route became vital later that year when on December 7 the U.S. Pacific Fleet was devastated at Pearl Harbor, and the Royal Navy warships at Singapore three days later. Hong Kong fell, and in a rapid succession of victories Japan secured control over southeast Asia. The winds of war blew closer to Canada, and isolation no longer suggested security but vulnerability.

Although even at the time military planners doubted that there would be a serious invasion from the North, Alaska was vulnerable

Building the bridge over the Sikanni Chief River on the Alaska Highway in north-eastern British Columbia, 1943. The original rough bridge has been replaced with a more permanent one. *U.S. National Archives, 111-SC-322949*

to attack: a fact made painfully clear when the Japanese captured the islands of Attu and Kiska in July 1942. Americans had wanted a highway to Alaska since the 1920s, but the Canadian government had refused to support a project that it felt would offer little benefit to Canada; it was a lot of money to spend on a road to the Yukon, which had only 4,000 or so residents in the 1930s. But the war swept aside considerations of cost.

In early 1942, the United States government, alarmed by the thought that Japanese submarines might cut the sea link between Alaska and the contiguous lower forty-eight states, drew up a plan to build a road link to Alaska. President Roosevelt approved it on February 11. This road, originally called the Alcan and later the Alaska Highway, was one of the greatest construction projects ever undertaken. Laid out to link the airfields along the North-west Staging Route, and thus winding a circuitous and treacherous course, the highway had a dramatic effect on northeastern British Columbia, the Yukon, and the Mackenzie Valley. The Canadian government cheerfully gave the Americans the right to build the road where they pleased, and to use whatever natural resources they needed, so long as the U.S. paid for it, and it was turned over to Canada after the war. It was not a sophisticated work of engineering: the original dirt road, opened to truck traffic eight months after construction began, had to be rebuilt immediately. Nevertheless, the Americans had conquered 2,400 kilometres (1,491 miles) of country, largely unknown to planners, in remarkably short order.

A major military-industrial project in the Northwest was more controversial. The Canol (Canadian Oil) project was initiated in 1942 to ensure a supply of oil to Alaska in case the maritime route was cut off. It was also designed to fuel defence efforts along the Alaska Highway and the staging route. Production was expanded at the small Imperial Oil facility at Norman Wells on the Mackenzie River, and a 1000-kilometre (621-mile) pipeline to a new Whitehorse refinery was built. American military officials pushed for the project, and a reluctant Canadian government went along, on the condition that the pipeline and facilities would be controlled by the Americans during the war, but the Canadian government would be given the first option to purchase them when the conflict ended. The project was plagued by morale and infrastructure problems, however, and the pipeline only operated sporadically for a year after it was finished in 1944. It was dismantled soon after. From today's perspective it may seem hard to understand why the Canadian government would permit tens of thousand of Americans to operate in the Northwest without any supervision, for it was not until 1943, more than a year after construction began, that Ottawa sent a single liaison officer to represent Canada's interests in the region. On the whole, Canada neither knew nor cared what the United States was doing in the region.

Nowadays, when the mere suggestion of the sale of water to the Americans sends Canadian nationalists into hysterics, such neglect of a large part of the country would be inconceivable. The reason for this wilful neglect was partly that the Canadian government felt that since the Americans were paying the whole cost and doing all the work, it had no moral right to question them. As well, the government was grateful for the security the presence of the American military guaranteed. Mackenzie King had spent his whole political career trying to detach Canada from its "British connection," and it wasn't until later in the war that he began to think that perhaps the rising power of the United States was more of a threat to Canadian sovereignty than the fading British Empire. When British High Commissioner Malcolm MacDonald and Vincent Massey, Canadian High Commissioner to Britain, raised the sovereignty issue, King replied that "we were going to have a hard time after the war to prevent the U.S. attempting control of some Canadian situations. [MacDonald] said already they spoke jokingly of their men as an army of occupation."[1]

The result of this neglect was that the Americans ran northwest Canada from early 1942 until the end of the war as a kind of friendly army of occupation. They changed the face of Whitehorse and the other small communities along the highway, building water treatment plants, theatres, baseball diamonds, and all sorts of other facilities. American military police enforced American law, sometimes on Canadian civilians. There were cases where First Nations women claimed abuse by soldiers that were never properly investigated—the men in question conveniently disappeared, and since environmental regulations were non-existent, there were quite a number of cases of serious pollution of lakes and streams.

These northern military projects raised sovereignty concerns for the Canadian government. Nearly 40,000 U.S. military personnel and American and Canadian civilians worked on the wartime projects in the Northwest. These transient workers represented more than three times the prewar population of the region. They also were given the right of extraterritoriality: American military and civilian employees were answerable to American, not Canadian, authorities. At first, this fit with Ottawa's "out of sight and out of mind" approach. By 1943, the government's "fit of absence of mind," to borrow Undersecretary of State for External Affairs Norman Robertson's apt characterization, was equalled by Washington's

African-American troops of the U.S. Army Corps of Engineers building a timber bridge on the Alaska Highway, summer 1942. *U.S. National Archives, 111-SC-139940*

ignorance of what was actually happening on the ground.[2] Prime Minister Mackenzie King told British High Commissioner Malcolm MacDonald in March 1942 that the Alaska Highway "was less intended for protection against the Japanese than as one of the fingers of the hand which America is placing more or less over the whole of the Western hemisphere."[3] If by that he meant that the Americans had plans to assert political control over northwest Canada, he was wrong. The Americans did not want to govern Canada; they simply wanted to build the highway and the pipeline, secure Alaska, and then go home, which is what they did soon after the war ended.

Canadian ignorance of and indifference to what the Americans were up to in the Northwest did begin to change in 1943. King appointed a special commissioner for defence projects in the Northwest, and Brigadier (later Major-General) W.W. Foster, based in Edmonton, became the eyes and ears of Canada in the region. Of course, he was only one man, really a token presence. More significantly, American plans to build more roads and air-staging routes were blocked, agreements were reached that American troops would leave the North after the war, and the Canadians agreed to buy back from the United States those facilities and installations that were already built or in progress in the North. The Americans, although sometimes begrudgingly, complied with each of these requests.[4]

To all but those who are pathologically suspicious of the United States, the Americans' attitude to northern Canada can be seen not as ominous, but as a reason for cautious optimism. American author-

The U.S. Army established control points along the Alaska Highway in 1942. Local traffic was monitored, and civilian traffic through to Alaska was forbidden until after the war. *U.S. Army Corps of Engineeers photo*

ities saw Foster's appointment as an effort to improve and simplify the Canadian-American liaison in the Northwest, centralizing Canadian authority in the area. According to the official American army historian, Stanley Dziuban, U.S. officials found Foster agreeable and cooperative, which suggests that he did not make a nuisance of himself, and they were pleased to have a Canadian counterpart with wide powers. The Canadian government, for its part, saw an opportunity for a show of control over American activities and protection of Canadian sovereignty. There were still occasions for Canadian concern after 1943, but the Cabinet War Committee had a representative in the field. American indiscretions were now dealt with through diplomatic channels.[5]

The highway and pipeline were the largest wartime projects in the Canadian North, but other activities also ushered in new modes of communication and transportation and reshaped social relations. Allied planners, with few offensive options in 1942 and overoptimistic faith in strategic bombing, believed that American aircraft production was the key to victory in Europe. With U-boat wolf packs prowling Atlantic shipping routes, the safest way to get airplanes to Britain was to fly them over an air bridge across northeastern North America. The hub of the Crimson Route, as this chain of air bases was called, was Frobisher Bay (now Iqaluit) on Baffin Island. Major airfields were also built at Southampton Island, Churchill, and The Pas.[6] By 1943, Goose Bay, Labrador (then part of the separate colony of Newfoundland), boasted the largest airfield in the western hemisphere. As the region's first large-scale development project, the military base changed life in Labrador. Radio sites were also established throughout the Canadian North, greatly facilitating communications over vast distances. Defence activities thus drew the Arctic increasingly into the southern web and highlighted the region's potential value to friend and foe.

Despite the amazingly passive attitude of the Canadian government, wartime developments actually strengthened Canadian sovereignty claims to its North by the end of the war. Physical development had occurred, the ownership of permanent facilities passed into Canadian hands once the war was over, and negotiations with the United States yielded various provisions indicating that Canada needed to be consulted and agreements reached before activities could be undertaken on or over its territory. Canada's *de jure* sovereignty had been asserted. While *de facto* sovereignty had been unclear at times, the withdrawal of American troops at war's end alleviated some of these concerns.

The war had revealed several fundamental aspects of Canada's security position vis-à-vis the United States. Given Canada's overseas commitments, it needed to be responsive to American concerns about continental defence, especially once the Cold War began. Northern development projects had been completed on a scale that Canadians could not have achieved alone, and fortunately, dismal failures like the Canol project wasted only American money. The Yukon had been given a boost in population and facilities that it never completely lost, and it continued to grow after the war. Most importantly, American compromises during the war demonstrated that the United States had no desire to mount a legal challenge to Canadian sovereignty. Why should they, when Canada gave them anything they wanted just for the asking? Why buy a cow, as the old country saying goes, when you could get milk through the fence?

There remained, however, a feeling that United States military commanders in Canada had been rather insensitive to the niceties of Canadian sovereignty and in a few cases had come close to regarding Canada as occupied territory. R.J. Sutherland later reflected, "Whatever the justification for this feeling—and it is true that the number of incidents was not very large—it has had a significant bearing upon Canadian policy and attitudes."[7] In reply, the Americans would probably have said that the middle of a colossal war was no time to worry about "niceties."

In 1945, the Cabinet War Committee decided that Canada would take full responsibility for defence measures on Canadian soil—a pledge easier voiced than implemented, given the shadow of the Soviet Union looming just over the northern horizon.

The Cold War

Before the war had ended, Canadian and American military planners began to think about possible Soviet-American conflict in the postwar world. When in September 1945 a cipher clerk in the USSR embassy in Ottawa named Igor Gouzenko defected, exposing Stalin's efforts to steal nuclear and other secrets from his allies, it was clear that the wartime friendship, never very warm, would not long survive the peace. Polar projection maps were hauled out, forcing Canada to rethink its strategic situation. "The war and the aeroplane have driven home to Canadians the importance of their Northland, in strategy, in resources and in communications," Lester Pearson (soon to be minister of external affairs) wrote in 1946. "We should no longer be deceived by flat maps and 'frigid wasteland' tales of our public school geographies. The earth remains round, and the shortest routes between many important spots on it lie across the Arctic ice and over the North Pole."[8]

Geography meant that Canada was now sandwiched between two increasingly hostile superpowers. History, ideology, and geography placed Canada in the American camp, and decision-makers in Ottawa had to take American views into account, even if they thought their fears of Russian intentions and capabilities were exaggerated. American security was inextricably linked to Canada's, and diplomats and military officials from both countries got together regularly to discuss continental defence. "The proximity of the northern land masses and the increasing range of aircraft are two factors which lead to the inevitable conclusion that the defense of North America must now be treated as one problem and not as the separate concern of either Canada or the U.S.," Major-General H.F.G. Letson, the Canadian army member on the Permanent Joint Board on Defence, noted in December 1945. "Canada is interposed between the U.S. and the polar sea and is therefore the buffer state for any attack which might come across the polar cap."[9]

The concept of "defence against help" is key to understanding Canadian defence decisions during the Cold War, particularly in terms of continental defence. This theory sees Canada as having a security dilemma based on the idea that the United States, in the process of guaranteeing Canada's safety, may itself become a threat to Canadian sovereignty. If Canada, constituting as it does the northern approaches to the United States, would not or could not defend itself from its enemies (or from the Americans' enemies), then the U.S. would be forced to help out in whatever way it believed necessary to ensure its own safety. If Canada was unable or unwilling to defend its territory, then the Americans would be compelled to take whatever measures they felt were needed, regardless of Canadian preferences. So Canada needed to defend against the Soviet Union, as well as its American ally.

If Canada allowed the U.S. to mount that "long polar watch" by itself, historian David Bercuson observed, "Would this not be an admission that whatever sovereignty Canada claimed in the polar regions was weak at best and nonexistent at worst?"[10] Canadian officials recognized this dilemma and stressed that the country could not retreat to an isolationist posture after the Second World War. Joint planning with the United States for peacetime defence was the only feasible way to grapple with the core dilemma: how could Canada help protect the continent against the Soviet Union, something it could not do alone, while, at the same time protect the Canadian North against the United States?[11]

Whatever the answer, it could not be allowed to consume significant government resources. The promised "peace dividend" to Canadians was the new welfare state, not military expenditures in remote parts of the country. Although some lessons had been learned during the war, Ottawa did not plan to spend much money on northern sovereignty and security. "Neither the United States nor Canada looked on the North as a *place* to be protected because of some intrinsic value," military historian Kenneth Eyre has suggested. "It was seen as a *direction*, an exposed flank."¹² If Canadian soldiers were needed to respond to potential diversionary attacks in the Arctic wastelands, Mackenzie King concluded that these did "not warrant the establishment of an elaborate defence scheme employing our resources in a static role." A small number of airborne forces, based in southern Canada,

The Mobile Striking Force, an airportable and airborne brigade group designed as a quick reaction force for northern operations, was an inexpensive solution to the question of how Canada could deal with an enemy in the Arctic. *DND photo PC-7066*

were more politically saleable—meaning cheaper—than permanent garrisons stationed in the Arctic. Thus the Mobile Striking Force (MSF) concept took shape. In theory, aircraft could fly specially trained paratroops into the Arctic, drop them in to counter any enemy presence on Canadian soil, and sustain themselves in the field. Assisted by the Canadian Rangers—untrained, northern volunteers given only a rifle and an armband—these forces would be Canada's front-line northern defenders.

The Americans' emphasis on developmental sovereignty contrasted with the Canadians' symbolic sovereignty. If the Canadian military built major installations in the North, particularly airfields, it would have to think about local defences. In the Canadian government's view, the simplest solution to the North was not to rush to build infrastructure that an enemy might use. As one senior officer remarked, Canada's northern regions offered, "from a military point of view, nowhere to go, and nothing to do when you get there." Lester Pearson, in a cheeky turn of phrase in the influential American magazine *Foreign Affairs*, called this the "scorched ice" approach.[13] If you left the Arctic alone, as a deserted wasteland of ice and snow, it would be useless to an enemy, which would have to fight the natural elements simply to survive, never mind mount an attack. This mentality certainly fit with the Liberal government's desire to keep defence spending and commitments to a minimum. At its core, government policy was to spend public money where the votes were, and there were not many of these north of the Arctic Circle.

Given the paltry Canadian resources devoted to continental defence, American decision-makers worried about the "gap between Alaska and Greenland," as U.S. Secretary of State Dean Acheson described Canada to President Harry Truman.[14] Almost immediately after the U.S. military left northern Canada at the end of the war, it asked to return to build airfields and meteorological stations. A leaked 1947 U.S. Air Coordinating Committee report, suggesting that the Americans should conduct reconnaissance flights to look for undiscovered islands that could be claimed as sites for weather stations, fuelled official Canadian fears of unilateral American action. Although much has been made of this memorandum, which hardly constituted general U.S. policy, a broader survey of the documentary record reveals that American officials recognized Canadian insecurities about sovereignty in the North[15] and actually made the solution to Canada's dilemma less difficult than it might have been. The State Department knew that it had to respect and attempt to soothe Canadian sensitivities. Although it occasionally acted too informally for Canadian tastes, it did not try to bully the Canadians when they were uncomfortable.[16] American military officials wanted bases in the North if these could be reasonably obtained through negotiation, but there was never any serious threat of moving unilaterally. Indiscretions by lower-level American officials (usually military) were always met by loud Canadian protests, and high-level decision-makers respected Canadian sovereignty concerns. After all, American members on the Permanent Joint Board of Defence wanted to ensure U.S. military access to specific Canadian sites, but they were committed to "'signing Canada on' as a faithful postwar ally" more generally.[17]

What Canada needed was a guarantee that the Americans would not defend the Arctic themselves and leave Canada out of the picture. But given the Liberal government's postwar focus on cutting defence expenditures, Canada could not afford to secure its northern front alone. It was not a choice between security or sovereignty: the solution had to offer both. When senior American and Canadian decision-makers met, United States representatives were much more open and flexible than the prime minister had anticipated. The idea of U.S. fighter bases in the Far North was dropped, and the emphasis shifted to mapping and meteorology. The proposed projects were of the sort that the prime minister could sell to the public for civil purposes. Mackenzie King gloated that "the Americans had come around to his own way of thinking," and the United States was pleased to have Canada "sign on" to the general principle of joint defence co-operation, especially in the North.[18] In fact, the "safeguarding principles" on sovereignty desired by the Canadians were deemed "immaterial from the standpoint of United States interests."[19] There was no secret American plot, and the general principles of U.S.–Canadian defence co-operation acknowledged Canada's sovereignty. No mention was made of the sector principle on which Canada had staked its northern sovereignty and to which the Americans remained noncommittal; the wording of the recommendation avoided contentious language. Instead, the Joint Arctic Weather Station (JAWS) agreement announced in March 1947 was a compromise that satisfied both parties. Liberal "minister of everything" C.D. Howe announced that nine Arctic weather stations would be built over the next three years, and the co-operative undertaking would be done on Canadian terms. "Thus ended," legal scholar Nigel Bankes noted, "what was the last potential legal threat to Canadian sovereignty over its Arctic *lands*."[20] But not, unfortunately, over Arctic waters.

Air defences and radar

So long as the Cold War was more bluster than bang, the pressure to invest considerable military resources in Arctic defences remained light. Once the Soviets detonated an atomic device in 1949 and war broke out in Korea in 1950, however, the perceived need to heighten continental defences became more acute. NSC–68, the American strategy report that served as "the blueprint for the Cold War," declared that the Soviet Union wanted "to impose its absolute authority over the rest of the world." Defence analysts noted that the Soviets were approaching technological parity in bombers and atomic weapons, and the most direct route for those bombers to the military and industrial heartland of North America was over the Arctic. R.J. Sutherland explained that strategists now grappled with the best means to achieve advanced warning of a strategic air attack. "By extending the air defence system northwards such bombers could be engaged before reaching their intended targets," he explained. "Almost equally important, by extending the area of radar coverage the risk of saturation of the defences could be reduced. Finally, by locating strike aircraft or refuelling aircraft on the northern bases, the range and speed of response of the strike forces could be improved."[21] In short, the North American allies sought defence in depth. By extending their military outposts to the farthest reaches of the continent, they might gain four to six hours' notice before Armageddon—enough time to get their own strategic bombers in the air and respond in kind.

As early as 1946, Canadian and American authorities began to consider the possibility of building a radar chain in the Arctic to give warning of any Soviet attack. At that time, the available technology could not guarantee complete coverage of the northern frontier or accurate tracking of aircraft, so investing huge sums in an ineffective early-warning system was ill advised. Conditions changed by 1949, however, and convinced the Canadian government that it should construct a radar line along the U.S. border. The United States decided to build a similar early-warning chain on its northern border that same year. Joint discussion led to a co-operative effort, the Pinetree Line, consisting of thirty-three radar stations across the mid-north from Vancouver Island to Labrador. This radar network was completed in 1954. By that time, the Soviets had upgraded their bomber force, prompting more ambitious plans to increase North American radar coverage by building stations farther and farther north. Longstanding Canadian minister of national defence Brooke Claxton had discussed the construction of an Arctic chain with the Eisenhower administration in early 1953, but no firm decisions were made. When the Soviets exploded their first hydrogen bomb that August, the question became more urgent.

As the spectre of Soviet long-range bombers delivering hydrogen bombs became more real, the Americans turned to a new defence strategy. In October 1953, U.S. president Dwight Eisenhower unveiled his "New Look" strategy based on "massive atomic capability, including necessary bases; an integrated and effective continental defence system; ready forces of the United States and its allies suitably deployed . . . and an adequate mobilization base." Continental defences would be critical to deter communist aggression. "We and our allies have and will maintain a massive capability to strike back," President Eisenhower proclaimed in his January 1954 State of the Union address.[22] "Massive retaliation" would depend upon adequate warning times so that the Americans could mobilize their strategic forces. Although building a complete radar "fence" around North America was out of the question, multiple radar lines extending northward—the only likely direction of an air attack—could provide adequate warning. The Liberal government in Ottawa was a willing partner. In June 1954, defence research scientists recommended the construction of a mostly unmanned Mid-Canada Line, along the 55th parallel, paid for entirely by Canada. This project was attractive for several reasons. First, the technology was available in Canada, and had been developed by Canadian scientists (hence its nickname, "the McGill Fence"). Second, building radar stations in the middle North would be less expensive than building an Arctic chain. Canada could afford to build and support a sub-Arctic network. Third, a Canadian project averted the troublesome issue of American presence on Canadian soil—sovereignty would not be an issue. Ninety-eight Mid-Canada stations were built by 1957 at a total cost of $250 million.[23]

The U.S. Air Force, however, insisted on more lead time to mobilize their deterrent than the Pinetree and Mid-Canada Lines could offer. It contracted American scientists to engineer a bolder solution that would use the vast, distant Arctic to provide maximum advance warning of an attack. The only contact that most of the scientists had with the actual North was maps and survey data, but this was enough for them to design radar systems to monitor the northern approaches. These "wizards of Armageddon" proposed a comprehensive long radar chain across the 17th parallel, and in June 1954 the Canada–U.S. Military Studies Group urged that a radar network be built stretching more than 8,000 kilometres (1,969 miles) from Alaska to Baffin Island (and eventually to Greenland). Under pressure from its American allies and the Royal Canadian Air Force, the Canadian government consented to these plans. The government felt that it was already stretched thin honouring its NATO commitments in Europe and could not afford the kind of defence installations required to satisfy its superpower ally. The Americans would have to pay for and build the Arctic radar network, even if three-quarters of it was in Canada.

In November 1954, Canada and the U.S. reached a formal agreement to build the Distant Early Warning (DEW) Line. In its press releases, Ottawa insisted that this radar network was part of the comprehensive continental defence system, not a stand-alone project, along with NATO, collective security, and the United Nations. Furthermore, Lester Pearson explained, military megaprojects were most effectively completed by placing responsibility with a single party: Canada would thus build the Mid-Canada Line, and the U.S. the DEW Line.[24]

Canadian negotiators reached an advantageous agreement with the Americans: the United States would bear the full cost of construction, but American firms would have to subcontract to Canadian companies and hire local indigenous labour to help with construction; Canada retained ownership of the sites located in Canada; and the major stations were to be commanded by Canadians. This was a major coup for Canadian sovereignty: the Americans officially acknowledged that all of the islands in the Far North explicitly belonged to Canada. "As a result of the DEW Line Agreements," R.J. Sutherland explained, "Canada secured what the United States had up to that time assiduously endeavoured to avoid, namely, an explicit recognition of Canadian claims to the exercise of sovereignty in the Far North."[25]

Although nationalist critics have often claimed that the DEW Line was a shameful example of how Canada's sovereignty in the North was undermined by American strategic priorities during the Cold War, the truth is quite different. In an article published just after the first press tour of the line, *Baltimore Sun* reporter Mark Watson painted a picture of a project that was co-operative, not dominated by Americans:

> It was obvious that the cost would be great (wild guesses went up to $2,000,000,000 and even higher) and that Canada, with one tenth of the population of the United States, could not pay as much in cash, however proud the Canadians were of paying their own way. . . . But there was more than cost to consider. Sovereignty was involved. That is why Canada, properly jealous of her own control of everything within her own borders, had properly insisted on building wholly from her own resources the Mid-Canada Line. . . . In the case of DEW Line

Canada was reluctant to yield, even to an ally, any aspect of her own sovereignty.

In the agreement, these old-time partners in joint defense recognized both sovereignty and budgetary facts. The United States would pay all the cost of DEW Line. . . Canada would make large contributions of items in which she was rich, in co-operation, reconnaissance, many supplies, policing, transportation by land, sea and air to a large degree, maritime support, and in personnel with a large and intimate knowledge of the difficulties to be encountered in the wild Northwest Territories over whose largely unexplored northern fringe most of the new line would run.

In an effort to make clear that this is Canada's soil, with all that is implied, the United States agreed that if in the future Canada desires to take over the whole set of installations, Canada can do so. Here is a dramatic working-out of one of the world's most enduring examples of international reliance, that shines like a good deed in an increasingly naughty world.

The agreement did everything possible to safeguard Canadian interests, but in the remote reaches of the Canadian Arctic "there could be no assurance that the fine print would be scrupulously observed."[26]

The 22-station DEW Line was completed in 1957, its creation an extraordinary feat of geographical engineering that altered the military, logistical, and demographic characteristics of the territorial North. Yet concerns about sovereignty continued to be voiced in the press. The U.S. acknowledged that Canada had legal owner-ship to the Arctic islands, but did we have any practical control over the North? Canadian reporters and politicians on the Opposition benches painted a disturbing portrait. "Stories of the impairment of sovereignty, sometimes true, sometimes partly true, sometimes wholly false, but always disturbing, began to trickle down from the north country into Parliament and the press," political scientist James Eayrs recounted. "Tales were told of American discrim-

ination against Canadian contractors; of violation of Canadian customs and immigration procedures
by American snow trains and aircraft bringing in men and equipment; of American flags flying
where Canadian flags (whatever
they might be) ought to have flown;
of American security regulations
forbidding Canadian journalists
and, occasionally, Canadian officials from visiting DEW Line stations." The "whatever they might
be" recalls that, at the time, there
was no official Canadian flag, so the
Americans can hardly be blamed
for not knowing what to fly. For all
the protections that the 1955 agreement offered on paper, and despite

The DEW Line raised concerns
about American encroachments on
Canadian sovereignty. Suggestions
that Canada would become "the
northernmost banana republic"
never came to pass, thanks to persistent Canadian vigilance to ensure
that its interests were protected.
DND image PCN-1656

satisfactory explanations or responses to each alleged American
transgression, concerns about American influence lingered, especially among people who were naturally inclined to suspect and dislike the United States.[27]

For example, Ralph Allen, the editor of *Maclean's* magazine,
wrote an article that asked the core question "Will the DEW line
Cost Canada Its Northland?" "It is the charter under which a
tenth of Canada may very well become the world's most northerly
banana republic," Allen asserted. "For a sum of money that has been
officially estimated at four hundred million dollars we have at least
temporarily traded off our whole northern frontier. In law we still
own this northern frontier. In fact we do not." In his view, we did
not simply allow our American allies to take control, but insisted
that they do so. This was not a passive loss of sovereignty, but the
Canadian government's decision to "thrust it on a friend who did not
really want it but who, having been forced to take it, must inevitably

use it in ways that will impair our friendship." For roughly the amount of tobacco taxes that Canadians would pay between 1954 and 1957, the country "handed the expense and operation of this radar network—perhaps obsolete already—to the United States," Allen lamented. In so doing, Canada also handed over part of its national independence.[28]

The U.S. did foot the bill, flew its flag at DEW Line sites, and exercised the right to turn away Canadian visitors without security authorization. Journalists and members of the Opposition in Parliament used these issues to generate controversy. For the most part, this was muckraking—searching for sensational stories to prey upon anti-American sentiments and discredit the government. Much of this was mere posturing. Of course journalists and members of Parliament couldn't wander about DEW Line facilities without permission, any more than they could wander about Canadian military bases elsewhere in Canada. When federal officials took their concerns to Washington, they reached mutually satisfactory solutions that showed the Americans were respectful of Canada's insecurities about sovereignty. "Nothing exists which one could call United States control in the north," minister Jean Lesage explained in the House of Commons on August 3, 1956. "It is Canadian control. Our northern service officers are constantly touring the line. The R.C.M.P. are . . . looking after order, peace and good behaviour on the part of everyone concerned. It is clear that Canadian law is applied and enforced, and that the control is in the hands of Canadians."[29] Partisan dialogue inflamed alleged irritants far beyond their actual severity. *Maclean's* journalist Blair Fraser admitted that journalists' allegations of American attacks on Canadian sovereignty had been overblown. "This has tended, in Washington, to magnify Canada's reputation for being a hypochondriacal fuss-bucket, a reputation not yet widespread, but growing enough to worry some Canadian officials who would rather see Canada hold her fire for things of more importance."[30] Canada's hypersensitivity over sovereignty in this context was largely a product of a long history of inaction and underdevelopment. It should not be misread as *caused* by American perfidy.

Like the journalists who harped on Canada's claims as though this would reinforce them, many historians have cited the DEW Line as an example of the Canadian government sacrificing sovereignty in the name of American security. This requires a selective and unbalanced reading of the historical record. The DEW Line contributed more to Canadian sovereignty in the North than it took away from it. It was run in the spirit of partnership, allowed Canada to "defend against help" (particularly after the Royal Canadian Air Force took over the management of Canadian sections of the line in 1959), and did not drive Canada into bankruptcy. Indeed, the employment of both Inuit and southern Canadian men, who represented 97 percent of the personnel along the Canadian section of the line by 1963, entrenched Canada's claims to "effective occupation" of its Arctic.[31]

In terms of its actual military usefulness, however, the DEW Line was questionable. It was designed to detect the approach of long-range Soviet bombers flying over the Pole, but critics suggested that its radar and communications could be jammed. The counter-argument would be that jamming would have sent a strong signal that the Soviets were up to something. In theory, Soviet aircraft could swing wide and come into North America from the Atlantic or Pacific. Given the range of Soviet aircraft in the 1950s, this was unlikely, particularly when "Texas Towers" (offshore radar towers) extended the range of the DEW Line. All told, the radar network did its job in helping the Canadians and Americans— united in the North American Air Defence Command (NORAD) after 1957—to meet the manned, long-range bomber threat.

By the time the DEW Line became operational, new threats emerged that proved more unnerving than bombers and drew strategic attention away from the Canadian North. In 1957, the Soviets placed *Sputnik*, the first artificial satellite, in orbit. This was a major technological breakthrough, raising fears that the Russians were winning the space race. If they could launch a satellite into outer space, they could also launch intercontinental ballistic missiles (ICBMs): nuclear-tipped missiles that could cross entire continents

Prime Minister John G. Diefenbaker speaks at the official opening of the town of Inuvik, 21 July 1961. Distracted by other divisive issues, Diefenbaker failed to deliver on his Arctic research, transportation, and resource development program. *LAC image PA-166413*

much faster than planes, thus overwhelming the existing air defence network. The bomber threat remained, but the superpower fight for technological supremacy had moved to the next round. In due course, NORAD implemented the Ballistic Missile Early Warning System (BMEWS) to work in conjunction with American satellites to detect a potential Soviet missile attack. Canada's geography was not needed for this system, which was stationed in Alaska and Greenland. As NORAD moved away from static radar lines, preferring to invest in more versatile satellites, the Mid-Canada Line was phased out of service in 1965, and most DEW Line and Pinetree stations closed. The DEW Line would maintain its lonely vigil for several more decades, just in case the Soviets launched a bomber attack, but the priorities of the U.S. and Canada had shifted elsewhere.

By the 1960s, the politics of defence in Canada were increasingly divisive. John Diefenbaker campaigned in 1957 partly on his "northern vision," but this was based on exploiting the natural resources of the region rather than on military preparedness. His tenure as prime minister, from 1957 to 1963, was marked by clashes with the Canadian military and with the Americans, with public debates over the cancellation of the Avro Arrow, the decision to acquire BOMARC and Honest John missiles instead, and the requirement to arm these weapons with nuclear warheads. The government's blundering during the Cuban Missile Crisis of 1962 led to a Cabinet crisis, and its failure to convince the Americans that it would fulfill its defence commitments promoted the outgoing NATO commander to tell a news conference that Canada was reneging on its alliance obligations. When the U.S. State Department called Diefenbaker a liar, and the American ambassador in Ottawa derided the Conservative government publicly, his government fell. In the ensuing 1963 election, Dief's vitriolic anti-American campaign held the Liberals to a minority government. There were still elements of "defence against help" in Canadian strategic thinking, and concerns about the sovereignty implications of being partner to the American behemoth, but these no longer included the threat of American soldiers and airmen occupying Canadian tundra against our will.

As continental defence priorities shifted to missiles and outer space, Canada's concerns over the American sovereignty threat to the Arctic diminished. Strategist Colin Gray observed that by the mid-1960s there was "no military incentive to urge the Canadian Forces to be active in the North."[32] The navy's northern cruises in the summer ceased, surveillance flights were scaled back, army exercises were cancelled, radio and highway systems managed by the military were turned over to civil departments, and the Canadian Rangers were virtually abandoned.[33] If the Americans did not have any pressing security needs that might cause them to act alone and jeopardize Canada's sovereignty, military activities seemed irrelevant. "The sovereignty of a great majority of modern states is in fact protected, not by their military power, but by international law and a somewhat more nebulous but important factor referred to as 'world public opinion,'" a defence paper on the role of the armed forces in maintaining Canadian sovereignty noted in 1968.[34] Nevertheless, the Canadian Forces would soon be called upon to help the federal government react to a new sovereignty threat, one posed by the commercial interests of our closest friend and ally.

The driving force behind Canada's approach to the Cold War Arctic was the need to "defend against help." As long as the Americans perceived the Arctic as a strategically significant approach to the North American continent, these security concerns placed Canada in an awkward situation. If it opposed American plans, its southern ally might take unilateral action to defend its own interests, thus undermining Canadian sovereignty. If Canada went along with plans that it could not conceivably carry out itself, however, it would still have to turn to the Americans for "help" that, in practical terms, might diminish its *de facto* sovereignty. Partnership, however, offered the Canadians a say in decision-making, solidified its alliances with the Americans, and could guarantee both security *and* sovereignty. It could not be an either/or equation. Cold War decision-makers knew that solutions had to offer both.

Canadians are ultrasensitive when American plans or actions seem to hurt their feelings or threaten their interests. This was equally true of the North, where Canada's passive approach of symbolic sovereignty ran up against American developmental sovereignty in wartime (both hot and cold). Canadian officials had some valid concerns, particularly about *de facto* sovereignty in remote regions. A balanced reading of the evidence, however, makes it difficult to fault the Americans unless one assumes, as all too many Canadians do, that every American foreign policy is malevolent. Certainly the Americans acted in their own interests in the Canadian North, often in what they saw as a power vacuum, and sometimes behaved as if the North was theirs to exploit. Given the lack of Canadian military presence, however, coupled with new continental security concerns, the American military could hardly be faulted for perceiving itself as discoverers of a new land. When Canadian government officials realized that they were acting in a "fit of absence of mind" and pressed their American allies to respect the Dominion's sovereignty, the U.S. observed the proper diplomatic niceties. Negotiated solutions allowed the two nations to reach mutually satisfactory outcomes to most problems they encountered. After all, the Americans did not wish to assert formal sovereignty over Canada's North, in this or in any period since the War of 1812. To suggest otherwise is to misread and misrepresent the evidence. The Americans had specific interests in the North as a strategic frontier that demanded attention, and Canada found ways to meet American needs and avoided spending itself into oblivion on defence projects, all the while quietly reinforcing its legal claims to its northern territories.

Although Canada's terrestrial sovereignty claims were not in dispute, the perplexing matter of the Northwest Passage remained outstanding. "Since World War II Canada has, for all practical purposes, acquired another ocean," political scientist Thomas Tynan observed in 1979. "Before that time the Arctic Ocean was impassable and unchallengeable. Now it is a major pathway for the exchange of hostilities between the two great superpowers, Russia and the United States, and Canada is caught in between. Moreover, the fragile environment of this region opens up the possibility that commercial pollution could cause it irreparable damage." As the next chapter reveals, the greatest challenges to Canadian sovereignty over the last fifty years have come from the Americans: the voyages of an oil tanker, the *Manhattan*, in 1969–70, and then the *Polar Sea* icebreaker in 1985. Canada's response has been to extend our jurisdiction over "our" Arctic waters, ahead of international law, and challenge American views of the passage as an international strait.[35] Peculiarly, throughout the Cold War, the military remained the instrument of choice to show Canada's commitment to defending its North, even when the "enemy" was not a hostile superpower but its southern neighbour and closest ally.

Chapter Three

INTERNAL WATERS
OR INTERNATIONAL STRAIT?

THE NORTHWEST PASSAGE
AND THE COLD WAR

*"Any American threat to this region . . . would be seen as
an assault upon Canada's very own heritage and identity."*
– THOMAS M. TYNAN, political scientist, 1979

By the end of the 1960s, sovereignty concerns had shifted from the
Arctic Archipelago—the offshore islands themselves—to the water
(ice) passage between the islands. No one questioned Canada's
sovereignty over the lands and islands. The status of the waters
between Canada's Arctic islands, however, remained contentious.
This should come as no surprise. Most land belongs to one state or
another, and is thus subject to its laws. Land conflicts are thus about
which particular state owns a particular territory. When it comes to
water bodies, however, the first step is to determine whether a particular region falls under the control of a particular state or whether
it belongs to everyone. In the case of the Northwest Passage—or
Passages, because there are seven routes from the Chukchi Sea to
the Atlantic Ocean through Canada's Arctic islands—no states challenge Canadian ownership of the waters. The question is whether
a strait runs through Canadian waters, in which case Canada has
limits on how much it can control access to the Passage. The doctrine of the "freedom of the seas" holds that state jurisdiction ends

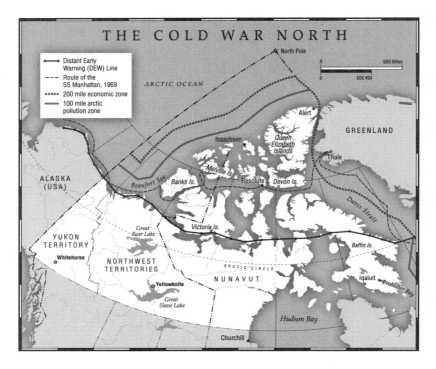

THE COLD WAR NORTH

Distant Early
Warning (DEW) Line
Route of the
SS Manhattan, 1969
200 mile economic zone
100 mile arctic
pollution zone

North Pole

500 Miles
500 KM

ARCTIC OCEAN

Alert

GREENLAND

Isaachsen

Queen
Elizabeth
Islands

Thule

Melville Is.

Banks Is.

Resolute

Devon Is.

ALASKA
(USA)

Beaufort Sea

Davis Strait

YUKON
TERRITORY

Great
Bear Lake

Victoria Is.

Whitehorse

NORTHWEST
TERRITORIES

ARCTIC CIRCLE

NUNAVUT

Baffin Is.

Yellowknife

Iqaluit

Frobisher Bay

Great
Slave Lake

Hudson Bay

Churchill

at the coast, and the high seas are open to everyone. Thus the rules governing the seas must be made by the international community under international law. Canada has always considered the Northwest Passage to be internal waters. Others view it as an international strait stretching 2,850 nautical miles (3,280 miles, or 5,280 kilometres) from Greenland's Cape Farewell to the Bering Strait in Alaska: 1,932 kilometres (1,200 miles) in the Canadian Arctic, 1,208 kilometres (750 miles) of Alaskan waters, and 1,449 kilometres (900 miles) of sea shared by Canada, Greenland and Denmark.[1]

The status of the Northwest Passage is a bone of contention between Canada and the United States. Canada maintains that the Northwest Passage is internal and thus subject to full Canadian "sovereignty," with no right of transit passage to any foreign ship. Canada welcomes domestic and foreign shipping in its waters, but retains the legal right to control entry to and the activities conducted in its internal waters as if these were land territory. The United States insists that the Passage is an international strait with the right of transit passage. The Americans are inflexible on this issue. They see it as a potential commercial route between the Atlantic and the Pacific, and insist that commercial and their naval vessels need full access to it. There is more at stake for the Americans than Arctic waters, however, for if they accept the Canadian position, a precedent may be set for more strategically valuable straits in other parts of the world. For its part, Canada has refused to budge on the issue. Challenges to Canada's sovereignty over Arctic waters have led Canadian governments to assert national rights, not by ringing claims over control of the Passage, but statements about the need to protect the delicate Arctic environment, the Inuit inhabitants of the North, and Canada's icy inheritance.[2] The federal government, hoping to demonstrate its commitment to defending Canadian sovereignty, ordered the Canadian Forces to "show the flag" and make a demonstration of Canada's presence in the North. This was ironic, given that our closest military and economic ally was also our main opponent in the matter. Of course, and to no one's surprise, the rhetoric about sovereignty and the military's role was mostly bloviating, for the government was not willing to spend money on the equipment or personnel needed to turn hot air into reality, so when the American ships went home and the mini-crises faded, the speeches stopped. One thing had changed, however: sovereignty, though still largely symbolic, was now vested in the Canadian Forces and the Canadian Coast Guard who now replaced the RCMP as uniformed symbols of southern Canada's willingness to safeguard its North from foes—and friends.

Canadian Confusion about Its Arctic Waters

Several commentators have noted how well defined Canada's archipelago is geographically. "The Arctic Archipelago is really a prolongation of the main mass of [the] Canadian mainland North of the

Hudson Bay in the direction of the North Pole, and the whole Archipelago is a clear unity with the continental mass," a British diplomatic document stated in 1958. Rather than far-flung, scattered islands, Canada's archipelago was more of "an island fringe off a mainland coast" far removed from the main commercial shipping routes or lanes. Its symmetrical, unitary appearance—"practically a solid land mass intersected by a number of relatively narrow channels of water"—distinguished it from other archipelagos around the world. (Neither Indonesia nor the Philippines are natural extensions of a continent, and the former is a long chain while the latter is a scattered group of islands. Both are on important shipping routes.[3]) Canadian External Affairs legal expert G. Sicotte wrote that the properties of Canada's Arctic waters made them even more unique. They were not open to navigation without extensive Canadian assistance, and because of their ice cover resembled land more than the open seas that covered much of the globe:

> A further consideration is that for most of the year the waters within the archipelago are completely frozen and form an integral part of the land areas. The sea ice is lived on and moved over in precisely the same fashion as the land masses. In fact, the sea ice is used to a greater extent for surface transportation and for hunting by the local inhabitants. For practical purposes the waters within the archipelago are, therefore, completely indistinguishable from the land during most of the year.

The Arctic Archipelago was not just physically and geographically united with the mainland. It was also closely tied to it economically. "The local inhabitants depend almost entirely on the resources of these waters for their livelihood,"[4] Sicotte noted. But as late as the 1950s senior Canadian officials admitted that Canada had not clearly formulated its position with regard to sovereignty over the waters of the Arctic basin and the channels between its Arctic islands, both from "narrow national" and international points of view.[5] This clarification would take decades to realize.

While Canadian nationalists are always quick to react to perceived threats to sovereignty, the nature and extent of Canada's claims have always been ambiguous. The sector theory introduced in the early twentieth century—which theoretically extended Canadian control over all the lands and waters in a pie-shaped wedge—never became official policy. The voyages of British explorers formed the original basis for Canada's claims in the Far North, and their concern was with land, not water. Bernier's 1909 declaration also referred to lands and islands.[6] Postwar military activities bolstered Canada's legal claims to the mainland and archipelago. The Arctic waters were an entirely different story.

As historian Elizabeth Elliot-Meisel has written, Canada chose to focus its postwar naval efforts on fulfilling its NATO obligations in the Atlantic—antisubmarine warfare and protecting shipping lanes—rather than "showing the flag" in the Arctic. As a result, Canada's early plans to control resupply of the Arctic weather stations were frustrated by a lack of resources.[7] Instead, U.S. Navy and Coast Guard icebreakers, sometimes with Canadian observers aboard, gained operational experience probing Canadian Arctic waters. The USS *Edisto* became the first ship to transit the Fury and Hecla Strait and to circumnavigate Baffin Island. The American navy and Coast Guard had free rein in the High Arctic, given the lack of Canadian maritime activity in the region, and there is no evidence that they considered this "a form of watery trespass." RCN Captain T.C. Pullen later noted that "somebody had to undertake 'icebreaker reconnaissance,' to make 'observations of geographical, navigational and aviation interest,'" and to conduct hydrographic, meteorological, and electromagnetic experiments.[8] Canada was incapable of performing these tasks, so they naturally fell to its superpower ally.

Beginning in 1948–49, Canada began to send naval vessels to the Arctic. That winter, five Royal Canadian Navy (RCN) ships undertook northern operations, and in January 1949 the navy let a contract to a Sorel, Quebec, shipyard to build a modified United States Navy Wind–class icebreaker capable of operating in the

High Arctic. This ship, christened HMCS *Labrador*, which first ventured north in 1954 and was the first naval vessel to transit the Northwest Passage, resupplied weather stations and the DEW Line and served as a platform for scientific research. By agreement, U.S. Navy and Coast Guard vessels that supplied the DEW Line applied for and received Canadian waivers under the Canada Shipping Act before they proceeded.[9] Captain Pullen, serving as the commanding officer of the *Labrador* at the time, was appointed U.S. Navy task group commander and reported to a U.S. Navy admiral during the 1957 sealift. One of his jobs was to ensure that three U.S. Coast Guard ships got safely through the Northwest Passage. "In those days, Canadians did not react as they would

HMCS *Labrador*, the first and only Royal Canadian Navy icebreaker, provided icebreaking and operational support for the task groups supplying the DEW Line during its construction. *Image courtesy of Canada Post Corporation*

now to foreign encroachment in their Arctic waters," he reminisced thirty years later; "but they had no cause. Great care was taken by the United States to respect Canadian interests. The joint security interest in the DEW line provided a shared incentive to devise arrangements that would avoid injury to either national position."[10] Indeed, journalists heralded Canada's supply efforts as a "big gain for sovereignty" in that it "immeasurably strengthens our claim to the waters between the islands."[11]

What were Canada's claims? Senior government officials in Ottawa scrambled to find out. In the mid-1950s, the government requested copies of the original British title documents to the Arctic islands and began to study its rights to the waters in the archipelago.[12] Before Canada formulated an official position, it had to ponder national goals and the international implications of claiming the waters and ice, as well as the underlying seabed and airspace above.

"In addition to any advantages," Gordon Robertson, the chairman of the Advisory Committee on Northern Development, explained, "sovereignty would imply certain obligations including the provision of such services as aids to sea and air navigation, the provision of any necessary local administration, and the enforcement of law"—in other words, the expenditure of public money. In response, the Soviet Union might either reject the claim or use it as a pretext to assert sovereignty over an even larger sector north of its mainland, and other countries would likely refuse to recognize a Canadian claim.[13] Indeed, reporters recognized that "the Russians would like nothing better than to stir up a row between Uncle Sam and Canada over who owns the Arctic ice and sea on our side of the North Pole."[14] "It is almost a certainty that the United States would not concede such a claim and that the world at large would not acquiesce in it," a legal appraisal at External Affairs explained. "It would therefore seem preferable not to raise the problem now and to implicitly reserve our position in granting permission for the U.S. to carry out work in Canadian territorial waters." It made more sense for Canada to reach agreements with the U.S. on "the unstated assumption that 'territorial waters' in that area means whatever we may consider to be Canadian territorial waters, whereas the U.S. does likewise. These two views may not coincide but this need give rise to no difficulty until something happens which might involve Canada asserting jurisdiction over an area which the U.S. considers to be high seas. Then, and only then, would it be necessary for Canada to state its claim or by implication from silence, relinquish it or seriously weaken it."[15]

The election of John Diefenbaker's Conservatives to a minority government in 1957 and a majority in 1958 suggested that the federal government would pay more attention to prioritize the territorial and provincial Norths. Although much of Diefenbaker's "northern vision" was foggy and was built upon the groundwork laid by his Liberal predecessors, his "roads to resources" policy led to the building of the Dempster and Mackenzie Highways, and his government continued to extend special social, educational, economic, and infrastructure programs to northern communities. Pearson, the Liberal Opposition leader, ridiculed the Conservatives for building roads "from igloo to igloo," squandering federal resources that might have been better spent elsewhere—a disgraceful and partisan sneer from an essentially decent man that one hopes he soon regretted. Nevertheless, the number of government officials in the North grew during the early 1960s, for the bur-

The *USS Skate* surfaces at the North Pole, March 17, 1959. The prospect of submarine-launched ballistic missiles reduced the importance of the DEW Line, designed to deal with the threat posed by manned bombers. *By permission of Ohio State University Libraries*

geoning social welfare state in Canada included igloo dwellers as well as everyone else, and the new schools, housing, and a cornucopia of government programs meant many new civil servants living north of the 60th parallel. At the same time, the military's relative presence diminished.[16] So too did its actual activity levels, particularly in Arctic waters. In the mid-1950s, the Royal Canadian Navy had pondered whether, to bolster Canada's claims, it should or could build nuclear-powered submarines or icebreakers.[17] Instead, it got out of the Arctic game altogether. The RCN's priorities lay with NATO antisubmarine operations, so in April 1958 it transferred the *Labrador* to the Department of Transport. Although criticized for this decision, the navy justified it on the grounds that the transfer of the *Labrador* would release 200 officers and men for duty in "fighting ships."[18] The government, focused on civilian administration and development initiatives, concurred.

"This great northland of ours is not ours because it is coloured red on a map," Alvin Hamilton, the Conservative minister of Northern Affairs, told the House of Commons on July 7, 1958. "It will only be ours by effective occupation." Nevertheless, what boundaries did Canada actually claim? And who was effectively occupying the Arctic waters? No one had a concrete answer, but the question of maritime sovereignty re-emerged when the U.S. launched icebreaker construction programs in the fifties. In 1958, the nuclear-powered submarine USS *Nautilus* crossed under the polar ice cap in its voyage from Pearl Harbor to Iceland. International law expert Maxwell Cohen wrote in *Saturday Night* magazine:

> [N]ow that the *Nautilus* has made the full undersea voyage that Jules Verne visualized for his readers and Sir Hubert Wilkins actually planned a few years ago—with much less manageable equipment—the Arctic seas have become another arena among the many that now provide military and strategic vantages in the continuing contest of East and West.
>
> For it will not be lost upon the Russians that atomic-fueled submarines can roam beneath the ice pack, not only under that portion of the pack regarded as the North American "sector" but also within the Soviet angle of "presumed" authority as well. How dangerous this may be to either side, with submarine-launched missiles such as the *Polaris* having a 1,500-mile range—and perhaps in the near future a 2,000 and 3,000–mile range—requires no great military imagination to understand. So the Arctic waters, now with Arctic air-space, are all a potential battleground while the romance of exploration and dog-team yields to the cruder demands of polarized power.[19]

The submarine USS *Seadragon* passed westward through the Northwest Passage in 1960, and the USS *Skate* transited eastward two years later. This tied back to Cold War technology. If radar systems like the DEW Line could detect bombers, then new strategic delivery systems would be deployed to change the strategic game. The Arctic Ocean, covered by a dense (and noisy) ice pack, offered protection from aerial surveillance and sonar detection. Using this logic, the U.S. Navy—or the Russians—could use the polar region to creep silently under the sheltering ice, and get close to enemy territory to launch a nuclear attack using submarine-launched ballistic missiles (SLBMs). Commander James F. Calvert of the *Skate* told public audiences that the United States could "best hold its world leadership by gaining superiority in the Arctic," and that the Arctic waters would soon become an "entirely nuclear sub-ocean." While this was not official policy, it indicated to Canadian officials that the American government would take "ever increasing interest" in the region.[20] Soon afterwards, U.S. international lawyers began arguing that the Arctic seas constituted international territory, belonging not wholly to Canada, or the Russians, or anyone else.[21]

What was Canada's stance? When in 1963 Ivan Head, a lawyer with the Department of External Affairs, surveyed the official record, he found confusion. "Few Canadian policies have been so inconsistently or unhappily interpreted over the years as that pertaining to the Arctic frontiers," he lamented. In 1946, Lester Pearson, then Canadian ambassador to the U.S., had written that Canada's northern territory included "the islands and frozen seas north of the mainland between the meridians of its east and west boundaries extended to the North Pole." Then, a decade later, Jean Lesage, the minister of northern affairs, stated that Canada's sovereignty extended to all the Arctic islands, but that "the sea, be it frozen or in its natural liquid state, is the sea; and our sovereignty exists over the lands and over our territorial waters." Did this include the Arctic waters? Prime Minister Louis St-Laurent responded a few months later that his government considered the waters between the Arctic islands to be "Canadian territorial waters." In June 1958, Alvin Hamilton clarified the position: "The area to the north of Canada, including the islands and waters between the islands and areas beyond, are looked upon as our own, and there is no doubt in the minds of this government, nor do I think in the minds of former governments of Canada, that this is national terrain." Hamilton's assertion rested on the idea of "effective occupation," which the government believed was consistent with international law.[22]

The essential issues had to do with international law. Maritime boundaries differ from territorial boundaries because they not only mark the place where one state ends and its neighbour begins, but also separate a state's jurisdiction from parts of the earth which belong to the world community at large.[23] There are three distinct types of water in international law that bear directly upon the Northwest Passage:

1. *the "high seas," the oceans of the world, are international waters over which no individual state can control the shipping of other states.* In short, the high seas belong to everyone and no state can claim them as their own. They are free to everyone.

2. *"internal waters" over which the state has full sovereignty.* There is no right to innocent passage—defined by the UN Convention on the Law of the Sea as passage that is "not prejudicial to the peace, good order or security of the coastal State"—through internal waters, which are either enclosed by land, harbours and waters surrounding coastal islands, or waters lying to the land side of baselines drawn by the state. The "mean low-water line" on the coast serves as the normal "baseline" to determine the outer limit of internal waters, measured out from this baseline. Of course, few coastlines are straight. So states have also drawn "straight baselines" across the mouths of deeply indented bays or archipelagos bordering a coast, claiming that the waters within them are also subject to full state authority. They have also claimed "historic title" to waters like Hudson Bay, but the question of "historical waters" has not yet been settled legally.

3. *"territorial waters," coastal waters of a country that extend seawards from either the coast or the baselines that enclose the internal waters of a state.* In the nineteenth century, the U.S. and Britain adopted a 3-nautical-mile (3.45 miles or 5.55 kilometres) limit on territorial waters, which became a standard in many parts of the world. By the 1960s, however, most states were claiming that their territorial sea extended up to 12 nautical miles

(13.8 miles, or 22.2 kilometres) off the coast, and some Latin American countries much more than that. The coastal state has limited authority over the "territorial sea" that is similar to sovereignty, except that foreign vessels have a right of "innocent passage" through territorial waters of any state. This right to innocent passage does not extend to the airspace above territorial waters, which falls under the sovereignty and jurisdiction of the state.

These definitions, coupled with the body of rights, privileges, practices, and customs that have evolved since the Middle Ages, form the basis of "the Law of the Sea."[24]

The status of the Northwest Passage can be read in different ways according to these criteria. Since 1985, Canada claims that the waters within the archipelago are historic internal waters that are part "of the natural unity of the Canadian Arctic Archipelago." In order for Canada's stance to hold, it has to withstand the challenge that the Northwest Passage constitutes an international strait: a body of water linking one area of the high seas to another, or connecting the high seas to a territorial sea that is used for international navigation. In straits used for international navigation, ships have a right to transit passage. The extent to which a passageway must be used for international navigation before it constitutes an "international strait" is unclear in international law, but evidence of foreign shipping is certainly necessary to claim that a waterway is an international strait. Furthermore, Canada maintained that entry into its Arctic waters could not be classed as "innocent passage" because the dangers of navigating ice-filled waters inherently threatened the northern ecosystem. This helps to explain why Canada moved cautiously to follow controversial international trends to widen its territorial sea and establish a contiguous zone of limited jurisdiction beyond that limit.[25]

In the 1960s, Lester Pearson's Liberal government continued to officially endorse a 3-mile (4.83-kilometre) territorial sea, but it also announced its intention to expand its control beyond those limits: "Following the failure of the 1958 and 1960 conference on the Law of the Sea to reach agreement on the breadth of the territorial sea and fishing, Canada decided to implement by unilateral action a nine-mile fishing zone adjacent to its three-mile territorial sea," an External Affairs statement declared on January 21, 1965. Although the government introduced legislation to this effect and instituted an exclusive fishing zone based upon straight baselines along the east and west coasts, it retreated from making any moves to do the same in the Arctic. The government knew that the U.S. would object to any action to any internal waters claim or to straight baselines, as it did everywhere in the world, but it hoped that the Americans might support an extension of Canada's claim to Arctic waters for reasons of defence and national security. The U.S., however, reacted sharply because any move in the Arctic could set a dangerous precedent. The Canadian government thus retreated from its plans, and Canada did not officially issue any geographical co-ordinates to delineate its claim to baselines in the Arctic for another twenty-three years.[26]

By 1970 it was resource development, not superpower security threats, that put the competing Canadian and American visions on the front burner. The search for petroleum had begun near Point Barrow, Alaska, during the Second World War, and large-scale exploration for new fields began in the Queen Elizabeth Islands in 1959. By the mid-1960s, an exploration boom drew unprecedented attention to the Beaufort Sea north of Canada and Alaska. Oil companies organized syndicates, secured exploration permits, conducted geological mapping and geophysical prospecting, and drilled at a few sites in the Canadian archipelago. "This has presented the first opportunities for use of part of the Northwest Passage for strictly commercial shipping," Trevor Lloyd noted in *Foreign Affairs* in 1964. "Even if oil in commercial quantities were to be discovered shortly, there might well be considerable delay before it could reach world markets as the method of transportation is still to be determined."[27]

When Robert Anderson, chairman of the Atlantic Richfield Company, announced the discovery of one of the world's largest petroleum deposits on the north slope of Alaska in 1968, Lloyd's hypothetical scenario became a reality. What was the most expeditious and cost-effective manner to get the estimated ten billion barrels of oil to southern U.S. markets? The oil industry immediately launched pipeline and transportation studies to determine the feasibility of various options, including the possibility of using tankers to transport oil through the Northwest Passage to East Coast refineries. In 1969, Atlantic Richfield, British Petroleum Company, and Standard Oil floated a plan to send an ice-strengthened vessel through the Passage, stating that "if successful, the test could result in the establishment of a new commercial shipping route through the Arctic region with broad implications for future Arctic development and international trade."[28]

The *Manhattan* voyage of 1969 had broad implications for Canadian-American relations, and has since assumed mythic proportions. If Canada's approach to Arctic diplomacy generally had, to this point, been marked by quiet diplomacy between close allies, its new activism signalled the changing times. By the late 1960s, Canada was differentiating its foreign policy from that of its southern neighbour. The Canadian social welfare state that blossomed during the Pearson years seemed very different from the American "warfare state" embroiled in Vietnam. Canadians now worried about their sovereignty for new reasons: the vulnerability of their economy, which was inextricably bound to American owners and markets, and disillusionment with prospects for continental cooperation generally.[29] "At no point had Canada in the past abandoned its sovereignty and jurisdiction in the Arctic. Indeed, it had taken considerable pains to affirm it diplomatically," political scientist Thomas Tynan explained. "In an era of heightened concern with Canadian sovereignty across the board, however, matters affecting the Arctic were drawn into the public sector and brought to high visibility. They could no longer be suitably dealt with through simply informal, or closed, diplomatic channels. A bold statement of national interest in the Arctic was needed to replace a merely quiet affirmation of it."[30]

The *Manhattan* was an ice-reinforced double-hulled tanker converted into the world's largest icebreaker, designed to test the feasibility of carrying oil from Prudhoe Bay north of Alaska to the American eastern seaboard. In the months before the voyage, oil company executives and the U.S. Coast Guard consulted with Canadian officials and even requested that a Canadian icebreaker accompany the ship during its transit. "Canada agreed, and gave the voyage full concurrence and

When the S.S. *Manhattan* tested the feasibility of carrying Alaskan oil to the American eastern seaboard through the Northwest Passage, Canadian nationalists reacted with alarm. Duncan Macpherson's cartoon in the *Toronto Star* showed how limited Canada's Arctic capabilities were.
Copyright: Estate of Duncan Macpherson. Reprinted with permission—Torstar Syndication Services.

support," navy captain Thomas C. Pullen observed. He served as the Canadian government's representative on the *Manhattan* during its voyage, acted as the Department of Transport's link with the tanker, and served as the ice adviser. The Canadian government also provided aerial ice reconnaissance and an on-board ice observer. "In return for this substantial Canadian participation," Pullen explained, "the valuable data on ice and ship performance acquired during the voyage were to be shared with Canada." Only six of the *Manhattan*'s forty-five tanks actually contained oil, so the environmental risk was minimal. Equally important, Pullen stressed that the *Manhattan*'s master, Roger Steward, "was meticulous in matters of protocol, and flew the Canadian flag as appropriate," and "the sponsors of the voyage did their best to offend no one."[31] Pullen was as surprised as the *Manhattan*'s crew when Canadian press reports began to depict the voyage as a direct challenge to Canada's Arctic sovereignty. He must have been unfamiliar with the ways of journalists.

"The legal status of the waters of Canada's Arctic archipelago is not at issue in the proposed transit of the Northwest Passage by the ships involved in the *Manhattan* project," Pierre Elliott Trudeau explained to the House of Commons on May 15, 1969. "The Canadian government has welcomed the *Manhattan* exercise, has concurred in it and will participate in it."[32] The government's position was that there were no sovereignty challenges to Canada's northern lands, territorial waters, or the continental shelf. But the U.S. refused to ask Canada permission to enter the Northwest Passage because this could be construed as recognition of Canadian internal waters. The nationalist media jumped on this attitude as a direct affront to Canada's claims, even though the Canadian government had still not defined "strait baselines" in the Arctic to enclose what politicians and journalists seemed to consider "internal waters." For all practical purposes, Humble Oil's request for Canadian co-operation seemed to imply that the passage was Canadian, even if it left official responses about sovereignty questions to the U.S. State Department, which would, of course, not say as much.[33]

Mitchell Sharp, the Canadian secretary of state for external affairs, responded in the *Globe and Mail* that "the *Manhattan* project would not have been possible without . . . extensive Canadian input, consisting of preparatory studies extending for many years over a vast area of the North. . . . It is wholly misleading, therefore, to portray the *Manhattan* passage as a test of Canada's sovereignty in the Arctic, the issue simply does not arise." He stressed that this was "no time for wide-ranging assertions of sovereignty—rather Canada must concentrate on specific objectives, the most important of which is the opening up of the Canadian Arctic region for development."[34] Unconvinced, journalists fed public anxieties about American encroachments and continued to press the government to take a strong stand, particularly after the owners of the *Manhattan* planned a second voyage the following year to test an alternate route. "*Manhattan's* two voyages," law expert Maxwell Cohen astutely noted, "made Canadians feel that they were on the edge of another American . . . [theft] of Canadian resources and rights which had to be dealt with at once by firm governmental action."[35]

In the *Manhattan* case, what was quickly perceived as a U.S. sovereignty challenge provided an important connection to the larger theme of Canada's custodial responsibilities in the North. "If the *Manhattan* succeeds," a *Globe and Mail* editorial predicted on September 9, 1969, "other oil laden vessels will follow in her wake. Before that happens Canada must be ready to receive and control them; for it is Canada's northland that would be devastated if the ice won and the tanker lost." What if a supertanker ran aground along the Northwest Passage? The Liberian tanker *Arrow* had run aground off Chedabucto Bay, Nova Scotia, in early 1970, discharging nine million litres of oil and polluting hundreds of kilometres of shoreline. Canadian scientists suggested that a similar accident in the Arctic Ocean would have catastrophic effects.[36]

In contrast to previous characterizations of the Arctic as an area through which to pass to get somewhere else, or as distant strategic space, or as a treasure-laden frontier, the idea of an ecologically delicate Arctic now became a convenient reason to extend Canadian jurisdiction northward. In his October 1969 Throne Speech to Parliament, Trudeau explained that

> Canada regards herself as responsible to all mankind for the peculiar ecological balance that now exists so precariously in the water, ice and land areas of the Arctic Archipelago. We do not doubt for a moment that the rest of the world would find us at fault, and hold us liable, should we fail to ensure adequate protection of that environment from pollution or artificial deterioration. Canada will not permit this to happen. . . .
>
> Part of the heritage of this country, a part that is of increasing importance and value to us, is the purity of our water, the freshness of our air, and the extent of our living resources. For ourselves and for the world we must jealously guard these benefits. To do so is not chauvinism, it is an act of sanity in an

increasingly irresponsible world. Canada will propose a policy of use of the Arctic waters which will be designed for environmental preservation . . . as a contribution to the long-term and sustained development of resources for economic and social progress.[37]

The prime minister's environmentalist spin on lingering nationalist concerns was innovative. The decision to frame foreign, particularly American, activities, as a threat to Canada, violating the country's territorial integrity and jeopardizing the broader human right to live in a "wholesome natural environment," was cited as a reason for the government to adopt extraordinary means to protect its environmental interests with unprecedented haste.[38]

In April 1970, the Liberal government introduced two bills into Parliament that indicated a new "functional" approach to Canadian sovereignty. Bill C-202, the Arctic Waters Pollution Prevention Act (AWPPA), was designed to allow Canada to regulate and control future tanker traffic through the Northwest Passage by creating a pollution-prevention zone 100 nautical miles (115 miles or 185 kilometres) outside the archipelago as well as the waters between the islands. "The Arctic Waters bill represents a constructive and functional approach to environmental preservation," Secretary of State for External Affairs Mitchell Sharp asserted during the debate in the House of Commons. "It asserts only the limited jurisdiction required to achieve a specific and vital purpose." It was not a full declaration of sovereignty. Rather, by putting aside but not renouncing any claim to sovereignty, the government claimed jurisdiction to ensure that "dirty" tankers did not pollute Canadian waters.[39] Bill C-203, the Territorial Sea and Fishing Zone Act, extended Canada's territorial sea from 3 to 12 miles (4.83 to 19.32 kilometres), which meant that any foreign vessels entering the Northwest Passage through Barrow and Prince of Wales Straits would have to cross waters subject to Canadian control. In explaining the bills in the House of Commons, Trudeau said that "the important thing is that we . . . have authority to ensure that any danger to the delicate ecological balance of the Arctic is prevented or preserved against by Canadian action. . . . It is not an assertion of sovereignty, it is an exercise of our desire to keep the Arctic free of pollution."[40] Both bills passed Parliament unanimously.

A key aspect of both pieces of legislation was that Canada did not claim outright sovereignty over the Northwest Passage. Instead, it asserted "functional" sovereignty: jurisdiction to regulate certain activities in Arctic waters. Trudeau acknowledged that, while Canadian governments considered the archipelago and the waters between the islands to be "national terrain," not all countries would accept that these were "internal waters over which Canada has full sovereignty. The contrary view is indeed that Canada's sovereignty extends only to the territorial sea around each island."[41] Although this was a statement of the obvious, the prime minister seemed to highlight the uncertainty surrounding Canada's position. Because the Arctic Waters Pollution Prevention Act did not assert full Canadian sovereignty, critics alleged that the government was actually diminishing Canada's sovereignty claim. Despite growing clamour from the Opposition benches and the popular media, Trudeau refused to concede to the "ultranationalists" and issue a straightforward declaration of sovereignty. His course, he suggested, was that of "legal moderation" with a clear focus on the popular issue of environmental protection.[42] After all, the prime minister explained, "to close off these Arctic waters would be as senseless as placing a barrier across the entrance to Halifax or Vancouver harbour." The government's commitment was to actively develop the Passage for safe navigation by any vessel that followed Canadian regulations and safety standards.[43] External Affairs documents, recently acquired under Access to Information, suggest that Canada's long-term objective was to lay the groundwork to apply the straight baseline to the system of the archipelago, even though this was strongly opposed by the U.S.[44] Indeed, as international lawyer Donald McRae observed, the legislation was a "manifestation of sovereignty" that was ultimately accepted by the international community, and thus "helped to consolidate Canada's authority over the

Prime Minister Trudeau in Igloolik, 1970. In response to the *Manhattan* voyage, the government adopted a "functional approach" to sovereignty in the Northwest Passage: it did not claim outright sovereignty but regulated commercial activities. *Glenbow Archives NA-4141-1*

waters of the Canadian Arctic Archipelago."[45]

Political scientist David Larson observed that the U.S. response, issued a week after Canada announced its new legislation, revealed how "this confrontation brought the United States and Canada squarely into conflict with each other over a number of law of the sea issues." The American position held that "international law provides no basis for these proposed unilateral extensions of jurisdiction on the high seas, and the United States can neither accept nor acquiesce in the assertion of such jurisdiction." The explanation was based on strategic considerations. If the U.S. did not oppose Canadian action, then it "would be taken as precedent in other parts of the world for other unilateral infringements of the freedom of the seas." This could affect merchant shipping, naval mobility, and heighten the potential for international controversy and conflict.[46] "We can't concede them the principle of territoriality or we'd be setting a precedent for trouble elsewhere in the world," a Department of State official had previously told the *Toronto Star*. All bodies of water connecting the high seas were international, making this an international issue that could "not be resolved by Canada's attempt to apply domestic law to ships plying these passageways."[47]

The Canadian position stressed that the Northwest Passage was not "high seas." While it acknowledged U.S. interests in free transit through international straits around the world, it maintained that the Northwest Passage was not an international strait and therefore could not serve as a precedent for elsewhere. The Canadian government thus proceeded with the legislation, despite American protests and counterproposals.[48] The Canadian ambassador in Washington and other senior government advisers had met with State Department officials in March 1970 and promised that American views "would be taken into account." It was clear, however, that "the Canadians were not interested in having [American] comments, suggestions, modifications, or alternatives," Theodore L. Eliot Jr. explained to President Nixon. "They admitted their embarrassment in giving us so little advance notification. It is equally clear that the Canadian presentation was in fact only a notification and that they did not anticipate real bilateral consultations before the legislation is a fait accompli." Canada said it was willing to open discussions to secure international confirmation for the legislation after it was in place, but not before. There was little ground for compromise. "The proposed Canadian legislation is in our view entirely unjustified in international law," Eliot explained. "There is no international basis for the assertion of a pollution control zone beyond the 12-mile contiguous zone; there is no basis for the establishment of exclusive fishing zones enclosing areas, of the high seas; and there is no basis for an assertion of sovereignty over the waters of the Arctic archipelago. The proposed Canadian unilateral action ignores our frequent request that Canada not act until we have had an opportunity for serious bilateral discussions."[49]

Rather than convincing Canadians to back down, American opposition "only buttressed popular support" for Ottawa's action. Thomas Tynan explained that it came "to represent a firm Canadian stand in the face of the American rush into the Canadian Arctic." Newspapers like the *Globe and Mail* took up the issue and tied it to diverging Canadian-American interests more generally:

> The United States objects to the Canadian bill. Let it. The ships that pose the greatest threat of oil pollution to the Arctic are American. And the Americans have been something less than a driving force in pushing for realistic international controls.
>
> This issue has a significant potential for confrontation between our two nations. But Canadians should realize that we are different nations with different interests and different

purposes. Inevitably, as we grow and develop, there are going to be conflicts.

And so Canadians should begin to prepare for a moving apart, not only on this issue, but many others affecting our economy, our culture, our approach to international affairs.[50]

The Northwest Passage became a litmus test for Canadian sovereignty. Here again was Canada's official "passive-reaction" tradition in response to perceived American threats to its northern sovereignty.[51] In the mid-1970s, it seemed, the stakes were higher than ever before.

If Canada's actions seemed hesitant to some commentators, they were ahead of international law and thus represented an important change in official direction. Legal advisers warned the government that the AWPPA might not stand up to an international challenge in the International Court of Justice. Nothing in customary law or in the UN Law of the Sea agreements to that time gave a country the right to implement pollution controls beyond its territorial waters. As a result, in 1973 the government reserved its pollution and fisheries legislation from the compulsory jurisdiction of the International Court of Justice—meaning it would not allow the Court to strike it down—thus pre-empting any foreign challenge to its legislation.[52] That same year, the Canadian Bureau of Legal Affairs issued the first official claim that the waters between the islands within the archipelago were "internal waters of Canada, on historical basis," a claim followed by a ministerial statement to the Standing Committee on External Affairs and National Defence two years later.[53] Through these actions, political scientists John Kirton and Don Munton explain, the government had accomplished "one of the largest geographic extensions of the Canadian state's jurisdiction in the country's history." It had also broken "with the liberal-internationalist traditions that had dominated Canadian foreign policy since the Second World War."[54]

Claiming jurisdiction was one thing; implementing it was another. How would Canada enforce its laws if foreign vessels decided to challenge Canadian controls? On April 3, 1969, Trudeau had identified "the surveillance of our own territory and coastlines—i.e., the protection of our sovereignty"—as the first priority in his government's defence policy. However, the specific nature of the Canadian Forces' role in asserting sovereignty remained ambiguous.[55] What exactly could the military accomplish as sovereignty soldiers? On April 30, 1969, Eric Wang, of the Department of External Affairs, emphasized that the sovereignty question related to Arctic waters was "a legal, political and economic problem. It is *not* a military problem. It cannot be solved by any amount of surveillance or patrol activities in these channels by Canadian Forces." Increasing Canada's military or non-military surveillance activities would neither strengthen its legal case nor undermine that of the U.S.[56]

The following year, M. Shenstone, of External Affairs' North American Defence and NATO Division, was still concerned because the rationale for the government's new defence policy had never been clarified in any classified or published document. "We are not aware of any current intelligence estimates forecasting a need for a greater level of military surveillance and capability in the North," he explained, but recent announcements showed that "the Canadian Armed Forces are moving in the direction of a significant reallocation of resources towards the North and away from other areas such as NATO Europe."[57] Why? The government insisted that there was no challenge to Canada's northern lands, territorial waters, and seabed, and that the only likely challenge was to the Northwest Passage—one that would be commercial and peaceful. "At the same time, Canada's Armed Forces had been given the primary mission of protecting sovereignty, with particular emphasis on the North," Ken Eyre explained. "Yet, by the government's own admission, the only possible challenge to Canadian claims—and that in a very specific and restricted area—was mounted not by an international rival or threat, but by the United States, Canada's closest ally and major trading partner." Given this confusion, he was not surprised that both the Canadian Forces and the broader public had difficulty discerning what the military's role should actually be in this "new North."[58]

Strategic planners at National Defence headquarters in Ottawa insisted that "apart from the threat of aerospace attack on North America, which can be discounted as an act of rational policy, Canada's geographic isolation effectively defends her against attack with conventional land or maritime forces."[59] Who, after all, was challenging our sovereignty, and what role could the armed forces play? The military eventually identified three classes of northern "anomaly" that could undermine Canadian control. The first, "tactical anomalies," were acts by foreign militaries such as overflights of Canadian territory, submarine or warship transits of Canadian internal waters, or the unlikely prospect of a military incursion in the North. The second, "commonweal anomalies," included disasters that threatened the ecological or social stability of the region and its people, such as floods, pollution, or air crashes. The third and most likely class, "sovereign anomalies," included foreign companies or individuals who, acting without direct government approval, contravened Canadian law but probably would not be detected given the vastness of the Arctic. Senior officials determined that the Canadian Forces should be able to respond to each of these anomalies from detection, to reconnaissance, to enforcement. In short, the military had to rethink its surveillance and reconnaissance role to incorporate non-evasive, non-hostile, and often co-operative "targets" that might undermine Canadian sovereignty.[60]

These were not primarily combat roles, of course, but reflected the complexities that the government faced in asserting sovereignty in the North. The minutes of an interdepartmental committee meeting on the Law of the Sea explained that

> The role of the forces is in many respects complementary to that of the civil authorities, but the proportionate requirement for the military is generally higher in the more sparsely settled regions until a more advanced stage of economic and social

development is reached and the associated expansion of civil agencies and resources occurs. Similarly where shortage of civil resources for the policing of waters off the coasts occurs, this requires an expanded role for the armed forces.

The Government's objective is to continue to occupy effectively and to have surveillance and control capability to the extent necessary to maintain authority over all Canadian territory, airspace and waters off the coasts over which Canada exercises sovereignty or jurisdiction. This involves a judgment on the challenges which could occur and on the surveillance and control capability required in the circumstances.

It is a complicated problem. The area to be covered is vast, in certain regions facilities are limited and weather conditions are often adverse. Indeed Canada has the longest coast line of any country in the world and fronts on three oceans. The problem would in a sense be simpler if defence were restricted to dealing only with the more traditional security threat of direct military attack from a predictable enemy. Instead challenges could arise in more ambiguous circumstances, from private entities as well as foreign government agencies. Incidents may involve, for instance, a fishing vessel, an oil tanker or a private aircraft. But the principle involved is well established. By creating a capability for surveillance and control which is effective and visible, the intention is to discourage such challenges.[61]

Other federal departments and agencies had lead roles in these areas, but the military bore ultimate responsibility for Canadian sovereignty. It had only meagre capabilities, however, to answer any challenges.

Defence initiatives also had to reflect Canada's broader northern policy agenda. A memorandum to Cabinet in early 1971 stressed that "the North has caught the imagination and attention of all Canadians and some people outside, which underlines the importance of the 'image of Canada' reflected in Government policies and activities there." By 1965, it argued, Canadian policy in the

North had shifted from "almost exclusive emphasis on defence matters to increasing concentration on people programs" such as housing and municipal services, education, health, and welfare. By the
late 1960s, the focus had turned to development. Then it had
shifted to environmental protection. The government was now
committed to "a systematic movement of all programs toward a
steady pace and rhythm for total development in the territories."
In addition to maintaining sovereignty and security, the federal
government identified three main goals: the provision of a higher
standard of living for northern residents; the maintenance and
enhancement of the northern environment; and the encouragement of economic development. The government's priority was to
strike a balance between people, ecology, and resource exploitation,
with a primary emphasis on the first two considerations.[62] The
Canadian Forces would have to operate within this new context.

The new look for Canada's Arctic patrols was "to see and be
seen."[63] In 1970, naval vessels sailed into Arctic waters for the first
time in eight years, initiating annual northern deployments or
NORPLOYs that continued through the decade. Maritime Command began Arctic-surveillance patrols using medium- and long-
range patrol aircraft, performing such tasks as surveying northern
airfields, examining ice conditions, monitoring wildlife and pollution, and documenting resource extraction and fishery activities.
The army began regular, small-unit "Viking" Arctic training
patrols, as well as elaborate paratroop assault exercises in the archipelago involving the Canadian Airborne Regiment. These activities
were transient and limited. So too were long-range air surveillance
patrols (which were limited by weather and the lack of northern airfields), and naval ships confined to select waters only in ice-free
months. To provide a permanent presence, the Canadian Forces set
up a new Northern Region headquarters in Yellowknife in May
1970, which boasted that it was responsible for "the largest single
military region in the world." To cover 40 percent of Canada's land
mass, the only resources at Northern Region's direct disposal were
the headquarters staff, two Twin Otter aircraft, 600 to 700 Rangers

in units that were being resurrected after their abandonment during the 1960s, and a few hundred personnel at communications research and radar stations.[64]

Strategist Ken Eyre has shown that the government not only avoided stationing regular forces in the North, it did not obtain any new equipment for the forces, such as special reconnaissance aircraft or surveillance equipment, ice-capable ships or submarines for the navy, or all-terrain vehicles for the army. "To protect sovereignty in the North, the government adopted a policy strikingly analogous to the situation that existed in Canada at the time of the 1922 Eastern Arctic Expedition," he noted. "In the 1920s, Canada established sovereignty in the Arctic with a symbolic presence of the Royal Canadian Mounted Police. In the 1970s, Canada prepared to protect that same sovereignty with a symbolic presence of the Canadian Armed Forces."

The Canadian Rangers (local residents who received a rifle, ammunition, and basic training) gave the military a permanent presence along Arctic coastlines. Here, Ranger Raymond Mercredi fires a rifle in a Nanook Ranger exercise. *DND photo ISC88-367*

An important difference, however, was that the southern military units that operated in the North were transient and their roles in national defence included much more than northern training. They were not able to stay for long periods, as the Mounties had done. Nevertheless, by 1975, "the Canadian Forces had re-established themselves in the North to an unprecedented degree." Perhaps more importantly, Eyre observed, "for the first time, the Department of National Defence was prepared to admit that the North had an intrinsic value to the country as a whole and that a military presence was required in the area."[65]

The intrinsic value of the region came to the fore during discussions surrounding the proposed Mackenzie Valley Pipeline. The difficulties encountered by the *Manhattan* convinced the oil industry that the Northwest Passage route was not commercially feasible at that time. Instead, U.S. president Richard Nixon authorized construction of the Trans-Alaska Pipeline from Prudhoe Bay on Alaska's North Slope to the Gulf of Alaska on the state's southern coastline. From there, tankers would transport the oil along the Canadian west coast for refining and distribution in the southern United States. Canadian officials, worried about the environmental and economic consequences of a tanker accident and oil spill in Juan de Fuca Strait or the Strait of Georgia, lobbied the American industry and government officials to try to convince them that an overland pipeline through the Mackenzie Valley region made more sense. J.J. Greene, the minister of energy, mines and resources, explained to the Vancouver Men's Canadian Club in February 1971 that

> the Canadian Government is not opposed to the construction of oil and gas lines from Alaska through Canada to the continental United States. . . . [T]he United States oil industry has been too hasty and too unplanned in its decision to move Alaska North Slope oil across Alaska from Prudhoe Bay to Valdez and then by sea to receiving points in the U.S. Northwest. . . . To us it appears that an oil line from Alaska through Canadian territory would have the advantage of ruling out a vulnerable tanker link to markets and would provide more economic transportation of oil to the U.S. Midwest. . . . Canada, for its part of the bargain, would undertake to ensure the uninterruptibility of the flow of Alaska oil down a Canadian "land bridge" line equivalent in volume to any flow which could be put through the [Trans-Alaska Pipeline system] lines.[66]

The Americans decided against the Canadian pipeline route because it was not "the most cost efficient, secure, economically beneficial and, in particular, expeditious."[67] The Trudeau government continued to explore the option, anticipating Canadian petroleum discoveries. Indeed, the prime minister likened the proposed Mackenzie Valley Pipeline to the Canadian Pacific Railway, which had opened the West after Confederation. The ensuing debate over the pipeline, however, signalled that the future of the northern frontier could no longer be decided in government or corporate boardrooms.

Chapter   Four

A   NEW   SOVEREIGNTY

*"What happens in the North will . . . tell us what kind of
a country Canada is; it will tell us what kind of a people
we are."*
— THOMAS BERGER,
  Northern Frontier—Northern Homeland, 1977

If Prime Minister John Diefenbaker's "Northern Vision" was con-
ceived—and faded—with little political controversy in the North,
Pierre Trudeau's version encountered regional resistance that
reflected the changing times. By the early 1970s the Native movement in Canada had mobilized, and Native leaders would no longer
tolerate being left out of discussions related to resource development in their homelands.[1] The most immediate danger that they
faced was not a Soviet nuclear attack or American encroachments
on sovereignty. It was posed by southern Canadians. Justice
Thomas Berger, hired to look into what the pipeline would mean
for the North, entitled his final report "Northern Frontier—
Northern Homeland." It highlighted competing visions of northern history and the future. "We look upon the North as our last
frontier," the report noted. "It is natural for us to think of developing it, of subduing the land and extracting its resources to fuel
Canada's industry and heat our homes. But the native people say
the North is their homeland. They have lived there for thousands
of years. They claim it is their land, and they believe they have a
right to say what its future ought to be."[2] These internal sovereignty claims by Native groups changed the political dialogue, and

meant that Canadian decision-makers had to grapple with northern perspectives even when it came to Canadian development projects.

With the issue of the Northwest Passage on the back burner, and Canadian attention directed to internal discussions over aboriginal rights and self-government, Canada and the United States seemed to agree, in the absence of any pressing need to fight for their respective positions, to disagree. As a result, official Canadian sovereignty concerns related to the Arctic waters lessened. This was typical. Canadian governments tended to react to perceived threats, and when immediate fears of losing the North—or, more importantly, of political embarrassment—disappeared from the public radar, so too did political commitments to defend sovereignty.

The Trudeau and Reagan governments had more serious differences of opinion in the early 1980s than the status of Arctic waters, such as the National Energy Program and the renewed Cold War.[3] Nevertheless, Canada's claims seemed stronger by the early 1980s than they had been a decade before. Both Canada and the United States were principal drafters of Article 234 of the UN Convention on the Law of the Sea (UNCLOS) which dealt with ice-covered areas. "Coastal States have the right to adopt and enforce non-discriminatory laws and regulations for the prevention, reduction and control of marine pollution from vessels in ice-covered areas within the limits of the exclusive economic zone," it read. Although Canada did not ratify the convention until 2003 (and the U.S. has not yet done so), both countries considered it customary international law on the subject. This vindicated Canada's Arctic Waters Pollution Prevention Act and gave it "the *de facto* right to legislate control over the type of commercial vessels that enter the Passage."[4]

Within days of taking office in 1984, Conservative prime minister Brian Mulroney had promised that "good relations, super relations" with the United States would "be the cornerstone of our foreign policy." When the United States Coast Guard icebreaker

Polar Sea transited the Northwest Passage in August 1985, however, Arctic sovereignty concerns precipitated another crisis in Canadian-American relations. The reasons for the voyage seem purely practical. The U.S. Coast Guard icebreaker *Northwind*, which usually resupplied the American airbase at Thule in Greenland, was immobilized by mechanical problems.[5] As a result, the U.S. Coast Guard decided to send the *Polar Sea*, based in Seattle, to complete the task instead. It used the Panama Canal to get to the Atlantic on the voyage to Thule, but it did not have enough time to take that route and still complete its Alaskan missions. A westward voyage by one of the world's most powerful icebreakers through the Northwest Passage would save both time and money. "Some Canadians suspected another Machiavellian plot on the part of the Americans," T.C. Pullen observed. "To others, the transit of the passage appeared to be a sensible operational redeployment by the U.S. Coast Guard. Maybe someone in the U.S. State Department was up to some sharp practice but to the coast guards of both countries, nothing sinister seemed to be afoot."[6]

In May 1985, the U.S. Coast Guard discussed its plans with the State Department and the Canadian Coast Guard, explaining that the purpose of the voyage was operational and it was not intended as a sovereignty challenge. Indeed, the Americans recognized that Canadians might be sensitive to the voyage and asked them to participate in the spirit of shared research. The two countries still disagreed over the status of the Northwest Passage, but the U.S. believed that it was "in the mutual interests of Canada and the United States that this unique opportunity for cooperation not be lost because of possible disagreement over the relevant judicial regime." Both countries should agree to disagree on legal issues and should "concentrate on practical matters" without prejudice to respective legal positions, the Americans suggested. The Canadian government's initial response was that the Passage was internal waters, but that it would cooperate. The two parties negotiated pollution controls to ensure that the transit would meet AWPPA requirements, and the American government reiterated that "the

Canadian nationalists reacted strongly when the *Polar Sea* transited the Northwest Passage on a 1985 resupply mission to Thule, Greenland. This prompted the Mulroney government to declare straight baselines to Canada's Arctic region effective January 1, 1986, enclosing the Northwest Passage as "historic internal waters." *US Pacific Air Forces photo 070105-G-9923N-004*

United States considers that this transit, and the preparations for it, in no way prejudices the juridical position of either side regarding the Northwest Passage, and it understands that the Government of Canada shares that view." Political scientist Rob Huebert, in his careful analysis of the *Polar Sea* controversy, concluded that the Americans did not intend the voyage to be an instrument to challenge Canada's claims. After all, three Canadian observers were accepted on board, and the Canadian Coast Guard ship *John A. Macdonald* escorted it during the early stages of the voyage. This practical co-operation between officials of both countries, however, was not mirrored on the diplomatic front.[7]

The Canadian government's position soon began to shift as a result of vocal opposition by what the British call the "chattering classes": academics, aboriginal spokespeople, national interest groups, politicians in opposition parties, and journalists. One of the earliest indicators of a budding controversy was University of Toronto professor Franklyn Griffiths's op-ed "Arctic authority at stake," published in the *Globe and Mail* on June 13, 1985. Although the article itself was sober and balanced, Griffiths correctly predicted that the *Polar Sea* voyage seemed "certain to rekindle a heated debate on Canada's sovereignty over its northern waters." The way he framed the issue—the Americans failed to ask for permission, thus challenging Canadian sovereignty and control over a region central to Canadian identity—helped to ensure that it did. Government officials took note. Other scholars reinforced the view that, unless the government took action, it was in danger of jeopardizing its claim to the Passage. Aboriginal groups like Inuit Tapirisat urged Ottawa to take a strong stand to protect their livelihood and the Arctic environment. "If the Canadian Government will allow a foreign ship passing through Lancaster Sound without permission, where do the Inuit stand?" Louis Tapadjuk asked. "It's going to be the start of something that we simply cannot allow to happen." The Council for Canadians, a left-leaning nationalist organization, chartered a plane and bombed the *Polar Sea* on August 7 with two canisters: one containing a Canadian flag, the other with the message that the voyage was "insulting and demeaning to our citizens and a threat to our sovereignty. It is not the action of a thoughtful, understanding neighbour." Liberal leader John Turner called the voyage "an affront to Canada," and both opposition parties used it as a pretext to castigate the Conservative government for its close relations with the U.S. The media also adopted a strongly nationalistic and highly critical view of the voyage, with editorials in leading Canadian newspapers chastising the government for its unwillingness to take action in the North and defend the country's sovereignty. This "transformed the voyage into a crisis," political scientist Rob Huebert observed, and the Canadian government responded not to the voyage itself but "to the actions taken by the various groups and individuals opposed to it."[8]

The Mulroney government thus changed its tune. It announced an "intensive review" of Canadian Arctic sovereignty on August 1, 1985, informed its southern neighbours that it considered all of the archipelagic waters to be "historic internal waters," and demanded that the U.S. seek official permission for the *Polar Sea* to transit the Passage. The Americans refused to make such a request, recognizing that this would prejudice their legal position. So the Canadian government simply granted the Americans permission as if they had asked for it. The U.S. retorted by denying that it had even given Canada prior notice. Prime Minister Mulroney declared that the American refusal to support Canada's Arctic claim was an "unfriendly act," but Canadian officials were just as unbending as their American counterparts. Canada's assertions went against the U.S.'s established position on the status of the Northwest Passage, which was tied to their strategic mobility around the world. Energy issues and new security concerns related to cruise missiles, the vulnerability of American land-based missile systems, and the ability for Soviet submarines with long-range nuclear missiles to hide in the Arctic ice pack further entrenched U.S. interests.[9]

In response to the alleged public outcry,[10] the Conservative government had to be seen to defend Canadian interests, and thus adopted a strongly nationalistic stance. External Affairs Minister Joe Clark's statement to the House of Commons on September 10, 1985, encapsulated the government's response to this latest sovereignty crisis. "Canada is an Arctic nation," he declared, and its "sovereignty in the Arctic is indivisible":

> It embraces land, sea and ice. It extends without interruption to the seaward-facing coasts of the Arctic islands. Those islands are joined, and not divided by the waters between them. They are bridged for most of the year by ice. From time immemorial Canada's Inuit people have used and occupied the ice as they have used and occupied the land. The policy of the Government is to maintain the national unity of the Canadian Arctic archipelago and preserve Canada's sovereignty over land, sea and ice undiminished and undivided. . . . Full sovereignty is vital to Canada's security. It is vital to the Inuit people. And it is vital to Canada's national identity.[11]

While the idea of the Arctic as an indivisible national space was not new, Clark's words suggested a shift away from Trudeau's ecological sensibilities and functional jurisdiction to a claim of full sovereignty over the Northwest Passage as "historic internal waters"—a claim based partly upon aboriginal use, rights, and protection. If the *Polar Sea* transit constituted a "psychological rape," as Member of Parliament Jim Fulton characterized it in a moment of hysterical hyperbole,[12] Canada was no longer going to lie back and accept it.

In the wake of the *Polar Sea*, the Conservative government took various formal measures to confirm and consolidate its legal position over Canada's Arctic waters.[13] First, it announced that Canada would apply "straight baselines" to the Arctic region as of January 1, 1986, effectively enclosing the waters of the Canadian archipelago to reaffirm their status as "historic internal waters." The Passage had never been part of an international strait, the government argued, and could not be considered high seas. By drawing straight baselines around the outermost islands of the archipelago, Canada would claim complete sovereignty and jurisdiction over everything within the baselines: it officially declared them internal waters. Furthermore, Canada's territorial sea, pollution zone, exclusive economic zone, and continental shelf would extend outward from these new baselines. Letters of protest soon arrived from the United States and European Community, but this did not deter Canada from reiterating its claim.[14]

This was a significant step. Trudeau had contemplated drawing straight baselines in the 1970s, but did not proceed because legal advisers suggested that international Law of the Sea was not sufficient to support this move. Things had changed, however, and the Mulroney government displayed more confidence. It withdrew Canada's 1970 reservation, so that the Arctic Waters Pollution Prevention Act could now be challenged through the International Court of Justice. Two main developments in international law justified this action. First, Article 234—the "ice-covered areas article"—in the 1982 Law of the Sea Convention suggested that state jurisdiction to prevent, reduce, and control marine pollution in ice-covered areas "far beyond those they could take in other ocean areas off their coasts" had become part of customary law. Second, the Law of the Sea now accepted exclusive economic zones (EEZ), granting states sovereign rights over the sea up to 200 miles (322 kilometres) from the coast in terms of exploring and exploiting marine resources. Both of these legal developments supported the AWPPA and made it less likely that an international court would find against Canada. The government also announced the Canadian Laws Offshore Application Act, which would apply Canadian law to all offshore resource activities within the EEZ and the continental shelf.[15]

To assert sovereignty, Canada adopted a "proactive and aggressive" plan to "exercise effective control" over its internal waters.[16] How could Canada claim sovereignty if it was unable to detect unauthorized, sub-surface transits, never mind respond to them? Ignorance might be bliss, but it is not a credible assertion of sovereignty. If Canada did not know what was happening in waters that it claimed as its own, it could hardly convince the world that it was exercising adequate functions of state in that region. Similarly, if it knew of foreign transits and did nothing about them, it would not be demonstrating credible authority and control. Moreover, if submarines transited the Passage on a frequent basis, this could support the argument that it was "used for international navigation" and thus constituted an international strait.[17] What options did Canada have, given that the only open challenger to its sovereignty claims in the preceding two decades had been the United States?

For seventeen years, Canadian governments had asserted the need for a large, all-season icebreaker that could operate in the High Arctic. In his landmark speech on September 10, Joe Clark announced that the government would build a "Polar 8" icebreaker—a vessel capable of maintaining headway at three knots through ice up to 2.4 metres (8 feet) thick. (By contrast, the *Louis St. Laurent*, Canada's largest icebreaker, was one-third the size and one-quarter as powerful, and could not break through ice half that thick.) The proposed icebreaker would be the world's largest and most powerful, and would "provide a year-round platform for hydrographic, oceanographic, and other marine science investigations in previously inaccessible areas," T.C. Pullen trumpeted. "In some many respects, she will be an ideal research platform, adding immeasurably to our knowledge in the polar environment . . . [and giving] Canada the opportunity to operate at any time of the year in the Northwest Passage and adjacent channels, straits, and sounds." For the first time, Canada would have the capability to respond to an emergency anywhere in its North. If a foreign submarine ran into problems, for example, Canada would not have to call on American or Soviet icebreakers for help and could thus avoid significant sovereignty questions.[18] The price tag would be steep— early estimates of $350 million soon ballooned to more than $500 million—and the project encountered many delays. Nevertheless, commentators tended to stress the symbolic presence and practical purposes it would serve. The Department of National Defence, by contrast, grew worried that the costs would cut into the naval modernization program it was planning without producing a vessel capable of responding to submarine intrusions in the Arctic.[19]

The boldest initiative, however, was the government's decision to acquire up to a dozen nuclear-powered attack submarines and lay a fixed sonar-detection system on the sea floor to monitor Arctic waters and identify foreign incursions in support of continental defence. "Our sovereignty in the Arctic," Minister of National Defence Perrin Beatty explained, "cannot be complete if we remain dependent on allies for knowledge of possible hostile activities in our waters, under our ice and for preventing such activities."[20] Questions, however, began to mount. Would an increased presence in the North not drain resources from Canada's NATO contribution to Europe at a volatile time? Did it not fly in the face of Canada's anti-nuclear image? Liberal defence critic Doug Frith complained that a non-nuclear power using nuclear-powered submarines for military purposes "would set a dangerous precedent." Cabinet ministers complained that the six-to-ten-billion-dollar price tag was too expensive. Pentagon officials were reluctant to transfer essential nuclear technologies that Canada would use to "build vessels that would be used to guard against unauthorized intrusions into Canada's Arctic waters by United States nuclear submarines." American defence planners suggested that Canada should leave submarine defences to the U.S. Navy and should focus on conventional forces.[21]

Canada's new Arctic policy was primarily about sovereignty, but it was framed so that it was not simply directed towards the United States. These initiatives coincided with a Soviet buildup in Arctic naval capabilities in the mid-1980s (especially their ballistic missile submarine fleet based at the Kola Peninsula, in the far north of Russia), as well as the Reagan administration's aggressive arms buildup. Canada did not officially participate in American plans for a "total defence" umbrella to thwart a full-scale Soviet ICBM attack (the Strategic Defense Initiative, popularly known as "Star Wars")—a stance possible because the American system did not require installations on Canadian territory. It did agree to help respond to the new threat posed by air-launched cruise missile technology through the North American Air Defence Modernization Program which would update the DEW Line.[22] This time, Canada contributed 40 percent of the construction and maintenance costs. Like other government initiatives of the era, even this co-operative endeavour was cast in terms that emphasized "the importance of fully exercising sovereignty in our north." Minister of National Defence Erik Nielsen explained to the House of Commons that "the DEW Line has served Canada well, but Canadians do not control it . . . The North Warning System will be a Canadian-controlled system-operated, maintained and manned by Canadians. Sovereignty in our north will be strengthened and assured for the future."[23]

Just as the RCMP had once been the agency of choice to assert Canadian sovereignty in the North, the Canadian Forces continued its role as the modern flag-bearer of choice. Many of the Mulroney government's supposedly new defence initiatives simply resurrected activities that had been introduced in the 1970s but had been allowed to wane when the earlier American sovereignty threat had diminished. Nevertheless, in the latter half of the 1980s, the army resumed company-level exercises in the Arctic each year, the air force increased its northern patrol flights (NORPATs), and naval deployments designed to show the flag in northern waters

(NORPLOY) were revived. Indeed, the Canadian Forces' role was core to the government's new northern maritime policy. The 1987 defence policy statement included three polar projection maps and reiterated that the government would allocate substantial resources to address northern security. A fleet of long-range maritime patrol aircraft and a new northern training centre would significantly augment the military's presence. Furthermore, the policy would upgrade five northern airfields so that these Forward Operating Locations (FOLs) could accommodate CF-18 interceptor aircraft. Critics suggested that even the latter initiative reflected "the now traditional sovereignty-presence concept" more than actual defence needs, but the important symbolism it offered in terms of Canada being able to project its air power over the Arctic was unmistakable.[24]

In the late 1980s, the Conservative Government promised a range of defence initiatives to defend Canadian sovereignty and security in the north. One of its pledges was to upgrade five northern airfields to accommodate CF-18 interceptor aircraft. *DND photo BN2006-0060-14*

As much as the Conservative approach to sovereignty assertion was nationalistic, the Mulroney government was the most pro-American in Canadian history. Part of its explicit Arctic strategy was to negotiate with the United States over Arctic waters. The kerfuffle over the *Polar Sea* highlighted incompatible interests and claims, and past reluctance of either part to concede on any points might have indicated that forward movement would be impossible. President Reagan and Prime Minister Mulroney, however, developed such a positive working relationship that after the two leaders met in April 1987, the president told his negotiators to reach a working compromise with Canada on the Northwest Passage issue.[25] In short, good personal relationships can make a difference in policy matters. On January 11, 1988, External Affairs Minister Joe Clark and Secretary of State George Shultz announced an agreement on Arctic co-operation. The United States agreed to seek Canadian consent before its icebreakers navigated in what Canada considered to be its internal waters, based on the principle that these were scientific missions of mutual benefit to both countries. This included, of course, the Northwest Passage. The agreement, however, was carefully framed to avoid prejudicing the legal claims of both sides. "Nothing in this agreement of cooperative endeavour between Arctic neighbours and friends nor any practice thereunder affects the respective positions of the governments of the United States and of Canada on the Law of the Sea in this or other maritime areas," it noted. The U.S. only agreed to disagree with Canada on the legal status of the Passage, thus ensuring that American national interests in international straits more generally were not jeopardized. "While we and the United States have not changed our legal positions," Mulroney explained, "we have come to a practical agreement that is fully consistent with the requirements of Canadian sovereignty in the Arctic." President Reagan also stressed that the agreement was "a pragmatic solution based on our special bilateral relationship, our common interest in cooperating on Arctic matters, and the nature of the area. It is without prejudice to our respective legal positions and sets no precedents for other areas."[26]

Though this agreement related only to icebreakers, and did not solve the core legal disagreement over "internal waters" versus "international strait," it did allow both sides to satisfy their basic objectives through negotiation. Canada could claim that U.S. icebreakers would not transit the Passage without Canadian consent, and the United States retained access to the Passage while avoiding recognition of it as Canadian. Developments soon confirmed that Canadian-American relations in the Arctic were co-operative and compatible, not competitive. In September 1988, two Canadian icebreakers were stuck in the ice off Point Barrow, and the USCGS *Polar Star* came to their rescue. When the task was complete, the *Polar Star* could not cross the Beaufort Sea. With winter fast approaching, the only safe route was back east through the Northwest Passage. In accordance with the 1988 agreement, the U.S. State Department sought and within hours received Canadian permission for the icebreaker to transit the Passage and to conduct scientific research along the way—while insisting that this action was not a recognition of Canadian sovereignty. Once again, a Canadian Coast Guard icebreaker accompanied the *Polar Star* and a Canadian officer was on board during its transit of the Passage.[27] This time, there was no political or popular backlash. The North American friends could, it seemed, agree to disagree about the legalities and work together.

From the late 1960s until quite recently, Canada's bark was much worse than its bite. Its northern foreign policy, if it had a coherent one, was to extend Canadian law and thus bolster the Canadian claim to waters seldom transited by anyone. As political scientist Rob Huebert observed, Canada's typical, *ad hoc*, reactive approach to sovereignty revealed that, despite tremendous political bluster, successive governments' actual activities in the North had been superficial through the last three decades of the Cold War.[28]

While Canada had come to view the North "as a place that, however remote and unknown, is still an inherent part of the nation," Ken Eyre concluded, the United States saw the North "as a direction of strategic approach."[29] In commercial terms, the Northwest Passage was something to pass through in the name of freedom of commerce. In military terms, it represented an international strait that, if designated any other way, could set a dangerous precedent for "innocent passage" through strategically important waterways around the globe.

"We cannot accept the assertion of a Canadian claim that the Arctic waters are internal waters of Canada nor can we accept their other proposals," Theodore L. Eliot Jr., executive secretary of the U.S. State Department, explained to President Nixon in March 1970. "Such acceptance would jeopardize the freedom of navigation essential for United States naval activities worldwide, and would be contrary to our fundamental position that the regime of the high seas can be altered only by multilateral agreement. Furthermore, our efforts to limit extensions of coastal state sovereignty over the high seas worldwide will be damaged when other nations see that a country—physically, politically and economically—as close to the United States as Canada, feels it can undertake such action in the face of United States opposition."[30] While Canadians are ultrasensitive about perceived U.S. incursions on sovereignty, or at least frustrated by American unwillingness to concede to Canadian national claims, they sometimes forget that we are not the centre of the U.S.'s strategic universe—one upon which we also base our security. Furthermore, as Joseph Jockel, director of the Canadian Studies Program at St. Lawrence University, remarked, "the Canadian emphasis on sovereignty protection places a premium on the presence of Canadians, rather than on the fulfilment of a defence mission." Indeed, Canada could devote resources to a presence precisely because it knew that, in the end, the U.S. could be relied upon to offer it security.[31]

Canada's 1987 White Paper on Defence was a classic Cold War document. The policy it espoused, and the assumptions upon which it was based, were rendered largely moot by the events of the next half-decade. On October 1, 1987, Mikhail Gorbachev called for "the North of the globe, the Arctic, [to] become a zone of peace." Western leaders were understandably skeptical, but did demonstrate room for circumpolar cooperation.[32] The 1989 fall of the Berlin Wall and the subsequent dissolution of the Eastern Bloc prompted western governments to re-evaluate their security assumptions. The Russian bear, although still untamed and potentially unruly, could no longer focus its primary energies on matters outside of its increasingly tenuous borders. Voices within the United States, bolstered by the confidence of "winning" the Cold War, began to preach about an expected "peace dividend" in a new era of liberal peace. The Mulroney government responded to the new realities by announcing, on April 27, 1989, that it would not proceed with plans to acquire nuclear-powered submarines. One by one, its other planned military acquisitions to serve the cause of

Arctic sovereignty were cut. Only the DEW Line modernization program and the expansion of the Canadian Rangers avoided the government's knife. More pressing national priorities—particularly a growing national debt—seemed to trump Arctic issues. Correspondingly, military activities in the North underwent a now-typical period of decline in the 1990s. The sovereignty crisis had passed, and so too had the imperative to deliver on Arctic promises. After all, what good could come out of allocating precious military resources to defend against the almost unthinkable possibility of American encroachments on Canadian sovereignty?

"Sovereignty is not a magic word which automatically requires or justifies a certain military set-piece. It is rather the political and territorial framework within which a state exists and functions. It is not made up of, or protected by symbols, tokens or gestures." So noted the Legal Division at External Affairs in August 1970.[33] Yet it seems that symbols, tokens, and gestures were indeed the main elements of Canada's reactionary approach to sovereignty until the 1980s. As historian Elizabeth Elliot-Meisel observed, "Canada has rarely allocated or committed funds, personnel, or equipment to monitor, defend, or protect the Passage."[34] When its conflicting maritime claims with the United States surfaced, the federal government seemed unwavering in its commitment to uphold Canada's interests. Of course, when both sides were unwilling to set aside their legal claims, there was no room for bilateral compromise. Captain Thomas Pullen, the retired RCN officer who had sailed on the *Manhattan*, published a sober reflection on the situation in September 1987:

> If push comes to shove, which is more important—Canadian Arctic sovereignty or U.S. security? When one shares a continent with a superpower, these are the facts of life; the issues of sovereignty and security are inseparable. To be squeezed between two superpowers is a costly and frustrating business. Canada should negotiate with its southern neighbour to find a mutually palatable solution to the issues of Arctic sovereignty

and North American security. Surely it should be possible for the United States and Canada—friends, neighbors, and allies— to come to some agreement.[35]

In 1988, a non-prejudicial, practical arrangement—necessary to overcome a longstanding legal impasse—proved that diplomacy could trump the politics of embarrassment so often played out in the press.[36] "The 1988 agreement represents a pause rather than an end to the Northwest Passage dispute as military, economic, and environmental pressures increase in the entire region," Philip Briggs, an American political scientist, concluded in a sober study of the *Polar Sea* affair. "Continued creative diplomacy and joint efforts will be necessary to avoid future problems . . . , however, diplomacy based upon mutual respect for each state's national interests and the growing interdependence between the two countries may yet yield a more complete solution to the Northwest Passage dispute."[37]

The time seemed right for a more co-operative approach. The West won the Cold War, or so it thought in the 1990s when the Soviet Union collapsed. As a result, radar defence systems, military outposts, and major security operations became obsolete. Preparing Canadian troops for sudden deployment in the Far North seemed much less important than training them for interventions in Africa and Asia. Canadians and their government lost interest in strategic questions—but soon found the national agenda once again crowded with northern concerns. The new issues—aboriginal land claims, northern self-government, and environmental concerns— were each stimulated in part by the dramatic impact of military and strategic measures over the previous fifty years. The greatest complication, and opportunity, rested with the fact that Canadian Arctic issues now played out on a circumpolar stage. The empowerment of aboriginal and other northern peoples, and growing connections between the Arctic regions, gave Canadian questions international meaning and Arctic residents powerful political platforms.

The end of the Cold War also meant that military considerations took a back seat to other concerns, particularly those relating to aboriginal peoples. Indigenous leaders objected to military manoeuvres on their lands, like those at Goose Bay, Labrador,[38] and the general presence in the North in general. Inuit and Dene leaders complained that military activities had harmed their communities. Mary Simon, president of the Inuit Circumpolar Conference (ICC), tried to redirect the sovereignty question, noting that "Arctic security includes environmental, economic and cultural, as well as defence, aspects."[39] "Inuit," she said, "have a legitimate, extensive and varied role to fulfill in international matters. In light of the increasing impact of the actions of the international community on Inuit rights, our culture and northern homeland, we have a compelling responsibility to become increasingly involved."[40]

The Inuit were the first of the international indigenous groups to bring effective pressure to bear on the government of Canada. The Inuit Circumpolar Conference, founded in 1977, promoted circumpolar co-operation, developed a pan-Arctic environmental strategy, advocated demilitarization, and pushed for northern autonomy.[41] Indigenous organizations like the ICC changed the debate from matters of national prestige and security to those of cultural survival, sustainable development, and political mobilization.

The collapse of the Soviet Union, as Rob Huebert has observed, shifted attention from traditional to new security concerns, particularly the protection of the Arctic environment. Canadian scientists, for example, uncovered extensive evidence of transboundary pollutants, such as fertilizers and insecticides, deposited in the Arctic region. Equally disconcerting, evidence mounted that the Soviet Union had done little to protect its Arctic regions from pollution and radioactive wastes.[42] An observer at the 1992 ICC meeting issued a sombre but realistic assessment: "Many Inuit have serious concerns about the long-term health of the Arctic environment and the course that future industrial development in the region, fuelled by Western investors, is likely to take. The Arctic environment, often mistakenly seen as pristine, is already polluted with rising levels of heavy metals, radioactive isotopes and industrial and agricultural chemicals."[43]

The Arctic political mobilization launched by the ICC soon spun off in several directions. In 1991, eight Arctic countries signed the Arctic Environmental Protection Strategy (AEPS), originally a Finnish initiative but largely drafted by Canadian officials, creating a forum to work on Arctic-wide environmental regulation and management.[44] Mary Simon, then president of the ICC, welcomed the step with cautious praise: "That has to come now. We can't keep signing these international agreements and have no action. The important part becomes the implementation and interpretation of the agreement and the work plan that has to follow."[45]

Canada, fittingly, played a significant role in pushing the international community towards a broader and more influential Arctic Council.[46] Prime Minister Brian Mulroney formally proposed the idea of a regional form for Arctic co-operation with Russian authorities in 1989. The idea picked up on a series of earlier initiatives, ranging from measures to protect polar bears, a Canada–USA co-operative agreement and the Canadian deal signed with the Soviet Union in 1989. The philanthropic Walter and Duncan Gordon Foundation pushed the idea of an Arctic Council, with an early panel calling for an organization with substantial aboriginal representation and a mandate "to make the circumpolar region into a domain of enhanced civility—an area in which aboriginal peoples enjoy their full rights, and where national governments that speak for southern majorities accord progressively greater respect to the natural environment, to one another, and, in particular, to aboriginal peoples."[47]

The concept of an Arctic council was more revolutionary than it seemed. National governments hesitated to elevate the role, stature, and decision-making power of aboriginal groups, particularly at the international level.[48] Although few people in southern centres paid much attention to the proposal, northern leaders saw in the Arctic Council the shape of a new North, working across national boundaries to solve problems of critical regional importance.

The proposal for an Arctic Council limped along, a high-profile commitment of the Mulroney government lacking the American support needed to proceed. Many observers, Franklyn Griffiths foremost among them, believed that the council had the potential to pull Russia into the circumpolar sphere and to help ease western worries about post-Soviet aspirations for the Far North. "It would be no small accomplishment for Canada to bring Russia onto the world stage in its first multilateral negotiation since the formation of the Soviet Union," he argued. "All the better if the purpose of the negotiation is to create a new instrument for civility and indeed civilized behavior in relations between Arctic states, between these states and their aboriginal peoples, and in the way southern majorities treat their vulnerable northern environment."[49] Tom Axworthy, principal secretary to Prime Minister Trudeau, agreed: "As Arctic neighbours and as the biggest members of the circumpolar North, Canada and Russia share many common interests and problems. We must do what we can to encourage Russian democracy and oppose the resurgence of ultra-nationalist and autocratic forces there. The creation of an Arctic Council will be a modest but real recognition that Russia has joined the democratic community of nations."[50] The Chrétien Liberal government, in office as of 1993, pushed the idea further, noting, "We have to stop defending what our countries are doing and start telling the truth even if it hurts."[51]

The Arctic Council came into being in 1996, with the United States reluctantly agreeing to join. Aboriginal people were assured substantial and separate membership. The new Arctic Council had an impressive—even daunting—set of marching orders. Russia, for example, needed help to eliminate radioactive waste in the Arctic, country foods had to be assessed for toxins to determine their suitability for human consumption, and climate change research encouraged. The council focused on sustainable human development in northern communities, and the need to balance resource development and environmental protection. In the international sphere, co-operation, trade, and cultural support were the orders of the day.[52] At the Americans' insistence, the council did not discuss military matters.[53]

Arctic collaboration quickly expanded in science and education, including the creation of the Circumpolar Universities Association and the University of the Arctic. The latter, a collaboration between 110 higher-education institutions and non-governmental organizations (NGOs), was officially launched in 2001 to deliver university courses to students across the circumpolar North. Scientific co-operation was spurred by the establishment of the International Arctic Science Committee (IASC) and the International Arctic Social Sciences Association (IASSA). In less than two decades, the strategic isolation of the Cold War era gave way to impressive collaborative enterprises in governance, learning, and research.

Canada declared itself pleased with these developments, and with the continued downgrading of military concerns. "Nothing illustrates more dramatically the link between domestic and foreign factors than the state of the Arctic environment," House of Commons Standing Committee on Foreign Affairs and International Trade chairman Bill Graham reported in April 1997. "That environment, so special and so fragile, is particularly sensitive to foreign influences." The report accepted that the concept of security had broadened from military issues to encompass an array of social and environmental issues. "This new agenda for security cooperation is inextricably linked to the aims of environmentally sustainable human development," the report noted. "Meeting these challenges is essential to the long-term foundation for assuring circumpolar security, with priority being given to the well-being of Arctic peoples and to safeguarding northern habitants from intrusions which have impinged aggressively on them."[54]

The most appropriate solution, the all-party committee recommended, was for Canada to push to make the Arctic a nuclear-free zone, and even to demilitarize the region. The environmental legacies of the Cold War also had to be addressed: abandoned military sites in the Canadian North required cleaning up and restoration, and the report recommended that Canada assist Russia with the dangers associated with its decaying northern fleet, such as radioactive contamination from illegal dumping of nuclear wastes and abandoned Russian nuclear-powered submarines rotting in the Arctic Ocean.[55]

This federal focus on international co-operation fit with the government's announcement of an "Aboriginal Action Plan" to foster healthier communities and partnership at home, even if they did not support demilitarization. The military played an important role in the region, particularly in communication, navigation, and transportation systems in the region. Furthermore, the Canadian Forces conducted essential operations, such as humanitarian assistance and search and rescue, which would be "difficult, and perhaps even impossible," for any other organization to provide. "Additionally, the cultural inter-play of service people serving in our North has an intangible benefit in promoting a sense of national awareness among the military and those northern residents who come in contact with the military," the response noted. "A military presence in the North also provides Canada's Aboriginal peoples with an opportunity to serve their country and community through participation in the Canadian Rangers." In short, Canada's existing activities to assert sovereignty (maritime surveillance overflights, Coast Guard icebreaker patrols, and the Canadian Rangers) were compatible with a constructive Arctic strategy. There was, however, no security crisis that warranted an *increased* military presence beyond a modest expansion in the number of northerners serving with the Canadian Rangers.[56]

The debates of the 1990s had convinced the government of Canada to reconfigure its approach to Arctic sovereignty. In 2000, the Department of Foreign Affairs and International Trade issued "The Northern Dimension of Canada's Foreign Policy." Its opening paragraphs showed how much the Liberal government's view of the Arctic changed from that of its predecessors:

Both the tradition of transnational co-operation and the new emphasis on human security are particularly applicable to the shaping of the Northern Dimension of Canada's Foreign Policy. The circumpolar world that includes the northern territories and peoples of Canada, Russia, the United States, the Nordic countries plus the vast (and mostly ice-covered) waters in between was long a front line in the Cold War. Now it has become a front line in a different way—facing the challenges and opportunities brought on by new trends and developments. The challenges mostly take the shape of transboundary environmental threats—persistent organic pollutants, climate change, nuclear waste—that are having dangerously increasing impacts on the health and vitality of human beings, northern lands, waters and animal life. The opportunities are driven by increasingly confident northern societies who, drawing on their traditional values, stand poised to take up the challenges presented by globalization. Whereas the politics of the Cold War dictated that the Arctic region be treated as part of a broader strategy of exclusion and confrontation, now the politics of globalization and power diffusion highlight the importance of the circumpolar world as an area for inclusion and co-operation.

Framed by principles of Canadian leadership, partnership, and ongoing dialogue with northerners, this rare foreign policy statement on the region was rooted in four overarching objectives. The first priority involved enhancing "the security and prosperity of Canadians, especially northerners and Aboriginal peoples." After all, the birth of the new territory of Nunavut in 1999 signalled that the North was changing in fundamental ways. Self-government and devolution, rooted in partnership with aboriginal peoples, required new economic opportunities that promoted northern interests.[57] While the government committed itself "to assert and ensure the preservation of Canada's sovereignty in the North," such efforts would take a new form, marked by the absence of traditional security and sovereignty threats. Canadian officials clearly believed

By the late 1990s, the Canadian Rangers' red ball caps and sweatshirts had become the most recognizable symbol of Canada's military presence in the far north, embodying a spirit of cooperation between northern communities and the Canadian Forces. *DND photo IS2004-2134*

that constructive engagement, not confrontation, would mark the twenty-first century.[58]

The focus on diplomacy and cooperation meant that traditional preoccupations with "defending" sovereignty slipped to the back burner. The Somalia affair of the mid-1990s and other scandals made the Liberal government wary of the Canadian Forces. Most military programs seemed to clash with agendas articulated by northerners. As a result, military activities in the North slowed. No sovereignty operations were conducted in 1999–2000. Aurora maritime patrol aircraft were scheduled to conduct only four sovereignty patrols in 2000, down from twenty in the mid-nineties. By the end of the decade, CF assets in the North were sparse indeed. The headquarters in Yellowknife, with seventy-seven personnel, lacked "the staff resources or situational awareness to coordinate more than a nominal level of activity." Although the four Twin Otter transport aircraft represented a CF presence in the North, they were small and slow, forcing the military to rely on commercial airlines. The Forward Operating Locations were seldom used for fighter-aircraft operations. The largely unmanned NWS radar sites, maintained by civilian contractors, and the skeleton staff at Canadian Forces Station Alert/Eureka on Ellesmere Island continued their quiet vigil. The Canadian Rangers, part-time volunteers in fifty-eight patrols across the territorial North, provided the most extensive and visible military presence in the North, as well as a constructive and intimate connection with northern communities. They did not, however, have the capacity to operate outside of their local areas nor the authorization to do more than report problems.[59]

By 2000, the Canadian Forces' "Arctic Capabilities Study" acknowledged that the nature of security issues had evolved to include environmental, social, and economic aspects, particularly in the North. Rather than diminishing the military's role, the commander of Canadian Forces Northern Area argued, the coming decades would make the North even more vulnerable to "asymmetric" security and sovereignty threats. "There is presently no immediate direct military threat to Canada," the study conceded, but "there remain many significant security/sovereignty challenges of a different nature emerging in the North" which could, over the long term, erode Canadian sovereignty. The Canadian Forces had to be prepared to respond to challenges related to environmental protection, increased shipping as Arctic sea lanes opened due to climate change, heightened commercial-airline activity, and "trans-national criminal activity" that would accompany resource development such as diamond mining. To meet its obligations in the North, Canadian Forces Northern Area argued, improved capabilities to monitor and respond to emergencies were needed.[60] The Department of National Defence decided, given its limited budget, that the equipment and programs proposed to address more than surveillance issues would be extremely expensive. Scarce military resources would, instead, go to more pressing priorities.[61]

If the North had been an "exposed front" during the Cold War, with perceived sovereignty threats prompting reactions at various junctures, nothing at the end of the twentieth century indicated a strong need for government action in the sovereignty or military-security realm. The government had to act in the North, Mary Simon explained in 1996, but the needs were social and environmental. "There is an image of this barren land that is very pristine and hardly anybody lives there, but in many ways it is not that," she explained. "You are talking about a much more severe climate, but it does not stop people from being concerned about the environment, about their livelihoods . . . their cultural identity, their language." Human and environmental security, sustainable development, and capacity-building were the new catchphrases of northern foreign policy. The direction of the twenty-first century, it seemed, would be broader and more progressive than the post–Second World War era.

As Lloyd Axworthy, Canada's foreign affairs minister, said at the inaugural meeting of the Arctic Council in Iqaluit in September 1998, "A true partnership has emerged where Arctic states and Indigenous peoples have, together, developed a vision for the Arctic where national agendas can be harmonized and cultural diversity encouraged. This has allowed us to work effectively on the substantive challenge of achieving equitable development in the Arctic while protecting and promoting its environmental integrity."[62] Promoters of the Inuit Circumpolar Conference, the Arctic Environmental Protection Strategy, the Arctic Council, and the University of the Arctic had stitched together a political and administrative trans-border network that, by the late 1990s, promised to make the Far North a place of co-operation rather than a resource and strategic battleground. The lack of southern interest, ironically, had created openings that northern and indigenous politicians had exploited with creativity and success. The result was that despite the huge stakes in the Arctic, the potential for actual conflict between states seems unlikely—something that stands in contrast to many regions of the world.

With each passing year, Canada's assurance about the Arctic seemed to build. Canadian legal experts expressed confidence that Canada's sovereignty claim to the waters of the archipelago was grounded in international law. Unique geography justified straight baselines to enclose the waters. The small number of ships that crossed the Passage hardly supported the contention that it was an "international strait" in legal terms, even if did connect the Atlantic and Pacific Oceans. But there was no justification for apathy. "Sovereignty can be lost; it can be abandoned," law professor Donald McRae warned. "And it can be abandoned by dereliction. Failure by Canada to exercise its sovereign authority over the waters will diminish the credibility of its claim of sovereignty." If foreign vessels continued to transit the Passage, it might become a strait "used for international navigation" and thus undermine Canada's claim to internal waters.[63] It would take a new threat—that created by a remarkable transformation of the Arctic environment—to make this possibility a likelihood and to once again transform the sovereignty and security concerns of the Far North.

Chapter Five

THE FINAL RACE
TO THE NORTH POLE:

CLIMATE CHANGE, OIL AND GAS
AND THE NEW BATTLE FOR THE ARCTIC

"The question of Arctic sovereignty is not a question. It's clear. It's our country. It's our water. It's the 'True North strong and free' and they are fooling themselves if they think dropping a flag on the ocean floor is going to change anything."

— PETER MACKAY, Minister of National Defence (2007)

Suddenly, after decades of being coffee-table conversation for academics, the Canadian Arctic is front-page news—in the *New York Times*, in *Time* magazine, and in papers around the world—and, because of the melting ice cap that according to Al Gore threatens to drown the coastlines of the world, has a prominent place in his documentary, *An Inconvenient Truth*. Overnight the Far North has become the canary in the mine shaft, a symbol of the impending catastrophe of global climate change. But there's more to the issue than melting ice. Developers lust after the oil, gas, and mineral potential of the region; there may be billions of dollars to be extracted from what have long been seen as ice- and snow-covered wastes. Russian submarines patrol the Arctic seabed, and a revitalized Russia is scientifically staking its extended continental shelf. Indeed, all Arctic Ocean coastal states have or are making submissions to delineate the outer limits of our respective continental

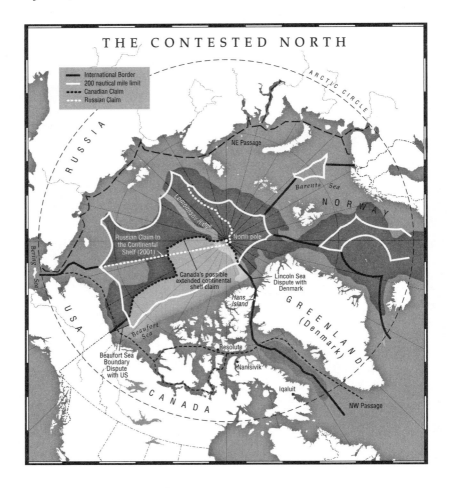

THE CONTESTED NORTH

International Border
200 nautical mile limit
Canadian Claim
Russian Claim

ARCTIC CIRCLE

RUSSIA

NE Passage

Barents Sea

NORWAY

Lomonosov Ridge

North pole

Russian Claim to
the Continental
Shelf (2001)

Bering Sea

Canada's possible
extended continental
shelf claim

Lincoln Sea
Dispute with
Denmark

USA

Hans
Island

GREENLAND
(Denmark)

Beaufort Sea

Resolute

Beaufort Sea
Boundary
Dispute
with US

Nanisivik

CANADA

Iqaluit

NW Passage

shelves. Russian submarines have been there for years, navigating the high seas, as they have every right to do under international law. But that same Russia, written off a few years ago as a declining superpower, is now flying patrols in the Far North, foreshadowing a remilitarization of the Arctic. Is this a new Cold War, the Hot Arctic, or some combination of both? Whatever the cause and the outcome, the Arctic has moved towards the centre of the international stage, fuelling misguided debates about the best means of protecting Canadian sovereignty in an area over which we previously had no rights. Confused by press reports of land extension and possible confrontation, the public's concern is really driven by its misunderstanding about the existing process. All Arctic states, Russia included, are engaged in a legally established United Nations process to delimit their extended continental shelves. States are not really enlarging their territory, but identifying the seabed area outside their 200-nautical-mile (230 miles, or 368 kilometres) economic zones where they have the exclusive right to exploit resources. Nevertheless, Canadian anxieties speak to the heightened tempo of activity and uncertainty in a changing Arctic region that will soon be more accessible to a resource-hungry world.

Climate Change and the Threat to the North

In a strongly worded October 2007 op-ed piece in the *New York Times*, Canadian scholar Thomas Homer-Dixon offered a sobering commentary on the threat posed by global warning. He used the Arctic as the symbol for the critical challenge facing the international community:

> The vast expanse of ice floating on the surface of the Arctic Ocean always recedes in the summer, usually reaching its lowest point in the last half of September. Every winter it expands again, as the long Arctic night descends and temperatures plummet. Each summer over the past six years, global warming has trimmed this ice's total area a little more, and each winter the ice's recovery has been a little less robust. These trends alarmed climate scientists, but most thought that sea ice wouldn't disappear completely in the Arctic summer before 2040 at the earliest.
>
> But this past summer sent scientists scrambling to redo their estimates. Week by week, the National Snow and Ice Data Center in Boulder, Colorado reported the trend: from 2.23 million

square miles of ice remaining on August 8 to 1.6 million square miles on September 16, breaking through the previous low of 2.05 million square miles, reached in 2005.

. . . One of the climate's most important destabilizing feedbacks involves Arctic ice. . . . Melting ice leaves behind open ocean water that has a much lower reflectivity (or albedo) than that of ice. Open ocean water absorbs about 80 percent more solar radiation than sea ice does. And so as the sun warms the ocean, even more ice melts, in a vicious circle. This ice-albedo feedback is one of the main reasons why warming is happening far faster in the high north, where there are vast stretches of sea ice, than anywhere else on Earth.

Homer-Dixon, and many others, believe that these changes foreshadow dramatic and potentially irreversible climatic catastrophe. The ringing of Arctic alarm bells represents a profound shift in global understanding of, and concern for, the Far North. In previous generations, the cold and ice of the Arctic was taken for granted. People knew the North was a forbidding place and understood that human life there was precarious. Few outside the scientific community paid much attention to the idea that there were strong connections between northern conditions and southern climate, or worried much that the environmental changes evident in heavily populated areas might have an effect on the Far North. Indeed, the Arctic was widely celebrated for its pristine nature, for being "untouched" by civilization and industrialization—although environmentalists such as Bill McGibbon, in *The End of Nature*, recognized decades ago that northern ecosystems were being transformed by global pollution.

Scientists interested in the Arctic have been at the forefront of the global debate about climate change. Given funding, alterations in northern ecosystems are easy to monitor and, because of the relatively uncomplicated nature of the Arctic environment, fairly easy to describe. One of the standard images in the global debate about climate change—useful because it is so simple and so arresting—

uses satellite images to document the retreat of the Arctic sea ice. Photographs comparing a surprisingly short period of time reveal a dramatic reduction in the once seemingly eternal polar ice cap. The ice cap used to be called "permanent," but these images show that it is not. More recent images, drawing on Homer-Dixon's evidence, show an even more rapid decline in the past few years. In 2006, John Falkingham of the Canadian Ice Service argued that the northern ice pack had shrunk at a rate of 3–4 percent per decade, accelerating to an 8 percent per decade decrease starting in 2000; others suggested a much more rapid decline. By September 2007, Mark Serreze, a senior researcher with the U.S. National Snow and Ice Data Center, declared: "The Arctic is on a fast track of change, and the Arctic sea ice is on a death spiral."[1] Both are moving faster than any of our previous models were telling us. We still don't understand what's happening up there." As scientists look for ways of documenting the extent and speed of climate change, they have found no better and more readily understood symbol of human-induced ecological transformation than in the Arctic Ocean.

Of course, it's not quite that simple. Much has been made, for example, of the rapid thawing of the Greenland ice sheet along the coast, opening up new areas for settlement and development (as well as potentially drowning Miami). Studies concluded in 2005, however, reveal that the loss of coastal ice was more than offset by additional snowfall at higher elevations. In fact, the total amount of ice and snow on Greenland actually increased, even though the highly visible thawing of ice along the coast suggested a significant decline in the Greenland ice pack. So, is this a bad thing for the world or a good thing? Scientists differ on this question.

Because of its stark beauty, the Arctic lends itself to provocative and attention-grabbing images of nature and the threats posed by global warming. *Time* magazine's eye-grabbing cover of April 3, 2006—a polar bear stranded on a small ice floe, seemingly heading off to imminent death due to rapid warming of the Arctic waters—is a perfect illustration of the age and the messaging about the vulnerability of the Arctic. It is a perfect match—the majestic polar bear, the ultimate symbol of the High Arctic, cast adrift by the environmental wickedness of a callous human race. As a graphical illustration of the end of the world—both geographically and metaphorically—it is hard to imagine a more attention-getting image. But it's also an image of the contradictions of the issue. It turns out that, far from legions of Nanooks drifting off to a dismal death, there are in fact more polar bears in the North than ever. Polar bears routinely live on the edge of the Arctic ice, where hunting is often at its best. They are fine swimmers and move easily between ice floes. But those pictures, however false the impression they may give, sell well at climate change conferences, and Nanook, perhaps happily off eating seal somewhere on the ice, has become the poster bear for global warming, appealing to our fascination with the exotic, our superficial affection for the North, and our need to reduce the scientific complexities of global warming to simple images and slogans.

Most northerners believe that climate change is only too real and they also believe, in the words of Mary Simon, "It's not about polar bears. It's about people."[2] The Inuit have no need for scientists to inform them of the major ecological transformations that they are living with. The reduced season for operating ice bridges—crucial means of getting supplies from the south to the diamond mines in the Northwest Territories—is but one example among many of the shifts in northern ecosystems. In 2006, De Beers Canada Corporation reported that warm weather had closed their ice roads for prolonged periods, leaving close to 25 percent of its supplies undelivered during the winter. Indigenous elders talk about changes in ice formation, the migration patterns of animals and birds, and the shortening of winter. While it may seem silly to complain when the North gets warmer, about a few more weeks of summer and fall weather, fewer weeks of –40-degree weather, more vegetation and animal life, northern residents realize that profound changes are under way. The fact that Kuujjuaq, a town in the far north of Quebec, bought air conditioners to help cope with summer temperatures above 30 degrees is certainly a sign of changing times. Traditional knowledge that has supported the region for many generations becomes less reliable when the herds do not show up as expected, when the ice does not freeze as reliably as in the past, and when precipitation levels change.

In some parts of the North, the Arctic thaw has become a matter of life and death. Baba Pederson of Kugluktuk, Nunavut, spoke about insects and birds never before seen in the region, changing ice and sea patterns, and new dangers for Inuit hunters. Speaking about two men from the community who died when their snowmobiles went through the ice, Pederson said, "I blame those deaths on global warming, and that is very scary when it causes people to die. They were going in an area where they should normally be able to go and everything that they had learned before says it's safe and it looks safe and they go over it and they drown. That's scary. All their knowledge didn't help them."[3] David Ooingoot Kalluk of Resolute Bay worried about global warming, observing that "the snow and ice now melt from the bottom," making travel much more dangerous than before.[4]

Because Canada claims so much of the Arctic Ocean, and because the polar ice cap has figured so prominently in Canada's self-image, the climate change debate has taken on an intensely Canadian focus. It is, after all, Inuit communities in the North that would bear the brunt of major changes in the Arctic climate. In August 2007, the leader of Canada's New Democratic Party (NDP), Jack Layton, two other NDP MPs, and a left-wing academic from Vancouver toured the Eastern Arctic to meet with northerners and to draw attention to their party's northern platform. As Layton observed at the end of his Arctic travels,

> After years of Liberal inaction and Conservative indifference, Parliament must tackle the growing climate change crisis now. Climate change is threatening the way of life for average northerners and that's undermining our sovereignty. We can't protect our sovereignty if we don't protect our land. As I've seen

and heard today first-hand, the effects of climate change are a reality for Northern Canadians. We cannot afford to wait.[5]

Layton heard, as other Canadian politicians have before and after, that there are observable and substantial changes in the North, that the pace of change is accelerating, and that the Inuit and other northern aboriginal peoples will likely bear the brunt of the negative changes. He learned of Arctic communities nervous about the prospect of unstoppable change and the realization that ecological shifts, which are already under way, have the potential to undercut their social and economic system. And because Layton was speaking to the Inuit—an aboriginal population that has a positive international image and that attracts a great deal of global sympathy—he managed to get great press for his venture into the Arctic, as well as make a few pro forma digs at the larger parties.

The Arctic has long held great symbolic importance for Canada and the western world—and it retains its hold on the public's imagination. Images of stranded polar bears, vulnerable Inuit villages, and despoiled northern landscapes play well with southern audiences. These same images, however, create space and distance from those same audiences. The number of southern Canadians who are going to trade in their SUVs, unplug their air conditioners, or take their bikes out of storage because new insects are making their way into the Arctic or because the harvesting cycles of a small number of Inuit are being disrupted is probably pretty small, though there are more of them every day. Put simply, Pangnirtung does not sell well in Lethbridge or Chatham; if it did, Canadians would have paid attention to the non-climatic crises in northern communities years ago. And if Canadians were truly exercised about threats to the polar bears, we would have had mobs on the streets thirty years ago, when the species did appear truly threatened. However much climate change in the Arctic plays on nationalistic and southern heartstrings, it is unlikely that the unique circumstances of the Far North will be the trigger that convinces Canada and other nations to revisit their emissions standards and to challenge their citizens to accept the drastic reduction in materialism and consumption necessary to address the real challenges of global climate change. Of course, the difference between Inuit children sniffing gas and houses sinking into melting permafrost is that the first problem is a northern one, while the second has implications that affect the south as well, which is the point of the picture of poor stranded Nanook.

The Opening of the Northwest Passage

If the prospect of doomed polar bears, the melting polar ice cap, and severe disruptions to Inuit communities will not galvanize the nation, having more foreign vessels sail through the Northwest Passage may do the trick. When Captain Henry Larsen sailed the *St. Roch* through the Arctic islands in the 1940s—twenty-eight months going west to east, eighty-six days on the return voyage—he completed an expedition that had long held the world's imagination. But even for Larsen, travelling during the Second World War, the voyage was more symbolic and exploratory than commercial and substantial. From the days of Martin Frobisher, Henry Hudson, and William Baffin, the world had known of the treachery and danger of the Arctic ice and had long since abandoned the idea of using the Northwest Passage on a regular basis. From the 1960s to the 1990s, the Northwest Passage was a playground for tourists, adventurers, and scientists. There were fascinating questions to be addressed about the movement and depth of the Arctic sea ice, seasonal variations in open water, and the safety of small- and medium-sized craft in northern waters. Only a few people kept thinking of the potential of a shipping route through the Arctic, much more profitable than the route through the Panama Canal, and plotted the commercial use of the Northwest Passage.

How quickly things change in public affairs. In less than a decade, the debate about the Northwest Passage has changed from one of symbolism and sovereignty to one of commercialization and

Canada's ability to protect its northern seas. The reason is climate change and the melting of the polar ice cap. As late as May 2006, scientists forecast that Arctic temperatures would rise slowly over the next century, and safe summertime navigation of the Northwest Passage would be possible by 2070. By the following year, 2007, some observers were suggesting that regular navigation might be possible by 2050. And towards the end of the year, the figure, in a northern version of Moore's law, had been cut again, to 2030 or earlier. In 2005, the Russians sent an ordinary ship to the North Pole without an icebreaker. Every few months scientists learn more about the pace of global warming and the rapid retreat of the Arctic ice. Passageways deemed all but impenetrable to northern navigation are now ice free for significant portions of the year. Five years ago few predicted that the Passage would be open this soon— twenty years seemed a radical estimate. Though admittedly on the basis of only a few years of data, the possibility of navigating the Northwest Passage regularly, reliably, and soon seems imminent.

Now, of course, Canadians, having paid little more than lip service to the matter for generations, seem keen to protect their northern waters. For years, Canada has not had to act decisively. It has the strongest set of regulations related to its Arctic waters of any Arctic nation, and has permitted zero marine pollution since 1970. But where Norway, Russia, Denmark, and the United States have substantial capacity for Arctic navigation—and where even Australia and New Zealand have substantial capacity for scientific navigation in Antarctic waters—Canada has an aging and underpowered Coast Guard fleet and only a small and scattered naval capacity in the North. In the past few years, submarines from the United States and Russia have been hard at work in the region. More prominently, cruise ships have come there, offering luxury travellers a unique opportunity to explore a part of the world previously available only to the hardiest adventurers. The cruise ships are bellwethers for the future: by making their way through the entire passageway without disaster, they have established the foundation for future commercial use of Arctic waters.

Now, suddenly, after decades of limited control, we are worried about the increased traffic into Canadian territorial waters. We have, for years, maintained that the Northwest Passage is part of our internal waters and not, as the Americans and others claim, a strait used for international navigation that must be available to all, like the Straits of Gibraltar and other critical passages. The UN Convention on the Law of the Sea spells out internationally accepted practices in such areas,[6] but the rapidity of climate change in the North has forestalled the standard Canadian response, which is usually to protest loudly and to announce impending plans to build naval capacity for the North that die on the order paper before the next election. National politicians know very well that Canadian interest in Arctic sovereignty issues is shorter than an Arctic heat wave—rarely outlasting the voyage of the offending foreign vessel—and that there are few, if any, consequences from backing away from commitments to protecting the North from future intrusions. Furthermore, such concern is limited to academics and political groupies. But the "announce northern infrastructure and then forget it" approach is woefully inadequate in the present situation, for development pressures on the Arctic are increasing steadily with little prospect of an end to demands for an open Arctic waterway.

CGS *Henry Larsen* sails alongside HMCS *Goose Bay* during Operation "Lancaster," August 2006. Prime Minister Harper declared that Canada's territorial integrity "takes a Canadian presence on the ground, in the air and on the sea and a government that is internationally recognized for delivering on its commitments." *DND photo AS2006-0515*

The prospect of regular navigation of the Northwest Passage has generated a great deal of debate. There's huge money at stake. The Tokyo-London journey would be shortened from 20,930 kilometres (13,000 miles) via the Suez Canal or more than 22,540 kilometres (14,000 miles) by way of the Panama Canal to only 16,100 kilometres (10,000 miles) if the Passage stays open. This highlights the fact that not all effects of global warming are bad— think of the fuel saved when voyages are reduced by 40 percent. There is also a risk substitution issue at stake in the Northwest Passage debate. The rapid growth of the Asian economy has sent shipping traffic through the Malacca and Singapore Straits sky-rocketing, with the number of transits expected to grow from 70,000 in 2007 to 140,000 in 2020.[7] The opening of the Northwest Passage would reduce traffic in this overcrowded waterway, thus limiting environmental risk in the area. Some businesspeople applauded the commercial opportunities that would attend shipping to the North, and the resulting stabilization of the northern economy. Scott Borgerson of the U.S. Coast Guard Academy highlighted the positive aspects of global warming, particularly the prospect that the Arctic Ocean could "become the common body of water linking the world's most important economies, all of which are located in the northern hemisphere."[8] For analysts like Borgerson, the opening of Arctic waters could easily match the construction of the Suez and Panama Canals in terms of the impact on global shipping and international trade, requiring only a suitable legislative and regulatory regime to protect national and security interests.

Other observers are worried about the potential environmental dangers—the sinking of a full-laden ship in the Arctic could cause severe ecological damage—particularly since, given the severity of Arctic storms, there's no assurance that the waterways would prove reliable and safe. Moreover, the prospect of dozens, if not hundreds, of foreign-flagged vessels in Arctic waters each year raises a variety of security and defence issues that Canada is ill prepared to address. The prospect of a wide-open Arctic passageway was, of course, a logical extension of the long-standing American belief in freedom of navigation for its navy. America's position that Canadian permission was not required to sail through the Arctic means that any "North Korean or Chinese ships [can] sail through North American waters without asking anyone's permission. From a national security perspective, that's a mad policy," commented Rob Huebert of the University of Calgary. Furthermore, he added, the fact that Canada did not require ships to seek permission to enter the area made little sense: "It's like asking speeders on a highway to report themselves."[9] For a smaller number of commentators, led by Huebert and UBC academic Michael Byers, the opening of the Northwest Passage also creates major security concerns. As Byers noted in January 2006, the creation of a major international shipping route could mean there was a "backdoor to North America that is wide open."[10]

Most observers paid little heed to such comments, which asserted that northern tankers would make an attractive target for terrorists. The suggestion that Al-Qaeda operatives, drug smugglers, illegal immigrants, or other miscreants would enter North America from the High Arctic struck many observers as far-fetched, although caution about underestimating the determination of America's opponents gave some credence to Byers's observations. Paul Cellucci, former U.S. ambassador to Canada, urged Canada to adopt more of a military presence in the Arctic: "That would enable the Canadian navy to intercept and board vessels in the Northwest Passage to make sure they're not trying to bring weapons of mass destruction into North America."[11] The more general warning about the opening of the waterway—that retreating ice would result in the testing of Canadian sovereignty and would likely show Canada's capacity in the North to be seriously wanting—struck a stronger chord: "I don't want Canadian policy to be decided on the fly," Byers observed, "under a timeline that's been set by some ship that's registered in Panama or Liberia with a Filipino crew."[12]

Many are inappropriately uncomfortable with the prospects of an open race to capitalize on the open waters of the Arctic. The Arctic Monitoring and Assessment Programme (AMAP) provides widely shared information on the state of the Arctic ice cap. Organizations like the Arctic Council and the Arctic Marine Shipping Assessment (AMSA) group call for unified research, monitoring, and self-regulation, in an effort to head off conflict and potential environmental catastrophes. The search for standards for Arctic shipping attracted interest from such diverse groups as the Russian Register, Lloyd's Register, and the American Bureau of Shipping, with considerable agreement that collaboration on ship design, crew training, insurance, and the use of Arctic passageways was in order.[13]

Not everyone is going to lose if northern waters get warmer, though. So much attention has focused on the opening of the Northwest Passage that there has been little comment on some of the other consequences of global warming. Consider, for example, the long-neglected port of Churchill, Manitoba. Opened in 1931 and intended to capitalize on the global demand for prairie wheat, the port was long plagued by the short season and difficult navigation in Hudson Bay. For decades the port limped along, underutilized, dashing hopes for a central North outlet to Europe, leaving the community to survive on polar bear tourism. In 1997, the government of Canada gave up on the port, selling the facility to an American entrepreneur, Pat Broe, and OmniTRAX for a measly seven dollars.[14] Broe's investment may prove to be a brilliant one. The further opening of Hudson Bay navigation will lengthen the shipping season, reduce the hazardous ice buildup in the bay and the often treacherous Hudson Strait, and convert the Port of Churchill into a going concern. Even the Russians are getting into the act, with Igor Levitin, Russian transport minister, offering to use icebreakers to keep Churchill open year-round, mirroring the aggressive Russian strategy of investing heavily in the Murmansk port facility to improve access to international markets. By shipping directly from the two northern ports—Murmansk to Churchill—ships could reduce the trip from Russia to North America from seventeen to eight days, revolutionizing ocean navigation and transportation across the Arctic waters. In the Western Arctic, the retreating ice cap will make the Beaufort Sea oil and gas wells easier and less risky to develop, and improve access to the fields, particularly for tankers supplying the burgeoning Asian market.

While political pronouncements garnered national attention, a small but highly symbolic event occurred at Churchill on October 17, 2007. The same day that Prime Minister Harper's government made bold statements about national commitments to the North, the *Kapital Sviridov*, a ship owned by Murmansk Shipping Company, arrived in Churchill. The *Kapital Sviridov* carried a load of fertilizer destined for the Canadian prairies. Using the "Arctic Bridge" route for the first time, the Russian vessel delivered its cargo at close to 10 percent less cost than the traditional southern Canadian option. Churchill mayor Mike Spence declared optimistically that the *Kapital Sviridov* was but the first of many ships that would capitalize on the retreating Arctic ice. Its arrival at Churchill provided one of the first and most tangible signs that, perhaps, a new North was emerging from under the retreating ice.

Arctic Resources: The New Imperative

In 1576, when Martin Frobisher first reached Baffin Island, he discovered impressive quantities of gold ready for easy collection. The gold turned out to be iron pyrites, and Frobisher ended up in disgrace because of his involvement with what his British countrymen saw as a massive fraud. Since the sixteenth century, the Arctic has become synonymous with a curious northern mix of overinflated expectations regarding resources and disappointment surrounding the reality of northern wealth. And so, through the post–Second World War era, there have been tentative but substantially unrealized efforts to develop Arctic resources. With a short-term but prosperous mine here and there, like Polaris and Nanisivik, promising oil fields in the Beaufort Sea and some meagre petroleum finds at Melville Island, the Canadian Arctic seemed destined to fulfill a pattern of glimmers of hope followed by crushing disappointments.

For decades, the Arctic presented a wide array of technological and climatic barriers to resource development. Thick ocean ice, difficulties with transportation, and high energy costs and wages were compounded by the lack of solid scientific data on the vast expanse of the region. But a conjunction of twenty-first-century developments has changed the equation with surprising speed. The rapid increase in resource prices has made once-marginal fields and properties commercially viable. Expanded scientific research and enhanced technologies have made it possible to define promising opportunities more precisely. The threat of shortages in southern areas, combined with the realization of the astonishingly huge untapped potential of the Far North, has given a sharp edge to the issue. The U.S. Geological Survey (USGS) originally estimated that the region holds up to 25 percent of the world's undeveloped oil and gas reserves—although the USGS has since retracted this estimate and is undertaking further studies. Helge Lund of Statoil, the state oil company of Norway, has estimated the Arctic basin resources at 375 billion barrels, saying "It will never replace the Middle East but it has the potential to be a good supplement."[15] Manoucheher Takin of the Centre for Global Energy Studies in London is more optimistic, claiming that there could be between 50 and 100 million barrels of easily extractable oil and gas, accessible within a decade.[16] An assessment by energy consulting company Wood Mackenzie in 2007 put the figure at 20 percent of the world's reserves, most of it natural gas and most of that, almost 70 percent, within Russian control. Add to this improved communications, growing sophistication in the development of fly-in mining camps and removable mining facilities, better search-and-rescue capabilities, and Arctic projects suddenly became commercially and logistically possible. Of course, climate change has expanded the exploration season, opened shipping lanes for longer periods of time, and reduced the costs of operation due to reductions in cold weather and snow and ice. As British commentator Carl Mortished noted about developing the resources, "The physical danger is great and the cost gigantic, with $1 trillion a low ball estimate to recover the resource . . . But whatever the price, the oil majors must push north. The door to the Middle East is shut, biofuels pose a threat to food production and coal is dirty. If Shell, BP and ExxonMobil are to remain open for business, the Arctic is the only frontier left."[17]

The northern resource rush, however, looks like none other in Arctic history. The Russians, ascendant in the North and looking for opportunities to enhance their economy, have increased their exploration activities, including along the seabed. American firms, aware that the Prudhoe Bay oil fields are running low, have eyed northern resources and the uncertain northern boundaries with growing interest. The traditional image of the lone wolf prospector—like Stuart Blusson and his partner, Chuck Fipke, who discovered diamonds in the Northwest Territories and founded the Ekati Mine—is giving way in the High Arctic to highly sophisticated multimillion-dollar exploratory teams, using satellite and other technologies to identify promising possibilities. Much of the work to date has been preparatory in nature, as oil and gas companies gear up for the gradual opening of the Arctic Ocean for full-scale exploration and development. There will be intense scrutiny of the environmental aspects of Arctic resource development, but most of the rich fields are a long way from the nearest indigenous settlement, so there should be none of the difficulties that have delayed the Mackenzie Valley Pipeline for over thirty years now.

Arctic resource potential can be readily seen in Hammerfest, a hitherto small outpost at the far north end of Norway that, remarkably for the North, achieved formal town status in 1789 and was the first in Europe with electric street lighting, in 1891. The construction of the Snohvit (Snow White) project, a close to $9 billion processing centre for liquefied natural gas, has drawn thousands of workers to the area. Snohvit, however, is intended to be the start, not the end, of Norway's Arctic oil and gas exploration activities, with hopes running high that explorations in the Barents Sea and farther north than Spitsbergen will uncover additional oil deposits. The combined Russian-Norwegian undersea Arctic play, designed to produce gas for exports to the American Northeast, is the largest and more promising of the northern resource initiatives. Hammerfest consultant Arvid Jensen noted, "Oil will bring a big geopolitical focus. It is a driving force in the Arctic."[18]

Hammerfest is not likely to remain the only Arctic hot spot. Russia's Yamal Peninsula holds an estimated 480 trillion cubic feet of natural gas, attracting the attention of companies like Repsol

YPF of Spain despite the formidable logistical challenges of operating in the Far North. Seasoned veterans cautioned against unrealistic expectations: "It will 'feel great' as the winters warm for the next 20 years and we start tapping the reserves in the Arctic. But it will still cost $100 to $150 a barrel for it. The ice may be gone—but the Arctic is a harsh environment—and a long distance from where the markets are."[19]

If this sounds like a booster advertisement for the happy side of global warming, consider the following vicious circle of events:

Greenhouse gas makes the climate warmer.

Warmer climate melts Arctic ice.

Less Arctic ice means that it's easier to find and extract more oil and gas.

More oil and gas burned means more greenhouse gas, and so on . . .

The Arctic has more than oil and gas on offer. In the summer of 2006, Prime Minister Stephen Harper joined an impressive array of bankers, mining executives, and others for the opening of Tahera Diamond Corporation's new Jericho Mine in Nunavut. Harper was roundly criticized for skipping an international conference on AIDS/HIV to attend the mine opening, but as one executive noted, "If he went to the conference, it would do nothing to speed up a cure for AIDS. [B]y coming here and announcing that the north is open for development, [Harper] will bring investment dollars to this part of the world."[20] The development of yet another diamond mine, with another opening in 2007 and other properties under consideration, fuelled southern investment in the North and generated near–Klondike-like enthusiasm for the Far North. Significantly, what set the new projects apart from their post–Second World War predecessors is that northern indigenous peoples played a significant role in the planning and operation of the mines.

It turns out that there is more than oil and gas under the Arctic ice, although the other resources have not yet attracted as much attention as the prospect of oil rigs and tankers working their way through the region. Preliminary investigations suggest that there are marketable mineral deposits and potentially coal on the Arctic seabed, though of course there's no shortage of coal easily accessible on dry land; furthermore, it's the worst possible fuel to burn from a global warming perspective. Moreover, the Arctic fisheries have barely been touched, raising the possibility of a major surge in activity in this area as well. Graham Shimmield, of the Dunstaffnage Marine Research Station in Scotland, and a leading scientist in the field, worries about the potential rush to exploit the hitherto untapped fishery: "There is strong evidence that there are still good reserves of fish such as cod and capelin in some regions of the Arctic. However, these are probably the world's last refuges. We should restrain ourselves from catching them on an industrial scale until we learn more about how strong they are."[21] The signalling of major fish stocks in a largely unregulated ocean is likely to spark a rush into the Arctic as soon as ocean navigation becomes reliable.

A long-standing joke about the Canadian Arctic is that the average Inuit family consists of a man, a woman, their children, and an anthropologist. According to Guy d'Argencourt of the Nunavut Research Institute, the demographics have changed. The anthropologists have been replaced by geologists![22] The Arctic has long been an area of promise and hidden potential. True, developable properties are few in number and widely scattered, and the prospects for finding substantial quantities of oil and gas in the region remain a matter of hope and conjecture. But with the world rapidly running out of known and potential gas reserves, hope springs eternal that the discovery and development of Arctic resources will postpone the day of energy reckoning for several additional years. There is the possibility, as well, that the Arctic seabed has a series of what are called "hot smokers, super-heated water jets containing valuable minerals such as manganese, platinum and gold."[23]

Rachel Qitsualik, an Inuit writer, offered a sarcastic commentary for those who assumed that the euphoria of the early twenty-first century would produce great wealth and opportunity. Writing from the imaginary perspective of 2020, she described the militarization of the North and major increases in sea mammal populations due to global warming, and then described a series of dashed dreams and unexpected twists: "It's amazing to think back on all the saber-rattling between the United States, Denmark and Canada over rights to the Northwest Passage only to have so many ships ripped apart by unanticipated icebergs. In 2018 there was much hoopla over Canada's new U.S. friendly licensing system for foreign usage of Canadian Arctic waters, even though America had already been using the waters since 2009. The issue only came to the forefront of public awareness in 2011, when [the *Rose of Texas*] an American oil tanker, was split open 300 kilometres from Gjoa Haven, ruining local fish stocks and poisoning coastlines." She continued in a similar vein, describing the resource-inspired boom, abandoned mine and townsites, and writing, "As they retreated to the South again, pockets empty and with bittersweet memories of a beautiful but strangely unprofitable land, they were haunted by a single, frustrating mystery: the knowledge that they could never say exactly why the Arctic hadn't been what they'd expected."

Qitsualik offered a perspective on the northern resource boom rarely heard in Canada: "The truth is that the Arctic is warming— but I fear more for how the South will react to it than I do for Inuit." The Inuit know, she said, that the Arctic is a harsh and unforgiving land, that the southerners' visions of northern prosperity rarely come true, and the Inuit will remain long after the newcomers flee, with Arctic wealth or impoverished by unrealistic dreams. Casting her thoughts back over thousands of years of Arctic history, which included other periods of Arctic warming and cooling, she believed her people would adapt once again: "And they will adapt, even as they whisper a prayer over the skeletons of those who refused to do the same. For Inuit have never owned The Land, having learned of old that it is no man's resource."[24]

Canadians woke up to the new Arctic realities when anxious commentators declared that the hitherto benign Danes, marketers of teak furniture and fairy tales, had dared to lay claim to Hans Island, suddenly a crucial piece of Canadian territory. The contested ownership of this barren rock, lying almost exactly mid-channel between Greenland and Ellesmere Island, had actually come to light in 1972 when Canada and Denmark met to negotiate an agreement to delimit their respective continental shelves. Rather than getting hung up on this minor matter,

Colonel Norm Couturier, Commander of Canadian Forces Northern Area, briefs the media on details of Operation "Kigliqaqvik IV," a long-range sovereignty patrol on and around Ellef Ringes Island in Nunavut, April 2005. *DND photo IS2005-0039*

the treaty negotiators simply left 875 metres (0.54 miles) of border in Nares Strait unsettled and concluded the longest shelf-boundary treaty negotiated to that time: a whopping 1500 kilometres (932 miles).[25] While Canada had done more to exercise sovereignty over the remote island than its northern neighbour, the Danes have not renounced their claim. This did not raise the spectre of sovereignty loss, however, and discussions with Denmark on the issue were marked by a notable lack of urgency. Far from fighting over the barren island, the countries collaborated on the management of the local environment. The realization that a Canadian company, Dome Petroleum, was using the island as a research base sparked a classic Arctic-sovereignty reprisal by the Danes—they flew by helicopter to the island in 1984 and deposited a flag, a bottle of schnapps, and a note: "Welcome to the Danish Island."[26] So there, Canada! Scarcely a handful of Canadians had heard of Hans Island before 2004, but in that year, Canada's ability to hold on to this tiny and isolated piece of windswept rock in Nares Strait became a test of national will and commitment to the North.

And then things got a little silly. Starting in 2004, the Canadian media began running stories about Danish designs on the tiny chunk of contested rock, claiming that Canada had neglected its northern territory and that the Danes were moving in. The opposition

Conservatives assailed the governing Liberal Party for their inability to defend the Arctic islands properly. The rhetoric inflated very quickly. Claims circulated that Canadian military exercises in the area were in response to Danish actions—they were not—and rumours circulated that the Danes had plans to move into the area. Canada's minister of national defence, Bill Graham, visited the island in July 2005, followed quickly by a formal Danish complaint about Canadian incursions on Denmark's territory. Further research concluded, appropriately given the slapstick nature of the "conflict" over Hans Island, that the island was neither Canadian nor Danish but probably belonged to both countries. The issue remains unresolved, with both countries still claiming sovereignty over the tiny piece of Arctic nothingness.

Canada, it must be noted, seems particularly drawn to conflicts with minor European powers, perhaps because we have too much sense to get into fights with bigger ones. In a 1994 controversy over fishing off Newfoundland, Fisheries Minister Brian Tobin actually ordered Coast Guard vessels to shoot over the bows of Spanish ships, arresting several and having them towed to harbour for impounding. The Hans Island affair fitted nicely with this pattern of Canadian sabre-rattling—a strong position over a seemingly inconsequential matter with a non-military rival whose own engagement on the issue was also haphazard. Few Canadians would have anticipated in 2005 that the minor squabble over Hans Island would be the opening salvo in a rapidly expanding conflict over the control of the Arctic.

Boundaries are assumed to be immutable. With a handful of exceptions—Kashmir between India and Pakistan, Somalia and several other failed African states—the lines drawn mostly in the nineteenth century have come to define the geopolitical outlines of the world. Funny, then, that the latest debate over the cartographic outline of the world would take place in two of the unlikeliest places in the world: underwater and in the High Arctic. Steve Gregory of Weather InSite commented in 2006 that "it's becoming more and more obvious that we'll be able to do drilling in the Arctic 161 to 322 kilometres (100 to 200 miles) off the coast, year-round. It used to be no one cared about borders and ownership up there, but now this leads to new problems, political fights. All the countries bordering the Arctic now care who controls particular areas and how do you draw those lines."[27]

The United Nations Convention on the Law of the Sea allows states to exercise exclusive jurisdiction over the resources on and under its extended continental shelf—the underwater extension of the landmass. (The technical wording is a "natural prolongation" of the continental shelf.) The recognition of the importance of the continental shelf through the creation of the EEZ had earlier allowed Canada to assert control over the fishery off the Grand Banks of Newfoundland, permitted Iceland to maintain effective management of its offshore fishery, and generally redefined the zone of national responsibilities around all maritime nations. Little public attention had been paid to the Arctic, primarily because of the doubtful value of underwater holdings trapped below many metres of solid ice, leaving the precise boundaries of the continental shelf in the Arctic undefined and hence unsettled. In fact, Canada has not yet completed the scientific research to delimit any of its shelf in the Arctic or in the Maritimes. The Convention gives us ten years from when we became a party to it, which happened in 2003. What is more, the complex underwater Arctic topography creates a formidable scientific challenge, as Richard Scott, a Cambridge University scientist observed: "The difficulty we have in the Arctic Ocean is that there are a lot of ridges and it is not clear whether they are attached to the continental shelves. The necessary data is missing at the moment. We have some information, but not very good information." And getting that data was no easy feat, as Andrew Latham, a British energy consultant, commented: "The technology to even explore in that sort of location is fledgling to put it mildly. If you've got to run icebreakers just to do a seismic survey, then you are into horrendous costs."[28]

In the summer of 2007 the public debate changed dramatically. In June, the Russians claimed that they had identified the precise nature of the Lomonosov Ridge, the underwater mountain range that rises some 3,500 metres (11,475 feet) from the ocean bed and runs between Ellesmere Island and Siberia. More dramatically, the Russians claimed that their discoveries documented the extension of the continental shelf in the Arctic. Eventually, they will make a submission to the UN Commission to assert their right to the resources within 1.2 million square kilometres (0.46 million square miles) of Arctic seabed. (Canada's claimed area may amount to as much as 1.75 million square kilometres [0.68 million square miles].) Political scientist Michael Byers reacted to the news with alarm: "The stakes are simply too high and time is running out." While some Canadian scientists described the announcements as "premature," David Hik, of the University of Alberta, advised Canadians to take the Russian scientists seriously, noting that they have a "very credible history of scientific research in the North. We have to remember that almost half of the Arctic is in Russia."[29]

A July expedition raised the symbolic stakes to the highest point yet. Reports surfaced that Russian scientists, working off the *Akademik Fyodorov*, the country's most important research vessel, and accompanied by the icebreaker *Rossiya*, would use submarines and cutting-edge technologies to descend to the seabed directly at the North Pole. The expedition, led by Arctic scientist Artur Chilingarov, himself a politician and Hero of the Soviet Union, included two representatives from the Russian Duma and sought, in the words of politician Vladimir Gruzdev, to "remind the whole world that Russia is a great polar and scientific power."[30] Chilingarov was more assertive: "The Arctic is ours and we should demonstrate our presence."[31] He declared that the expedition ranked among the greatest of all human feats of exploration: "We face the most severe and risky task, to descend to the depths, to the seabed, in the harshest of oceans, where no one has been before and to stand in the centre of the ocean on our own feet. Humanity has long dreamt of this."[32] The hyperbole suited the overheated rhetoric of the modern Arctic, for of all the world's great geographical challenges, this one had probably fuelled more fantasies than any other. The Russians played the exploration metaphors to the point of excess, likening the descent to the first step on the moon—and even linking the submariners with Russians in outer space. The descent went as planned, using submersibles MIR 1 and MIR 2 to check out the seabed some 1300 metres (0.8 miles) below the surface. The scientists deposited a Russian flag, encased in a titanium container, on the sea floor, bragging that evidence of the Russian presence would be around for hundreds of years. Chilingarov and his team were treated to a hero's welcome when they returned to Russia, a striking sign of the intersection of nationalism, science, and the Arctic in modern Russia.

Closer examination revealed some odd elements in the Russian expedition. The lustre of their accomplishment was tarnished subsequently when it was revealed that the television footage used by Russia to document the journey actually came from the movie *Titanic*. Furthermore, foreign businessmen Fredrik Paulsen of Sweden and Michael McDowell of Australia had paid upwards of $3 million for the privilege of joining the Chilingarov project.[33] Indeed, despite the inflated rhetoric of the summer of 2007, international co-operation and the mingling of business, science and sovereignty seemed to be the order of the day. Almost all of the expeditions launched to explore the seabed involved more than one country—an oddity in the so-called race to the Arctic ocean floor.

However, the Russian activities did grab Canada's attention. Foreign Affairs officials declared that the country's sovereignty was long-standing, well established and based on historic title. As for continental shelf extension, Canada was just in the process of conducting its science. All submissions are subject to review and counter-evidence, which was being collected by Canadian and Danish scientists (a co-operative endeavour that showed how much Canada was getting along with Denmark, despite all the hoopla over Hans Island). For some observers, Canada was best served by falling back on its informal arrangements with the United States. Michael Byers argued that Canada and the United States should finally resolve the boundary line in the Beaufort Sea, collaborate on scientific research, and support each other's claims to the Commission on the Limits of the Continental Shelf, created under the UN Convention on the Law of the Sea. Favouring a combination of a "serious investment of money and personnel as well as imaginative and proactive diplomacy," Byers questions: "Is Canada a serious Arctic country? Are we in this race to win?"[34]

While Canadians dismissed the Russian activities as hollow symbolism and rejected the argument that Canada's sovereignty over the region had been diminished, the reality was that Russia had taken a huge leap forward. Canada lacked both the icebreakers and submarines necessary to match Russia's feat and was years away from having the capacity even to monitor the Arctic properly, never mind do anything there. Joe MacInnis, a Canadian diver with long-standing interest in the Arctic, described the Russian manoeuvre as "the world's wildest land claim" and noted, "I've always taken the position that it's one thing to claim sovereignty. It's another thing to be able to go to the place that you claim. The Russians at least have got a sub that takes them to the bottom, that's the place that they're claiming."[35] MacInnis had participated in a Canadian expedition to the North Pole in 1974 where he swam under the ice and left a Canadian flag underwater. He returned in 1979, this time surveying the Lomonosov Ridge. He was not impressed with the Russian effort: "In the high Arctic Ocean, the rules of the land do not apply. The six months of sunless winter skies, the grinding ice, the fearsome winds, the freezing depths and the remote seafloor make this a place where sovereignty has a different meaning from sovereignty on land."[36]

Peter MacKay, Canada's foreign affairs minister, reacted angrily to the Russian manoeuvre: "This isn't the 15th century. You can't go around the world and just plant flags and say, 'We're claiming this territory.'"[37] MacKay's confident assertions tried to allay serious questions inside the country about the security of Canada's claims to the Arctic, and he was definitive: "The question of Arctic sovereignty is not a question. It's clear. It's our country. It's our water. It's the 'True North strong and free' and they are fooling themselves if they think dropping a flag on the ocean floor is going to change anything." The U.S. State Department dropped the bluster in favour of sarcasm: "I'm not sure of whether they've put a metal flag, a rubber flag or a bedsheet on the ocean floor" scoffed a spokesman.[38] The Danes dismissed the Russians' actions as a media stunt, an opinion, interestingly, that appeared to be shared by Russian scientists exploring the ocean floor. As the *Daily Telegraph* observed, "Mr. Chilingarov's stunt was a provocative but humorous challenge. Canada and the United States spectacularly rose to the bait."[39] So did much of the world's media, including *The Independent* (London), which devoted the front page to the story and greeted the descent with a large headline on July 31, 2007: "The North Pole A New Imperial Battleground." But this is more serious than scoffers think. Of course it was a stunt. Stunts make news and set precedents. Was it less of a stunt than the various attempts at the Passage in the nineteenth century, the hunt for the source of the Nile, or the race to the North and South Poles? Sovereignty claims can grow from the seeds of such stunts.

The contest—portrayed in the press and the political arena as a race to the Pole—is really nothing of the sort. In truth, Canada's claim on Arctic lands and maritime areas is as solid as international law provides. There is no question about Canadian ownership: neither Canadian lands nor our maritime area are in question. No foreign state claims them, with the exceptions of Hans Island and parts of the Beaufort and Lincoln Seas. Delimiting our extended continental shelf will take place according to international rules which all countries are respecting. Of course this means that Canada will have to negotiate on its northern boundary issues, just like hundreds of boundaries still being negotiated around the world. But the bottom line is that Canada's ownership of its Arctic Archipelago and the water within it is without question.

Canada's adoption of the UN Convention on the Law of the Sea set out a new time frame and process for recognizing control of its extended continental shelf. Countries have ten years from the point of adoption to make their submissions. Canada ratified the Convention in 2003, so the country has until 2013 to assemble its case, which will be placed before a non-partisan panel of scientists for adjudication. Signatories to the deal further agreed that claimants could bring forward evidence that documented the actual nature of the continental shelf. The research would be evaluated and, if a country's case was scientifically proven, the claim to the extension of the continental shelf would be accepted and the national boundary expanded accordingly. Five countries—Canada, Russia, Denmark, the United States, and Norway—all have Arctic claims, although the United States is not a signatory to the Convention and therefore is not bound by the process. (Iceland, although generally viewed as an Arctic nation, is not deemed to have any northward claims on the Arctic seabed.) The 2007 debate about Russian claims to the Arctic altered American positions on the Law of the Sea and appears likely to result in the United States signing on to the accord, largely to ensure that the country has a means of securing its interests in the Western Arctic.

The Arctic countries have all started to survey the Arctic seabed to determine where their shelves reach. Norway has already made its submission. Russia is also very active, which is understandable because its new deadline expires in 2009. The United States also has made substantial research commitments in the High Arctic, despite not yet being a party to the Convention. Canada has also been active in the lead-up to our submission in 2013. The Russian government took a large step forward in 2006–7 when submarine explorations allowed it to demarcate the outer edges of the continental shelf in the Arctic. Media commentators in other nations with interests in the area, such as Denmark, Canada, and the United States, resented what they construed as Russia's intrusion. But the bottom line is that Canada's ownership of its Arctic Archipelago and the water within it is without question.

In truth, Russia made its claims in accordance with applicable rules, though the Commission on the Limits of the Continental Shelf did not approve its application as presented.[40] To back their claim, the Danes added millions of dollars to the funds devoted to

In March and April 2008, scientists and members of the Canadian Forces conducted research on the Ellesmere Island ice shelves. *DND photo IS2008-3984*

surveying the ocean floor.⁴¹ Canada has done the same. New scientific expeditions were launched to provide surveys of the polar seas, partially as a matter of national pride, but also to defend potential economic interests to the oil, gas, and mineral resources that might be found underwater. In February 2008, Andy Armstrong, an official with the American National Oceanic and Atmospheric Administration, announced a "big discovery" concerning the sea floor off the coast of Alaska—the sea floor stretched more than 100 nautical miles (115 statute miles) farther out than had previously been thought—and commented that Canada and the United States were on a "collision course" over seabed rights in the Arctic Ocean.⁴²

As debate rages on the ownership of the seabed, some commentators suggest that Canada's claim is far from secure. Rosemary Rayfuse, of the University of New South Wales, Australia, offered a cautionary comment: "As a matter of legal principle, Canada has no greater claim on the Arctic than any of the other . . . Arctic states, or indeed any state in the world, quite frankly. Depending on the geological realities, Canada may have a geological claim on some extension of the continental shelf, although I think that Russia and Norway have the greatest amount, from what I've seen."⁴³

Who would have thought five years ago that the world would be squabbling over the undersea Lomonosov Ridge and that Canada, Denmark, Russia, and the United States would be jockeying for stature in the Far North? Perhaps lawyers who read the Law of the Sea, which explains the rights of coastal states to their continental shelf,⁴⁴ or foreign policy specialists who acknowledge that states can have conflicting interpretations on boundaries, have their facts right. But the debate is important for a number of reasons, not least the fact that it has important security overtones. The British, anxious to assert their military presence, have run submarines under the Arctic ice since the mid-1980s, and they knew that the Russians were re-establishing their submarine capacity and extending operations in the region. The Arctic debates, surprisingly, alerted countries with Antarctic claims and responsibilities to the possibility of commercial and other opportunities there as well. By the fall of 2007, Britain was asserting continental shelf claims to a vast area of the southern seas, sparking an angry response from the Argentinians and likely signalling the start of a southern undersea land rush paralleling the Arctic furor. There are, however, fundamental differences between the two polar regions: "The South Pole is an expensive place to exploit and it was realized that if everyone agreed not to touch it, they could all rest easy about pouring millions into the area. This is not the issue with the Arctic. It is becoming easier and easier to exploit. Nations aren't going to give up on these rich pickings."[45] Suggestions that the Antarctic model—governing the region through an international agreement that controlled development and protected the environment—be applied in the North have attracted little support.

Largely missing in the debate over the Arctic is the global nature of the continental shelf controversy. The UN Convention, often cited as stimulating the latest race to the North Pole, has wide international implications, for countries from Russia to Australia, Brazil to Australia have already made their claims to continental shelves, with many others soon to follow. As Scandinavian scientist Lars Kullerud observed, "This will probably be the last big shift in ownership of territory in the history of the earth," with total claims exceeding the size of Australia. Yannick Beaudoin, a colleague of Kullerud's at GRID-Arendal Foundation, noted, "Many countries don't realize how serious it is. 2009 is a final and binding deadline. This allows you to secure sovereignty without having to fight for it."[46] Only Russia has a 2009 deadline in the Arctic, but many commentators are playing up the need for urgent action by other circumpolar states, preying upon fears that they will lose out in "this great Arctic gold rush."[47] While media attention focused for a time on the Arctic, subsequent disputes in hotly contested areas like the South China Sea, Easter Island, and Madagascar have the potential to make the Law of the Sea a hot topic in the coming decade.

Article 77 of the UN Convention explains that coastal states already have sovereign rights over their continental shelf in terms of exploration and exploitation of natural resources, regardless of occupation or "any express proclamation," but this does not give pessimists much comfort. Other commentators, such as Hans Corell, who was responsible for supervising Law of the Sea matters at the United Nations, are less sensationalist. "The United Nations Convention on the Law of the Sea is the comprehensive multilateral regime that applies in the Arctic," Corell observes, and "there is nothing to suggest otherwise. As far as the rights of coastal states are concerned, the convention distinguishes between territorial sea, the exclusive economic zone [EEZ] and the continental shelf. Apart from the territorial sea, which extends 12 nautical miles (13.8 statute miles) from the baselines, the questions that arise in the Arctic are definitely not about territory over which states have sovereignty." Although states have the right to exploit the resources in or on the seabed itself in their exclusive economic zones or on their continental shelf, they do not have a legal right to control the freedom of navigation on the high seas. Sea areas in the Arctic that lie beyond the exclusive economic zones and continental shelf of circumpolar states "are referred to in the Convention as the common heritage of mankind. There are clear provisions to the effect that no state shall claim or exercise sovereignty or sovereign rights over any part of this area or its resources." In Corell's view, ideas that competing powers are "racing to carve up the region" which could "erupt in an armed mad dash for its resources" are "not only misleading" but "utterly irresponsible."[48]

Why is it, then, that Canadians are so concerned about losing their Arctic inheritance? Canada has relied so long on the assumption that the 141st meridian that divides the Yukon and Alaska simply extends to the North Pole that it has prepared minimally—psychologically and militarily at least—for any challenge to its sovereignty in the area. As earlier chapters revealed, Canada reacted to various sovereignty and security crises during the Cold War out of fear that our circumpolar neighbours threatened our national interests. Because Canada has generally neglected the region in terms of development and defence, focusing on southern Canadian priorities whenever it could, this meant that any perceived encroachment was bound to trigger a reaction. Often these anticipated "threats" reflected our inability to acknowledge that our Arctic counterparts also had interests, and that we'd have to negotiate with them when those interests conflicted with ours. The current debate, it seems, is based on similar confusion. Canadians have interests, as do our neighbours, but we're worried that we're falling behind in a "race" to protect ours. The debate has practical issues as well. Neither Canada nor the United States has the scientific capacity to match current Russian investigations of the Arctic. The possibility remains that if the Russians are as prepared and determined as their actions to date suggest, they will move unilaterally into the area and will test the old adage that possession is nine points of the law.

A *Globe and Mail* report on the status of Canadian capacity in the Arctic, published in October 2007, revealed the puny nature of Canada's military presence in the Far North. A map of land-based defences shows a tiny base at Resolute Bay, a small camp for the cadets and Junior Canadian Rangers in Whitehorse, and the Joint Task Force North headquarters in Yellowknife. The map also identified all of the RCMP stations in the North, most of them with only a handful of officers on station. Aerial defences included a substantial advanced radar detection system, major bases in the south (Cold Lake, North Bay, and Bagotville) with northern responsibilities and a series of Forward Operating bases, to be used in times of emergencies, at Yellowknife, Rankin Inlet, Kuujjuaq, and Goose Bay. Canada's Arctic naval capabilities, most depressingly, consist of ships stationed at Esquimault, near Victoria, B.C., and Halifax, Nova Scotia—plus a proposed Arctic deep-water port at Nanisivik,

Nunavut. Despite the hugely expensive second-hand submarines bought from Britain a few years ago, the report noted that Canada had no Arctic submarine capabilities.[49] One need only to contrast Canada's meagre presence in the region to the American military establishment in Alaska or, more appropriately, given the size of the country, Australia's mili-

Military operations in the Far North are resource intensive. Far beyond the national highway and rail network, heavy transport aircraft provide essential support to sustain exercises. *DND photo IS2008-3002*

tary facilities in the Northern Territory. By any appropriate international standard, Canada's capacity to defend and protect its northern region is woefully weak. It is hardly a surprise, consequently, that Canadians are worried about a major challenge to Canada's control over the region.

The Conservatives and the New Northern Policy

"Use it or lose it" is how Prime Minister Stephen Harper summed up Canada's options in the Far North. The blunt message is characteristic of the Conservative government's approach to sovereignty issues, although the policy and investments have, so far, lagged behind the rhetoric. The reality is that Canada has not had a significant presence in the Arctic for years. As political editor Andy McSmith commented in *The Independent* (London) in July 2007, Canada "looks like being the loser in a race to conquer planet Earth's final frontier."[50] There have been useful steps in the past—supporting the creation of the Arctic Council, the establishment of Nunavut and land claims settlements in the Northwest Territories, assisting with the early development of the University of the Arctic— but the overall level of commitment has been minimal compared to Canada's circumpolar neighbours. The Arctic sovereignty debate has dovetailed nicely with the Conservatives' growing concern about the state of national defence, a desire to improve the facilities and capacity of the Canadian military, and a stronger belief than previous governments in the importance of independent action in the North.

The Harper government has held to the long-standing Canadian position that the Northwest Passage is internal waters and consequently under Canadian control. Brad Morse, a leading legal scholar, says of the Canadian position: "Canada's claim is reasonably strong but far, far from being airtight as Canada has consistently paid little attention to the Northwest Passage and the High Arctic."[51] In a bad case of the revenge of the past, the country's long-standing neglect of the Far North has the potential to shape Canada's future. Alex Wolfe, of the University of Alberta, puts it simply: "The current levels of interest and activity would make such a claim at present laughable to other polar nations. Canada has neglected the North, its people and its relevance at large for generations. We are simply paying for it now."[52]

Other commentators believe that Canada should be more confident, emphasizing that Canada's relationship with the United States has been generally positive in the North, and that the Americans do not have malevolent designs to usurp Canada's Arctic regions. In this vein, "agreeing to disagree" remains a feasible strategy. There is no conventional military threat in the Arctic, nor will Canada solve its boundary disputes with the force of arms, but Canadians need to invest in military capabilities in the North so that it can operate in all parts of the country. Furthermore, the Canadian Forces plays a supporting role to civil authorities, namely, the Coast Guard and the RCMP, which have a limited presence and capabilities to deal with criminal activities or emergencies in the region. The rationale for a more robust military presence should not be so that Canada can stand up to the United States and its circumpolar neighbours with modern naval ships, intimidating them into submission with the latest weaponry. Everyone in the region has national interests at stake, but that should be self-evident. Instead, being a good neighbour means having the ability to control your territory and waters so that you don't have to rely on your friends to do so, which, in Canada's case, usually makes us jittery and launches another round of sovereignty crises!

For his part, Prime Minister Harper has discovered what all Canadian politicians learn in the cradle: that standing up to the Americans makes both for great theatre and successful Canadian politics, particularly for a party considered to be far too chummy with the Republican administration of the despised George W. Bush. As the Toronto *Star* editorialized, "Still, it's all grand politics. Canadians—even those who have never traveled north of Bloor St.—maintain a sentimental attachment to the Arctic. Nothing gets the blood stirring more than the idea of nefarious Yankees trampling all over this particular national icon."[53] Rob Huebert, of the Centre for Military and Strategic Studies, summarized the situation succinctly: "Some issues go beyond rationality. Any sign of an affront to northern sovereignty is absolutely guaranteed to get on the front page of all the newspapers."[54] Historian Jack Granatstein weighed in with his thoughts: "The Danes are trying to get Hans Island, and do not accept our claims in the Arctic—they claim the North Pole. The protection of the Arctic is a key national interest."[55]

The government's position largely ignored a crucial reality, described in detail earlier: the fact that Canada had for decades tolerated American military incursions into the Arctic, in kind of a "Please Ask, Do Tell" approach to Canadian sovereignty. As U.S. president Ronald Reagan indicated, the sovereignty issue should be put to the side, with the Americans agreeing not to act in the Arctic without Canadian permission. John Noble, a Canadian diplomat assigned to the U.S. Relations Branch, observed of the growing problem: "Rather than trying to make a big issue out of this matter, both countries should be proclaiming that the Arctic is an area where we do co-operate and have come to a pragmatic solution to a difficult legal problem."[56]

In December 2004, Prime Minister Paul Martin issued a comprehensive northern strategy. The policy called for more money for northern affairs, but little change in direction. The goals were all laudable—protect fragile Arctic ecosystems, expand research activity, and empower aboriginal communities and regional governments—but the strategy lacked both a sense of scale and urgency. The audience for the strategy was internal; it was designed to demonstrate to Canadians that the federal government was serious about the North. While Prime Minister Martin had a strong personal commitment to the North, the policy represented a small advance on long-standing approaches to the Arctic. It did not, in any real way, represent a bold assertion of Canadian interests in the Far North. Martin, like prime ministers before him, was hamstrung by a simple political reality: there are precious few votes in the Arctic region and little southern interest in the North generally. Until and unless Canadian control of the Arctic is questioned, Canadians are generally very happy to continue in a "fit of absence of mind" about their vast northern lands.

Stephen Harper, elected in January 2006, made the defence of Canadian sovereignty a significant part of his pledge for "Canada's New Government." Harper addressed Arctic questions in the first press conference after his January 2007 election, mincing few words in sending a strong message to the United States. He criticized U.S. ambassador David Wilkins for repeating the long-standing American rejection of Canada's claims to the Northwest Passage. "The United States defends its sovereignty. The Canadian government will defend our sovereignty," Harper said, laying down a firm challenge to his American counterparts. His minority government had strong plans for the Far North, promising to build military icebreakers, upgrade underwater and aerial surveillance capabilities, build a deep-water port, and expand Canada's military presence in the area. Gordon O'Connor, Harper's defence minister, commented, "There certainly is a need for us to play in the world and represent Canada in the world, but we also had to make sure that at home we had enough resources to ensure reasonable security, and to protect our sovereignty. In the south, we've got to think about terrorism, but in the north, there are issues of sovereignty."[57]

At the same time, Canada stepped up military activities in the North. As one soldier, Master Corporal Chris Fernandez-Ledon, observed, in a classic statement on the nature of Canada's military approach to the North, "Down there [Afghanistan] it was war fighting we were doing. Here you don't have to worry about people shooting you and ambushing you. You just keep an eye on each other and have fun."[58] National Defence also launched Operation Nunalivut ("the land is ours") in the late winter of 2006. The expedition involved forty-six military personnel, including over thirty Canadian Rangers, travelling in five separate patrols over land and ice to reach Resolute Bay. Major Chris Bergeron then led an even smaller seven-person group to Alert Bay, at the tip of Ellesmere Island, where the Rangers deposited a metal Canadian flag—yet another symbolic assertion of Cana-

Members of 1 Canadian Ranger Patrol Group at the magnetic north pole off Isaachsen, Nunavut, in 2002. Enhanced sovereignty patrols encourage Rangers to extend their surveillance over parts of the Arctic that are rarely visited by human beings. *Photo 1 Canadian Ranger Patrol Group*

dian sovereignty, of the sort that has been made for the past hundred years. It was, for Canada, an impressive $1-million display of national interest in the North, and a symbolic training exercise for a country that had questionable capacity to respond to military or civilian crises in the North. Compared to the growing Russian military presence in their Arctic and the formidable air and land resources stationed in Alaska by the Americans, critics saw our military effort as pathetic—a pitiful reminder of Canada's limited capacity to operate in the Far North.

The Conservatives had proposed a major investment in defence in their 2006 election campaign and, in office, announced their determination to proceed. They proposed to spend over $5 billion on the surveillance system and a port in Iqaluit—although subsequent

Conservative budgets did not set aside the required funds. It was not immediately clear if the government would opt for icebreakers—used primarily for civilian purposes—or for naval vessels designed for military operations. Canada's aging and small fleet of Coast Guard icebreakers, none with the capacity to operate in the thick ice of the High Arctic, had become a national embarrassment, leaving the country as the only Arctic nation without the capacity to work properly in the region. The government committed $720 million in its February 2008 budget for a new icebreaker, which would give Canada the capability to go "anywhere, anytime" in the Arctic, but critics told journalist Bob Weber "that splashy polar programs have been promised before, only to be quietly cancelled once they've been milked for political gain."[59] If it takes Canada as long to develop a military presence in the North as it has to replace its Sea King helicopters, there will be no ice at all, and perhaps palm trees, in the High Arctic before any troops arrive at their new base. Norway, in contrast, is investing heavily in new-generation Arctic vessels, under development at the Aker Yards, which will have enhanced capacity to navigate in thick ice conditions. President Vladimir Putin indicated that Russia intended to play in these waters as well, declaring an intent to expanding facilities for the construction of ships capable of working in the Arctic Ocean.

Growing concern about Arctic warming and the increasing Russian presence in the North is increasingly attracting the attention of the Canadian government. Prime Minister Harper made his government's concerns clear in August 2006: "It is no exaggeration to say that the need to assert our sovereignty and take action to protect our territorial integrity in the Arctic has never been more urgent." Newly elected Liberal leader Stéphane Dion ensured that partisanship enlivened the debate. Drawing on his credentials as a committed environmentalist, and skating around the obvious point that he was a long-time member of a government that had done little to advance Canadian interests in the region, Dion argued that Canadians had to show they were "good custodians" of the Far North. He called on the Harper government to focus on environmental questions, through the creation of parks, extending protection to vulnerable maritime areas, and increasing scientific research in the area.[60] The prime minister took a harsher line, focusing more on security and sovereignty. He dismissed the all-too-familiar Canadian concerns about the Americans, saying, "I'm less concerned with the U.S., who . . . while not formally acknowledging our claim, at least acknowledges that we make the claim and cooperates with us on the defence of North America. I think the greater worry is some of the other nations that we believe have been paddling around up there and not necessarily acknowledging their obligations to communicate with the government of Canada."[61]

Politically, the North's time appears to have arrived—although this has been said many times in the past. A Leger Marketing poll on the Arctic released in February 2007 offered the hardly surprising observation that Canadians want the North protected. Over 50 percent favoured diplomatic and legal tactics, fewer than 20 percent supported military buildup, and slightly more than 10 percent preferred the status quo. Canadians viewed environmental issues as the greatest threat, followed by American incursions on the Arctic. Around 10 percent cited one of two other possible threats: foreign claims to Canadian territory and terrorist attacks.[62] Of course, the pollsters didn't ask, "Would you accept an increase in your taxes to support a greater presence in the Arctic?"

The Conservatives' strong interest in matters of national defence made the emerging debate about the future of the Canadian North a natural for the minority government. As the prime minister commented in February 2007: "We believe that Canadians are excited about the government asserting Canada's control and sovereignty in the Arctic. We believe that's one of the big reasons why Canadians are excited and support our plan to rebuild the Canadian Forces. I think it's practically and symbolically hugely important, much more important than the dollars spent. And I'm hoping that years from now, Canada's Arctic sovereignty, military and otherwise, will be, frankly, a major legacy of this government."[63] Harper's government responded within a few months. In July 2007, the government announced the expenditure of $3 billion for the construction by 2013–14 of six to eight medium-sized, helicopter-carrying vessels designed for use in the North, and another $4.3 billion to operate them over a quarter of a century. These would replace Canada's ailing and aging Arctic fleet—one large and four mid-sized icebreakers, all more than thirty years old—which were not up to the twenty-first-century Arctic challenge. The Liberals, predictably, attacked the Conservatives for not doing enough, blandly disregarding, with the straight faces only politicians can assume when asserting the preposterous, the fact that they had allowed military activities in the Arctic to wane for over a decade. Harper's plan was a retreat from his election promise, but the investment was in accordance with the Canadian military's needs and recommendations.

The plan was a significant upgrade over the existing national capacity to patrol the Far North, but fell far short of the large icebreakers promised earlier. The country, or more properly, the chattering classes, engaged in a loud exercise in rivet counting, with some arguing that the ships were too small to break through the thick ice in the region and others finding fault with the decision to base the ships on the east and west coasts rather than to commit to the construction of an Arctic port to service them. Michael Byers described the ships as merely "ice-strengthened" and pointed out that Canada would still lack the capacity to operate year-round in the Arctic, unlike Russia and the U.S.[64] Some critics referred to these modest vessels as "slushbreakers." Others argued that the lower-key approach was more suitable to the real challenges in the Arctic, which included monitoring resource development, northern tourism, and environmental assessments. The Toronto *Star* applauded the effort: "It is Canada's urgent need to affirm its presence across the North's land, sky and sea that is driving Harper's agenda, and rightly so. For too long, we have relied on Inuit Rangers to assert our claims, on overflights by Aurora patrol planes and on the occasional military manoeuvre or scientific expedition. This is benign neglect."[65] A month later, the Toronto *Sun* was more aggressive, urging the Harper government to declare its control of the North Pole: "Ownership of resources beneath the North Pole is not an issue Canada should ignore. From our point of view, any minerals this side of the North Pole are Canada's—part of our sovereignty, regardless of what the UN or any international court may say. What's on the Russian side of the Pole is theirs. End of argument." Showing a heightened level of Canadian assertiveness, the editorial concluded, "Let the world know that this side of the North Pole is ours, and anyone who messes with it will risk annoying Santa Claus."[66] Perhaps Santa has the clout to back up such aggressive talk; certainly Canada doesn't, not yet anyway.

For many Canadians, the investment in medium-sized ships represented a continuation of southern, short-term thinking. Peter Wilson, who had formerly worked for the Nunavut Planning Commission, called the plan an "embarrassment" and suggested that the new strategy represented little more than a monitoring exercise. Instead, he argued, Ottawa should have committed itself to long-term environmental monitoring, improved wildlife management in the Arctic, expanded its search-and-rescue capability (again drawing attention to the hundreds of transpolar flights that cross Canadian airspace each day), revamped northern regulatory procedures, and empowered the territories to control the region's affairs directly. For much less than the cost of the ships, Wilson observed, the country could get a much more effective means of asserting its sovereignty: "So here's the plan. For a tiny fraction of what taxpayers will spend on Mr. Harper's patrol vessels, the federal government could operate a northern-based Arctic aerial monitoring program. Inuit and other northern residents could be trained to fly Canadian-built planes from community bases across the Arctic, from Labrador to Yukon. These small northern-based teams could provide regular, low cost, sovereignty patrols, general environmental monitoring, ice patrols, land-use permit inspections and enforcement, search and rescue, aerial photography and wildlife surveys."[67] This is an example of so-called soft power. Many questions arise from it: What Canadian-built planes are these? Presumably not military planes, since we don't build any. Something from

Bombardier? How long would it take Inuit and "other northern residents" to be trained to the point of being able to fly these planes? Why do civilians flying Dash 8s on monitoring expeditions or helicopters (Canadian ones?) on search-and-rescue missions demonstrate sovereignty better than icebreakers do? What difference does it make if the territories control the region's affairs directly? What affairs are these anyway? And so on.

Mary Simon, president of the Inuit Tapiriit Kanatami (Canada's national Inuit organization) and one of the most important aboriginal leaders of this generation, offered a similar assessment. Establishing meaningful sovereignty in the North, according to Simon, required a great commitment to meeting the needs of the Inuit: "The bedrock of Canada's status as an Arctic nation is the history of use and occupation of Arctic lands and waters by Inuit for thousands of years. Inuit are, and expect to remain, the permanent majority population of the Arctic. This is helpful for Canada when defending claims of sovereignty against other nations. Coherent policy-making for the Arctic must commit to two things: A credible power-sharing partnership between Inuit and the government; and a determination to overcome the obvious gaps in basic measurements of well-being that separate Inuit from all other Canadians." Like Wilson, Simon argued for an expanded role of the Canadian Rangers and the use of local residents to conduct environmental assessments. She urged the prime minister to move beyond the construction of expensive ships and, instead, to focus on improving facilities for smaller vessels.[68] In fact, Simon's and Wilson's ideas are simply examples of how such issues become transformed, in typical Canadian fashion, into another job creation project: use Canadian planes (to create jobs), train locals (to create jobs), monitor the environment (to create jobs), and on and on.

NDP leader Jack Layton criticized Harper roundly for his plans and called for greater attention to regional issues, particularly on the social, ecological, and economic front. For Layton, predictably, climate change was the issue, not Arctic sovereignty. "Yes, we need some military capacity here but we're not going to win the battle for northern sovereignty with military might. We're going to win it through strong communities that are sustainable and viable and have an economic future, and Mr. Harper doesn't seem to get it."[69] He made no suggestions as to how these communities might be made sustainable. In a letter to the editor in the *Globe and Mail*, Kitchener resident Dick Moutray wrote: "What Canada needs right now is a little flair and imagination to quickly defuse this Russian initiative. How much would it cost to whip up a stainless steel replica of the CN Tower, fly it to the North Pole, drill a hole in the ice and lower said replica to the ocean floor? This CN Tower would be equipped with a rotating webcam to capture the arrival of the Russian sub and broadcast to the world we have been there all along."[70] Eric Posner, an American law professor, proposed a different solution: "If the U.S. supports Canada's claims to the Northwest Passage, in return for some sort of guarantee of U.S. military and civilian access, the two countries will strengthen their position vis-à-vis Russia."[71] Canadian law professor Ed Morgan, of the University of Toronto, countered Posner's argument: "Canada's problem in all of this is that for so many years we had a foreign and defence policy premised on what Lloyd Axworthy dubbed 'soft power.' Our soft power, however, turns out to have been nothing more than soft thinking. We enacted long-arm environmental legislation to protect the Arctic, but have no means to get there to police potential polluters; we embraced peacekeeping as our primary military goal, but deprived ourselves of the forces needed to fill in the space between warring parties; we endorse humanitarian intervention as a military mission, but deprived ourselves of the transport aircraft needed to fly personnel and equipment to the world's inhospitable regions. The government of Canada finally appears to have turned the corner on its long lapse of focus, and is now pushing a version of hard power. It's about time. If we're going to savour the international law rights of a sovereign state, we have to crack some ice."[72]

The prime minister, it turned out, was not finished with the North—and some of the major criticisms of his government's plans were soon answered. He declared, again, that the Arctic was "central to our identity as a northern nation" and sought to position his government as a defender of national interests in the Arctic. As one government official noted, "The Russians sent a submarine to drop a small flag at the bottom of the ocean. We're sending our Prime Minister,"[73] although not, presumably, to the bottom of the Arctic Ocean. Harper travelled across the North in August 2007, visiting research stations across the Northwest Territories and Nunavut and drawing attention to federal plans for the defence of the North. NWT premier Joe Handley used Harper's visit to lobby for the completion of the highway from Inuvik to Tuktoyaktuk; Harper demurred. Harper visited Resolute Bay and announced the development of an Arctic training facility in the community and a $12-million-per-year expansion in the Canadian Rangers that would add 900 Rangers to the 4,100-member volunteer force. He also declared that Canada would spend $100 million upgrading the port at Nanisivik, near Arctic Bay on Baffin Island, to improve the country's capabilities in the region. Harper reached back into the bag of Canadian nostalgia to support his actions: "Even Canadians who have never been north of 60 feel it. It's embedded in our history, our literature, our art, our music and our Canadian soul. That's why we react so strong when other countries show disrespect for our sovereignty over the Arctic. And that's why we're gathered in Resolute, a community whose very name expresses our intent and purpose here today."[74]

For Defence Minister Gordon O'Connor, the announcements tugged at Canadian heartstrings: "This remains a place where the principal forces of nature still hold sway, a place where men and women are braced into vigour by the huge trackless landscapes and the other harsh elements. And a place so stunningly beautiful that no Canadian can experience it without feeling an overwhelming sense of romantic patriotism for our country."[75] Other federal initiatives followed in 2007: the announcement of the final $40 million in scientific research grants to complete the government of Canada's $150-million commitment for research funding for the International Polar Year, $8 million to up-grade the Port of Churchill, and $60 million (shared with Manitoba and OmniTRAX, the U.S. owners of the port and railway) to improve the Hudson Bay Rail Line leading to the port.

Not since the Klondike gold rush had the North figured as prominently in Canadian political life. The throne speech of October 17, 2007, raised the stakes even further, committing the government of Canada to a comprehensive strategy for addressing the needs and challenges of the North:

Iconic Arctic symbols such as the Inukshuk being recorded by a Canadian Forces videographer in this photo are prominent in Canadian national imagery. *DND photo IS2004-2108*

The Arctic is an essential part of Canada's history. . . . Canadians see in our North an expression of our deepest aspirations: our sense of exploration, the beauty and the bounty of our land, and our limitless potential.

But the North needs new attention. New opportunities are emerging across the Arctic, and new challenges from other shores. Our Government will bring forward an integrated northern strategy focused on strengthening Canada's sovereignty, protecting our environmental heritage, promoting economic and social development, and improving and devolving governance, so that northerners have greater control over their destinies.

To take advantage of the North's vast opportunities, northerners must be able to meet their basic needs. Our Government will work to continue to improve living conditions in the North for First Nations and Inuit through better housing.

Our Government will build a world-class Arctic research station that will be on the cutting edge of Arctic issues, including environmental science and resource development.

This station will be built by Canadians, in Canada's Arctic, and it will be there to serve the world.

As part of asserting sovereignty in the Arctic, our Government will complete comprehensive mapping of Canada's Arctic seabed. Never before has this part of Canada's ocean floor been fully mapped.

Defending our sovereignty in the North also demands that we maintain the capacity to act. New Arctic patrol ships and expanded aerial surveillance will guard Canada's Far North and the Northwest Passage. As well, the size and capabilities of the Arctic Rangers will be expanded to better patrol our vast Arctic territory.[76]

The combination of international attention to the Arctic and a federal government committed to national defence and regional autonomy provides one of the strongest northern alignments in Canadian history. Territorial governments are pushing the government of Canada to invest more heavily in the North—moving away from the long-standing position that fighter planes based in Cold Lake, Alberta, and other southern locations are the appropriate means of defending Canadian sovereignty in the region. The Inuit, in particular, offer the Canadian Rangers as a foundation for a northern-centred strategy for protecting Canadian interests in the region. Security analyst Rob Huebert said of the situation: "I've come to the point after studying this for so long that it's not about sovereignty, it's about security. For a lot of people it's about chest-thumping, but when you talk to an Inuit [sic] or any northerner, what sovereignty means is for them to have protection."[77] Journalist James Travers had stronger words: "It's a shocker, but the pressing Arctic issue isn't really about sovereignty. It's about control. . . . Sure the earnest Rangers wander about and the military makes noise, occasionally mushing around on snowmobiles. Still, the real action is at sea and under the ice where from time to time those damned Yankees twist our beaver tails by sailing a tanker or a nuclear submarine through waters we claim as our own."[78]

Even as Canada prepared itself for the largest-ever Arctic initiative in the country's history, a potential crisis loomed. To meet the 2013 deadline established under the United Nations Convention on the Law of the Sea, Canadian scientists had only five research seasons to complete their work and submit a complex and detailed case on the northward extension of the continental shelf. Jacob Verhoef, of the Geological Survey of Canada, pointed out something Arctic scientists know all too well—given the vagaries of Arctic conditions, it is not uncommon to lose one or more research seasons. "If everything goes right, it can work. You can make all the plans you want, but you can't predict the ice conditions," Verhoef explained. "Any work you do in the Arctic is high risk. We've tried to come up with a plan that might work. It's the best we can do." Then he offered the killer possibility: "If anything goes wrong, and we lose one or two field seasons—which we very likely will because of conditions in the Arctic—we are in trouble."[79] International scientists had more general worries about the politicization of their work. Fraser Taylor, of Carleton University, argued, "If you start seeing science as a servant of national political interests then you're on a slippery slope."[80] If that is indeed the case, then Arctic science has been sliding for years, for many of the current advocates for enhanced scientific activity in the North have framed their arguments in terms of national sovereignty concerns.

It is not, however, clear that the final decision would rest with the scientists, as most observers assumed. While the countries had to make their submissions to a scientific tribunal, there were limits on the Commission's ability to reconcile conflicting claims. Ted McDorman, a University of Victoria specialist on the Law of the Sea, declared that "the commission can't deal with information presented where there is a conflict. It has no power to decide . . . so like other ocean boundary disputes, it will ultimately come down to some level of negotiation. Political negotiation."[81] Just, in fact, like the Alaska Boundary Dispute of 1903. And you can bet your mortgage that the scientific information will clash, and that boundary disputes will be resolved by tough negotiations, in which the standard of living in Nunavut will be of no importance at all.

What should be most disturbing to Canadians is that, when we actually sit down to negotiate with our neighbours, we might face a situation where everyone else seems prepared to invest more money and effort in their Arctic regions than we do. Mikhail Leontyev, a major Russian political commentator, applauded Canada's actions to beef up its military capabilities: "The Canadians are absolutely right. They are doing what we should be doing. One must use sovereignty or lose it. The fact that the Canadians are undertaking military efforts is also totally correct. If any claims are at stake, any disputed territory, especially those which are interesting because of their mineral resources, no evidence or international law would help one ensure that rights are respected, if they are not backed by military and political power." Leontyev mocked American responses, particularly their suggestion that the region be made international: "The Americans are promoting humanitarian ideas along the lines of 'let's make everything international' because the size of the shelf they may end up with does not correspond to the size of their ambitions." He continued that "surrendering this zone would be similar to surrendering one's own territory [and] would merit execution by firing squad."[82] By the fall of 2007, Russia was increasing Arctic flights by its TU-95 bombers and supersonic TU-22s, heightening tensions and reminding the world of the country's formidable military and strategic resources and history. Charles Langton, of London's International Institute for Strategic Studies, put the Russian moves in a broader context: "We have to look at this in the context of an increasingly assertive Russian relationship with the United States, NATO and the west in general. Russia is displaying an increasing willingness to show its people that it is powerful again."[83] Paul Kennedy, director of International Security Studies at Yale University, described the Russian assertiveness more bluntly: "Actually, Russia's actions are rather predictable. They are the steps taken by a traditional power elite that, having suffered defeat and humiliation, is now bent upon recovery of its assets, its authority and its capacity to intimidate."[84] Canadian and American fighter planes had scrambled in response to Russian aerial activity, providing a quick reminder of post–Second World War conditions.

Russian observers resented the attempt to paint their country's actions into a Cold War mural. Yury Fedetov, ambassador to the United Kingdom, argued that the West had seriously misunderstood Russian intentions: "For those living and growing up in Russia, the receptions of the country perpetuated by cold war thinkers living [in] the post–cold war world seem utterly at odds with the reality of the country today. Our claim to part of the Arctic sea bed serves as the latest illustration of this. Russia's submission made in 2001 is based on the understanding that the limits of the continental shelf disputed by two or more states should be the subject of negotiations between relevant countries. We have been clear all along that the future of the Arctic cannot be resolved through unilateralism, but only through international law and negotiation where required. Those seeking to address the Arctic issue on the basis of cold war dichotomies will do little to promote a successful resolution to the stewardship of the region."[85] President Vladimir Putin poured ice-cold water on the growing contretemps, apologizing to Prime Minister Harper about the escalation of tensions. As Harper reported the conversation, "President Putin assured me that he meant no offence, nor had any intention to violate any international understanding or any Canadian sovereignty in any way."[86] As Anatoli Sagalevich, the commander of one of the submersibles, commented, "I don't really know why some people are so nervous about [our] placing the Russian flag there. The Americans placed their flag on the moon, and it doesn't mean the moon became theirs."[87] True enough, but laws and regulations seemed to offer little comfort when the unruly Russian bear looks like it has crawled out of its post–Cold War hibernation and prominent commentators suggest that it is once more on the prowl.

Once again, national embarrassment about being caught with our sovereign drawers down has conditioned Canadians to be temporarily more receptive to Arctic investments, albeit with countervailing demands from various politicians that the real money be spent and used in their constituencies. As Prime Minister Harper asserted, "Protecting national sovereignty, the integrity of our borders, is the first and foremost responsibility of national government."[88] At present, but admittedly based on a very short window of political engagement, it appears as though Russian and American interest will not soon wane and that debates about climate change, the opening of the Northwest Passage, fears of environmental degradation, and worries about the vulnerability of Canadian sovereignty in the High Arctic will keep the issue in front of the Canadian and international public. The prospect of major resource discoveries, sufficient to sustain an oil-based industrial world, is what has really pushed the southern nations to look to the Arctic as a final frontier. As Dr. Pete Ewin, of the World Wildlife Federation, noted with sadness, "We are pushing into the frontiers of both knowledge and resources. It is easier to go into the extremes than to change your lifestyle."[89] *National Post* columnist Terrance Corcoran viewed the matter similarly: "But it does highlight the obvious absurdity; Governments that have signed a UN climate convention to curb carbon emissions are battling to use a UN law of the sea convention to get control over oil and gas that could massively expand carbon emissions."[90]

Canadian paranoia over the potential loss of our sovereignty is just that: paranoia. But even if we do not stand to lose our North, Canada—apart from northern indigenous groups—has a poor track record in actually using its Arctic lands and waters. Prime Minister Harper is discovering that is impossible to overturn a century-long approach to the Far North within a few years. And so, like his predecessors, he has been responding to the pressures on the Arctic with nationalist enthusiasm and bold promises. Only time will tell if he can deliver on them, and whether they will have an on-the-ground impact.[91] It takes money and commitment to be a northern nation, and it takes a national belief in both the potential of and the responsibilities towards Arctic regions. Other circumpolar nations have built up their northern infrastructure—universities and colleges, research stations, tourism operations, investments in roads, airports and the like—over decades. In each case, they have used military expenditures as a crucial element in regional economic and social development, strengthening the North through long-term defence commitments. In the current situation, as in past crises, Canada finds itself responding to a long-term problem with short-term solutions and without the base of public interest and commitment that is necessary to assume full responsibility for the Far North. While this may have been sufficient in the twentieth century, it will not be in this one.

When she was running for the leadership of the national New Democratic Party in 1989, Yukon Member of Parliament Audrey McLaughlin routinely spoke of Canada as stretching from "sea to sea to sea," an obvious dig at the national motto, *A Mari usque ad Mare*. Ms. McLaughlin did not get very far in changing the national phraseology, although the triple-ocean message is commonplace in the North. Perhaps now, with Arctic sovereignty competing with the country's interminable debates about Quebec's future as the focal point for national worry, Canada will begin to understand its geographic reality as a nation framed by three, not just two, great oceans. Maybe once Canada has established a serious presence in the Arctic, when it has truly become a polar nation, the country can talk with pride about being a nation from sea to sea to sea.

REALITY CHECK:

WHERE DOES CANADA
STAND IN THE ARCTIC?

"Sovereignty Begins at Home."
— MARY SIMON,
President of Inuit Tapiriit Kanatami, 2007

The Arctic Ice in Retreat

Only a fool would try to predict where Canada will stand in the Arctic in 2028. Twenty years from now, Canada could have an expanded military presence in the North, major research facilities in the High Arctic, a renewed national commitment to things northern, the ice-breaker capacity to patrol the now-open Northwest Passage, vigorous territorial governments in Yukon, the Northwest Territories, and Nunavut that have expanded their activities in and along the Arctic Ocean. Canada could finally emerge as a truly northern nation, committed to the region and determined to assert and preserve Arctic sovereignty in the area.

Or not. We've been through much of this before. Canada has spouted the rhetoric of Arctic engagement in the past and then done nothing. The current crisis could quickly pass. Two cold winters could dampen interest in the Arctic and slow the panic about global warming. Southern Canadians could once again lose interest, for the national attention span about things northern in this country tends to be very limited. The highly touted oil and gas

exploration activity in the Far North could produce dry wells or inconsequential returns. Ships going through the Northwest Passage could hit ice and sink, scaring off repeat usage of the route. Rogue nations or terrorists might try to use the Arctic. In other words, no one knows what lies ahead.

Although Canadian sovereignty is not on thinning ice,[1] the country has neglected the North and has failed to integrate the region into the broader national society. For many Canadians, the Arctic is out of sight, out of mind, a place to enjoy vicariously if at all, a marginal part of the nation to the vast majority of citizens. Put simply, Canadian nation-building is incomplete, with the provincial and territorial North still outside the Canadian family. Canada has made efforts over the past thirty years and some, particularly land claims, aboriginal self-government, and the creation of Nunavut, have begun to transform the region. But compared to our circumpolar neighbours, we have started the race in last place. And so, in contrast to the Nordic countries, Russia, and the United States, we have exercised little oversight over the High Arctic and have developed little capacity to control our lands and waters in the region. The Arctic sovereignty debate keeps reappearing precisely because of misperception and ignorance, born of tentative and reactionary measures in the North that reach back over a century and a quarter. If this country is going to defend its interests in the Arctic, it will have to rethink the very fundamentals of its approach to the region. In the final pages of this book, let's give our country a northern report card:

Canada's Arctic Track Record: F

Giving a failing grade is a harsh assessment—especially in a country that hates to give this mark in its school system. No grade inflation here, however, for this is the real world. The reason for the failing grade is simple:

- Of all the polar countries, Canada has been the weakest in developing the potential of its Arctic regions and in responding to its full range of responsibilities there. While the case can be made that Canada has preserved its sovereignty in the North—for its control of the land and sea has not been seriously or successfully challenged—it is abundantly clear that the overall Canadian presence in the area has fallen far short of circumpolar norms.
- Canada is the weakest of all polar countries in integrating the northern regions into the nation as a whole. While there have

been major improvements over the past quarter century, the long delays in responding to the needs and aspirations of the North have put the region far back in its evolution compared to other northern regions.

- Previous governments, both Liberal and Conservative, placed their emphasis on improving regional social, economic, and political developments. We have territorial governments that increasingly are powerful and creative; the commitment to local control and forward-looking development is impressive, and improvements over the past twenty years have been more dramatic and important than most Canadians appreciate. This is the most impressive area of Canadian policy towards the North, but it remains a work very much in progress. For the most part, the emphasis has been on resolving social, cultural and economic crises within aboriginal communities and not on developing a stronger north-centred approach to infra-structure and regional integration.

- There have been occasional positive steps from the govern-ment of Canada, from Diefenbaker's Roads to Resources pro-gram to the Chrétien government's early-stage commitment to circumpolar collaboration, but these have never been fully implemented nor followed up properly.

- There are, sadly, few connections between northern and southern Canada, and little commitment from the south towards the North. Our science is not where it should be. Canada's military presence and capacity is limited, and our ability to exercise our sovereignty over more than one-quarter of our land mass and surrounding water is woefully inadequate.

- We are not properly situated to monitor the effects of global warming and Arctic climate change. Because of inadequate research funding, we rely more on anecdote than hard scien-tific fact. What little we do focuses on monitoring and identi-fying changes, not problem alleviation.

- Canadians talk a good talk—our poets, novelists, artists, and filmmakers have done a better job than our politicians and business leaders in responding to the Far North. But image-making and symbolism mask the shallowness of the Canadian commitment to the Arctic.

- Despite the recent rhetoric, Canadians are not much interested in the Arctic. Go back five years and see what people were saying about the Far North before the current debates started—not much. Recognize, too, that a large percentage of the population has little experience with the region, no historical or cultural connections to it, and thus very little interest in the North. Our national commitment to diversity, to doing your own thing, means that young Canadians and new Canadians are not required to absorb our history into their culture. Incredibly, in some provinces, Canadian history is not taught in high schools. It's possible that a younger generation will read "The Shooting of Dan McGrew," but if it chooses not to, that seems to be fine with Canadians.

- The Canadian Arctic often disappoints its boosters, with heightened expectations of resource wealth and opportunities often disappointed. This helps explain the country's divided response to the area, for Canadians know that it will cost a great deal, at great risk, to develop resources in the region. There is no consensus that the effort can be justified on sovereignty grounds alone.

- The idea that Canada needs to possess exclusive control of the Northwest Passage (translated as being able to do everything ourselves to defend the region militarily) to uphold our Arctic sovereignty is unrealistic and should be replaced by an ideal of practical co-operation—an ideal which, historically, we have done well at realizing. Canada has successfully controlled navigation in the Northwest Passage, and our laws are respected by foreign countries, including the United States. We need to develop more Canadian capabilities, but cannot lose sight of the practical and financial benefits of working with our allies. The proposal to link with the United States on matters of regulation and control, so quickly dismissed at the national level, is the only sensible solution. We have precedent in "agreeing to disagree" with the Americans, thus safeguarding our essential interest. In turn, the United States has not sought to steal our North from us. Failure to negotiate and work with the Americans may lead other countries to use the route with impunity. The hasty rejection of this option is a classic example of rhetoric and symbolism overcoming good sense. The Americans have strategic interests in the region, and so do we.

The Government of Canada's Current Response: B-

The Harper government has made significant progress—at least in terms of defence commitments—to improve Canada's defence capabilities in the Arctic. Although the Mulroney government made significant steps towards an Arctic strategy, the Harper administration appears far more serious than most in responding to both the threats and the opportunities in the Far North.

- The construction of smaller ice-strengthened frigates lacks the dramatic and symbolic flair that the construction of a major icebreaker would have had, but it is a reasonable response to the challenges and opportunities facing the country. They are versatile and flexible and, moreover, they reflect the government's willingness to follow the recommendations of the Canadian Forces, which have many other military needs to address.
- The idea of a major research station and a major mapping exercise gives Canada a chance to get the science right, but the timing is very tight. This is a case of the right thing started a decade too late; only a concerted effort by the country's Arctic scientists and government officials will produce the desired result.
- The military response, overriding frantic calls for the creation of a stronger Arctic defence capability, actually meets national

needs rather well. The Canadian Rangers, well placed across the North, provide precisely the kind of regional surveillance capacity that Canada requires in the Far North. It is true that Canada currently has greater capacity for working in desert environments than Arctic ones, but this is a situation that reflects the country's global strategic interests and commitments.

- Canada, unlike the other Arctic states, has taken strong regulatory steps to control shipping. The civilian Coast Guard, not the navy, enforces these regulations. The government's commitment to replace one of its two heavy icebreakers by 2017 is therefore a positive step towards maintaining Canada's Arctic presence. Designing the ship to accommodate a Canadian Forces helicopter (rather than the light helicopters that can operate with the current icebreakers) will expand its intelligence, surveillance, and reconnaissance capabilities.[2]

- The Conservative approach, so far, is lopsided, emphasizing military initiatives over the integration of the territories into the country at large. These two elements—making the North more Canadian—and Canada more northern—and improving our strategic capacity in the region—are required in equal measure if the country is to take the North more seriously in the future. Just as the NDP is too quick to reject strategic concerns in favour of improved housing, the Conservatives have bet heavily on the military side while providing less emphasis on the need to improve living conditions and opportunities for northern residents. The government's Arctic strategy will provide greater attention to social and economic development, however. The regional development strategies of the Liberal and Conservative governments of recent times are moving in the right direction and provide a substantial amount of federal funding to assist the North. The region has long since learned that money is not a replacement for attention and dedication to the internal development of the North. The North needs the money, but it requires commitment and vision even more.

- The current stance on the Northwest Passage and sovereignty "crisis" is more bluster than substance. Other countries have better resources and more of a presence, and Canadian officials know it. They must be praying that nobody tests the national resolve. More to the point, it is very likely that two other routes—across the North Pole and along the Russian coast—will open for reliable navigation well before the Northwest Passage is routinely clear of ice. A lot of the anguish about Canadian internal waters is likely to be superseded by developments elsewhere in the Arctic. The Russians, incidentally, are embracing the prospects of Arctic shipping and work very hard to promote the northeast route as the most logical connection between Asia and Europe.

- The Conservative plan is government focused, not nation centred. It lacks the transformative elements needed to convince and remind Canadians that they are an Arctic nation. Our current capabilities in the North lag well behind other countries. It takes decades, if not generations, to convince a country to make a full and lasting commitment to a new national agenda. Canada has, at best, a few years to discover its legacy and its responsibility in the Far North. Despite the rhetoric and issues of the present, the sense of national urgency is limited. The government's response is measured not against the need and the concerns, but against the country's capacity to care for the Far North. In the end, Canadians will devote more energy and debate to the question of where to put the shipyards to build icebreakers (Quebec? Not in Quebec? Why not New Brunswick? And what about British Columbia? Thankfully, Saskatchewan will make few claims to a share of the icebreaker contracts. We hope!) than they will to the question of whether the country is properly positioned in the Arctic.

With the current government's approach as a starting point, it remains clear that a great deal remains to be done. Truth be told, Canada has few options. The basic problem is that, at the most fundamental level, Canada lacks the northern outlook of other polar nations. The nation is becoming more southern and more urban all the time; a great deal of the professional and skilled work under way in the North is being done by people who do not live there and who commute to work from southern homes. Large numbers of Canadians have little connection to the region and feel little responsibility for its past and future. Other polar nations have a solid, modern, and substantial presence in the North. Canada has a region that is isolated, impoverished, but nonetheless proudly Canadian; the Inuit commitment to the country should not be underestimated.

Ideally, all Canadians would rally around the North. The country can certainly become energized in the right circumstances, which typically involve the discovery of major resources, and therefore national economic opportunity. But this really works only for gold, diamonds, oil and gas. Other minerals, like lead, zinc, iron ore, tungsten, and the like are less compelling; witness the systematic neglect of the Voisey Bay development after the initial euphoria and debate about the discovery and mine opening. The country can also get agitated when there is a perceived threat to national sovereignty, as the debates in the past two years have demonstrated. Realistically, however, Canada has difficulty maintaining its enthusiasm, first because the resources are hard-won and rarely as glorious and dramatic as promoters would have us believe, and second because the threats to sovereignty have all proven to be either imaginary, in which case interest quickly fades, or subject to American intervention and control, as with the installations during the Cold War. In either case, Canadians have no choice but to agree to the requests of the powerful nation and eat humble sovereignty pie.

On the resource front, it is hard to believe that the North will not once again disappoint its promoters, at least in the next two generations. There may well be a great deal of oil under the Arctic, most of it in Russian and Norwegian waters, but it will be difficult to extract. Developing safe technologies, overcoming severe climates, and coping with the climatic realities of the Arctic will take time. Some scientists are sounding cautionary notes about the prospects for sizable quantities of Arctic oil—and remember that rigs have been active in the Canadian Arctic islands for several decades with disappointing results. But the speculators and politicians are gripped with twenty-first-century oil fever, driven by skyrocketing prices, growing demand, and a desperate optimism that the energy foundations of the western industrial world can be sustained for a few generations more. There may be huge quantities of fossil fuels in the Arctic (most of it gas), but it is at least as likely that economic prospects in the Far North will not match the excitement and assumptions of our times.

Canada's role in the Arctic, dire forecasts predict, will be challenged—and very soon. If the Northwest Passage remains open in the summer—and signs point strongly in this direction—test ships will start working their way through the Arctic islands. Canada's legal position is untested, and we lack the independent capacity to enforce our regulations and preferences in the region. Expect to see several ships, likely American and Asian, testing the waterway in the next two years, and expect to see Canada change its strategy from asserting control over the Northwest Passage to collaborating with the United States on the monitoring, environmental supervision, and servicing of the commercial shipping through the Arctic. The most pressing sovereignty issue, from the Canadian perspective, is defining the limits to the continental shelf, and not northern shipping, because other Arctic routes between Asia and Europe will open sooner and with less risk, and because the long-term economic benefits rest more with ensuring an extension of territorial control than limited Arctic shipping. The pace and extent of Arctic shipping rests to a considerable extent on the climate, though also on uncharted waters, reefs, and nervous insurance providers. The smaller the ice pack, the lower the risk, and the greater the number of ships going through the Passage and over the polar route.

At a certain level, Canada's approach to the Arctic reflects basic geographic realities. Canada's northern regions are not like those of other countries. Alaska, for example, has a much more temperate climate in its south, and most of the state's 670,000 people live in the southern quarter of the state, with Anchorage accounting for 270,000 alone. Those parts of Alaska that are like Nunavut and the Northwest Territories are as sparsely populated and underdeveloped as the Canadian regions, with two exceptions. The North Slope has been developed extensively, based on a substantial Inuit community at Point Barrow and a largely transient non-aboriginal population. The other exception relates to the scale of American military operations in Alaska. The U.S. maintains major air and army posts near Fairbanks and Anchorage and many smaller installations. Norway's warm ocean currents mean that coastal communities like Tromso and Alta, although northern by any test of latitude, have gentler climates and richer economies than Cambridge Bay or Gjoa Haven. Most of the northern reaches of Norway, Finland, and Sweden share more in common with the northern parts of our provinces than they do with the Arctic regions, including climate, resources, large non-indigenous populations, more advanced civic institutions, and a stronger economic base. Greenland matches closely, in climate and geography, the circumstances facing the people of Baffin and the Arctic Islands. Like Nunavut and the NWT, it subsists on generous subsidies from its southern guardian, in this case Denmark. Unlike the Canadian territories, however, Greenland has a strong history of literacy and academic attainment, extensive biculturalism, and a more diverse economy, one that is potentially being strengthened by global warming.

Russia's Far North shares a lot in common with the Canadian Arctic—bitterly cold winters, a previously unnavigable Arctic coastline, large but scattered indigenous populations, and an uncertain economic base. Russia also has a long history of Arctic engagement, particularly through the construction of plants during the Second World War, notorious use of the Siberian labour camps, the militarization of the region during the Cold War, and accelerated (and uncontrolled) resource development. As a consequence, Russia has a formidable presence in the Far North. There are 35.5 million people in Siberia, more than in all of Canada, with many of them in large urban and industrial centres. Yakutsk, in the middle of the Sakha Republic, is a fast-growing city of more than 210,000 people—or twice the entire population of the three Canadian territories. The marginal areas in Russia, however, are much like those in northern Canada. Chukotka, in the far northeast corner of the country, has only 55,000 people in an area of 770,000 square kilometres (297,297 square miles) (the NWT is 110,000 square kilometres [42,471 square miles]). The largest city, Anadyr, had slightly more than 11,000 people in 2002, a sharp decline from the more than 17,000 living in the area in 1989. The drop in population is emblematic of the rapid out-migration of ethnic Russians and Ukrainians from the region, following the collapse of the subsidized economy in Siberia.

There are some good reasons why the Canadian approach to the North lags far behind that of Scandinavia, Alaska, and Russia—and not all of them point to southern neglect or the colonial mindset of old. The imperative of real and potential armed conflict has driven the other Arctic states (with the exception of Iceland) to integrate—economically, socially, militarily—their northern regions into the body politic. Their northern regions are not merely frontier, politically, economically, and socially; their northern regions exist within the constitutional and social borders of the nation.

Canada, by contrast, has not faced similar historical politico-military challenges to its sovereignty in its North in the same way as Russia, the United States, or the Nordic countries. Sweden has lived with the threat of the Russian bear for centuries. Norway confronted hundreds of thousands of Soviet troops only a few kilometres from its border—in the North. Finland was invaded by the Soviet Red Army in the Second World War and many of its towns and cities were razed by the retreating German army. The United States feared first a Japanese invasion of Alaska, and later, a potential Soviet threat only a few kilometres across the Bering Strait. Russia is surrounded by states that have invaded it at one point or another in its history, including western armies that invaded through the Russian North to try to topple the Bolshevik government established after the 1917 revolution. Even neutral Sweden has developed its own state-of-the-art military forces, including Saab fighter aircraft, to defend its sovereignty.

Canada has not faced serious territorial threats on its northern flank, and in response to what threats have existed, our country has relied heavily on the United States for its defence. In many ways, our North is treated like many countries in Africa. Stability in the international system and the protection of borders of states has meant that many African states have not had to fight major international conflicts. As a consequence, many African states have weak governments and frontier areas. When Chad was invaded by Libya in 1983, France sent troops to help counter the offensive and protect Chadian sovereignty. Like Chad, and countries like it, we never completed nation-building. The threat of the United States to our southern border helped prompt the construction of a railway linking Canada from sea to sea and the constitutional and political development of the western provinces, transforming them from colonial territories into equal partners in a federal state. Without a comparable threat to the North, Canada has been able to neglect the region, leaving it politically, constitutionally, economically, and socially on the periphery. Canada needs to complete the mission of nation-building from sea to sea to sea.

Canada's meagre northern military presence prevented the country from artificially propping up its northern economy, as the Russians and the Americans have done with theirs. However, our approach to economic development, focusing on the free mobility of labour, has created a skilled workforce much like that on Alaska's North Slope and radically different than the forced and massively subsidized labour that sustained the mines and industrial plants in Russia's Arctic until glasnost and the collapse of the USSR. Canada's Arctic trajectory, therefore, is closer to that of Greenland, albeit a little less successful, and that of Arctic Alaska.

Northern Nation-Building: Completing Canada through the Arctic

Canada clearly needs to do more to solidify its presence in the Far North and must become a serious player in the long-term management of the Arctic. The country remains oddly incomplete, a northern nation more in physical geography and symbol. Current sovereignty concerns are a product of both rapidly changing circumstances and Canada's long-standing indifference to a major portion of the country. If, as politicians now assert, our future once again lies to the north, then significant steps are required to move Canada in the right direction. Movement is required on all fronts if the country is to assume its full responsibilities in the North and become a true and active member of the circumpolar world. Canada's options and requirements fall into six general categories. There are strong connections between these initiatives; should Canada move aggressively and competently on them, the North would assume its rightful place within Canada and, equally, Canada would assume its rightful place within the circumpolar world:

1. **Knowing and Defending the North**: In order to protect Canadian sovereignty, Canada must know the region better and extend its military capacity in the area.

- **Military Strategy**: In general, the Harper government's military strategy is moving in the right direction, strengthening practical capabilities without militarizing the North.
- **Northern Research**: The scientific initiatives, particularly the Arctic research station, are too small (and way too late). Canada needs the capacity to understand the Arctic better, requiring a truly national effort to know the North. This will require a much stronger research capacity in the region.
- **Arctic Waters**: Canada needs an open debate about the nature of the Arctic waters. While much of the discussion has focused

on whether the Northwest Passage is internal waters or an international strait, Inuit, including Paul Okalik, premier of Nunavut, have argued that the waters in the Arctic Archipelago are best understood and protected as internal waters to Nunavut and the Northwest Territories, subject to local control and local use.

- **Opening the Northwest Passage**: Canada had best prepare for the rapid expansion of Arctic shipping. Attention must be paid, immediately, to the development of shipping facilities, monitoring networks, rescue capabilities, and environmental-cleanup systems. In all likelihood, the ships are coming. Pretending that they are not will only delay the country's ability to protect the region, capture economic benefits for the North, and ensure that an appropriate level of control is exercised over navigation in the area.

- **Canada–American Arctic Strategy**: In the final analysis, Canada will not be able to overcome American designs on the Arctic. We can pontificate about this endlessly, but the reality is that the United States has the will and resources needed to secure access to the Northwest Passage. Americans' long-standing belief in the need for their navy to have unfettered rights to navigate international straits around the world means that they will not concede on the status of the Passage for fear that it will set a precedent elsewhere. Canada can head off an unseemly contretemps by working with the United States to develop a shared strategy for the control, regulation, and use of the Northwest Passage.

- **The Canadian Rangers**: The Rangers are a national success story and need to be enhanced. They provide an excellent opportunity for northern capacity-building, with participants provided with training in first aid, search and rescue, and emergency response, as well as increasing opportunities to operate outside of their local areas in "enhanced sovereignty patrols."

2. **Removing Irritants to Regional Development**: The North has been a political, legal, and constitutional battleground since the mid-1970s. It is high time that the basic conflicts in the region are resolved, and the North permitted to get on with the business of responding to the challenges and opportunities that lie before it.

- **The Subsidy Claim**: The North is constantly told that it is massively subsidized and that it already costs the country too much. But the North is expensive and always will be. We should drop the language of subsidy (how much of a subsidy is required to maintain Ottawa or the Atlantic provinces?) and focus instead on the legitimate costs of building a national presence in the North.
- **Settling Outstanding Claims**: The remaining northern land claims must be settled as soon as possible. That the task is almost complete is a wonderful testament to the efforts of aboriginal groups, federal authorities, and the territorial governments.
- **Implementing Settlements**: Settling land claims is only part of the story, for Canada does not do particularly well implementing them once they are signed. Success stories, like the Inuvialuit, are offset by the tangled history of the James Bay agreement in northern Quebec. The country needs a rapid and reliable dispute resolution system, likely through an arm's-length authority, that has the capacity deal with the complex and often controversial issues arising out of land claims settlements.
- **Regional Aboriginal Self-Government**: The 2007 Nunavik (Arctic Quebec) agreement on regional self-government may well prove to be the most important development in aboriginal autonomy in recent decades. This approach should be replicated across the provincial Norths and in the territories. The current pattern of aboriginal groups seeking to concentrate decision-making at the community level is rife with problems and will not provide viable and sustainable solutions.

Nunavik holds great potential for aboriginal groups wrestling with the difficult administrative challenges in their regions.

- **Northern Provinces?**: The idea of the territories becoming provinces has largely been taken off the table in recent decades, and northern demands have receded. The territories do need province-like authority—an arrangement that is already in place for the Yukon. The Northwest Territories and Nunavut need to move in this direction as well. There is a current tendency in the south to criticize Nunavut, in particular, for its widely decentralized administrative structure, which is enormously expensive, and its political shortcomings. Few people remember that the new jurisdiction, poor and with monumental administrative challenges, is less than a decade old. The pace of innovation and change in the Arctic has been nothing short of remarkable, and this must be allowed to continue in the coming years.

3. **Being Circumpolar**: Canada has a growing reputation for being a circumpolar nation in word rather than deed. This has to change.

- **Canadian Follow-through**: Canada needs to put its money where its mouth is on circumpolar issues, including initiatives such as the working groups of the Arctic Council and the University of the Arctic. Here our per capita commitment pales in comparison to the funds devoted to this enterprise by Norway or Finland—under the Liberal government Canada's investment in UArctic was 25 cents per northern resident, whereas Norway's was $1.58, even though Canada has no university in its North, whereas Norway has at least six. Canada has been strong on the rhetoric and weak on delivery, but this must end. The country needs to make firm and clear commitments to Arctic initiatives.
- **Increased Multilateral Engagement**: Canada has placed a great deal of emphasis on unilateral planning, with occasional

forays into bilateral discussions and negotiations. The future of the circumpolar world rests in multilateral engagement, through circumpolar associations and organizations. This country should be a world leader in multinational partnerships and collaborations relating to the circumpolar world, but this will require a marked change in direction and emphasis.

- **Regional Circumpolar Engagement**: Para-diplomacy—the engagement of sub-national jurisdictions and organizations in international affairs—has a crucial role to play in the North. Indigenous organizations, like the Inuit Circumpolar Conference, are of fundamental importance in charting the future of the region. Nordic countries support regional participation in northern forums and organizations; Canada generally leaves this up to the small and cash-starved regional governments. The future of the Arctic will largely be defined in the Arctic—and Canada must have the territories, municipalities, indigenous groups, and other organizations engage across national boundaries.

4. **Completing the Nation**: Aboriginal leaders complain that many northern settlements have Third World living conditions. They are right. The North needs to be integrated into the country as a whole and brought up to the standards that are taken as a given in the rest of Canada.

- **Building Northern Cities**: The North requires permanent, substantial cities in the region, with sufficient social infrastructure and other resources, that will compete with comparable communities in the circumpolar world. Whitehorse, Yukon, a delightful community, falls far short of Fairbanks, Alaska, in size, activity, and complexity. Similarly, Inuvik is not Alta, Norway, and Iqaluit is not Akureyri, Iceland. Canada does not have a northern Tromso as yet. Whitehorse and Yellowknife both have growth potential, as do Inuvik, Iqaluit, Baker Lake, and Rankin Inlet, but growth depends on long-term, serious

southern commitment to developing strong regional centres,
with the capacity, opportunity, and resources to sustain prosperous, active cities.

- **Making the North Attractive:** Northern living has to be
  attractive if it is to sustain population growth and provide
  the level of stability and opportunity that Canadians take for
  granted. Oddly, places like Alaska, northern Finland, and the
  like are viewed more positively as places to live than are northern Canadian communities. The country should not, as it
  does at present, focus on salaries—which leaves the impression of bribing people to come North. Instead, effort should
  focus on ensuring a comparable level of basic services (broad-
  band Internet, health care, education) with roughly comparable prices. Canada does this in some areas—northern post
  office and telephone services, for example; the concept needs
  to be broadened and entrenched within government and private sector operations.

- **Solving the Housing Crisis**: Housing remains of fundamental importance for the Canadian North. The shortage of
  suitable accommodation is unacceptable, and the slow and in-
  cremental manner in which the issue is being addressed remains
  a major brake on social and community development. Canada
  needs, as a matter of high urgency, a new approach to Arctic
  housing, one that capitalizes on architectural innovations, new
  approaches to home ownership for indigenous peoples, and a
  commitment to meeting demonstrated need in the area.

- **Northern Research Capacity**: Canada desperately needs a
  university physically located in the North. Post-secondary
  education in Canada has always been driven by real or perceived student demand. That is not sufficient. Canada should
  build off the partnerships created through institutions like the
  University of the Arctic, calling on its major members to create
  a collectively owned university centred in the North. The
  emphasis would be on building research capacity related to the
  Arctic but with strong ties to southern expertise. The university

could include a focus on graduate studies and research that would enable the country to become, once again, a world leader in Arctic research.

There is a great irony in the urgency of the scientific research around the continental shelf project. Cuts in funding to the Polar Continental Shelf Project, a body advising the government on Arctic-research matters, resulted in substantial cutbacks in Arctic research—precisely the kind of science that Canada now urgently needs. Canada needs to recommit to northern science, beyond the Arctic Research Station proposed in the budget. The Arctic matters, and it matters in the long, as well as the short, term. Steps must be taken to create a substantial northern research capacity, related to both the natural and human science aspects of life in the North. While the current climate change agenda and sovereignty debates create an opportunity to expand our northern presence, much more has to be done to make Canada truly credible in Arctic research. This involves facilities, support for faculty and students, and extensive engagement of the private sector and government agencies in the research and dissemination of results.

- **Northern Capacity**: Two issues—capacity building and migration—represent the greatest barrier to sustainable northern development. Aboriginal groups are acutely aware that they need additional administrative and organizational strength; non-aboriginal groups, including territorial governments, speak less often about this safe issue. The rapid turnover of personnel, largely because of the poor facilities and service challenges in the region, compounds the difficulties. The North requires a sustained and purposeful program of capacity building, designed to ensure that the region has the leadership and support personnel necessary to handle the multitude of tasks being assigned to the region. This holds equally for the private sector, incidentally, where northern capacity is noticeably deficient.

5. **Building an Identity as a Northern Nation**: For the vast majority of Canadians, Franklin is a cartoon turtle, not an important historical figure representing the best and the worst of the Arctic experience. Vancouver, the least northern city in Canada (after Victoria), took the Inukshuk as a symbol for the 2010 Olympics. Canada is not now a northern nation, and it is rapidly becoming more southerly and urban in orientation. It is a fantasy to imagine that substantial numbers of people will move into our Arctic, but the current approach of wrapping ourselves in northern symbols while rarely venturing into the region needs to stop.

- **Accepting Winter**: One of the hardest things for Canadians to contemplate is the need to embrace winter. Compared to other northern nations, Canada has an inadequate northern architecture, little enthusiasm for cold and snow, and a bunker mentality about the most dominant season of the world. Like it or not, though, Canada, even with global warming, will be cold, snow covered and therefore quite beautiful for large portions of the year. It is time to recognize this basic reality and start to celebrate this central fact of national life.
- **Towards a Canadian Architecture**: Architecture is a great place to start. Take two of our northernmost universities—the University of Northern British Columbia, designed specifically and successfully for a northern environment, and the University of Alberta, a wonderful institution that is making a belated attempt to recognize its climatic setting. Canada needs more of these. The country requires urban places that reflect their setting, not a strong desire to be southern in appearance and structure. A major initiative of the country's architecture schools and a commitment by governments to rethink their architectural investments in northern settings is essential.
- **Taking Canadians North**: Canada urgently needs an increased presence in the North—and not just of government organizations and the military. The region is fascinating and

magnificent—few areas in the world match its beauty and uniqueness. But very few Canadians go there. Canadians need to connect with their North. We have done the symbolism part well, but we need to go the next step. Where is the Canadian interest in Arctic tourism? The Germans, Americans, and Japanese appear more interested in our North than we do. For every Canadian who has visited the national parks in Nunavut, there must be tens of thousands who have visited Walt Disney World. Efforts must be made to get Canadians, particularly new Canadians, to see the Arctic as part of their country and their future—and not just as a potential source of wealth or security threats.

The country needs mechanisms—north-to-south student exchanges, special vacation packages—designed to bring thousands more southern Canadians into the region. Imagine the impact if Canadian lotteries used just a small portion of their prize pot to award holiday excursions to the North— within a few years, thousands of Canadians could have a personal experience of the North. Canadians need to know their North to be proud of it, and they need to experience the North to understand in full the costs and issues associated with defending, protecting, and improving the region.

- **Arctic Journalism**: Canadian journalism about the North— like national journalism generally—tends to be Ottawa and Toronto focused, with a crisis orientation towards understanding the rest of the country. The tragic murder of two police officers in 2007, one in Hay River, NWT, and the other in Kimmrut, Nunavut, attracted more attention to the North than a decade's worth of aboriginal self-government and improvements in northern educational achievement. Global climate change has really captured the southern imagination—images of polar bears trapped on ice floes and Inuit hunters falling through the ice have proven much more intriguing than stories about commercial joint ventures, land claims implementations, and new approaches to resource management. Canadian news authorities, particularly the CBC and the two national newspapers, the *Globe and Mail* and the *National Post*, need to upgrade their routine coverage of northern issues and get away from the current crisis and conflict orientation towards Arctic issues. Northern media outlets, including aboriginal broadcasters and publications, provide ready access to northern stories that will likely attract a great deal of attention in the country.

6. **Planning for the Twenty-first Century**: The dynamics of northern life are changing rapidly. Even as Canada catches up for decades of neglect, it needs to look forward to a world dominated by global climate change, the resource stampede to the Arctic, and the dynamics of the new world economy.

- **Arctic Climate Strategy**: The Canadian Arctic has become the bellwether for global climate change. The country should capitalize on this international attention immediately, using global interest to draw attention to the urgent need for collective action. To do this properly requires extensive baseline research so that change can be monitored effectively. It requires on-the-ground capacity, both scientific and local, to chart the impact of global warming. The Arctic Climate Strategy requires forward-looking planning to address potential social, cultural, and economic changes associated with environmental realities. And the whole initiative requires high-profile coverage so that the world understands that the full effects of global environmental abuse are being felt first and hardest in the Canadian North.
- **Resource Development**: The country has a test run at Arctic development within its grasp. The Mackenzie Valley Pipeline is still on the drawing board, and construction could be under way within a year or two. Lest there be too much concern about environmental questions, it is crucial to remember that

a northern oil pipeline, stretching from Norman Wells, in the Northwest Territories, to the Alberta pipeline grid, has been in operation since the mid-1980s; this installation has, by existing accounts, been well managed in terms of environmental and socio-economic impacts. The Mackenzie Valley Pipeline will bring the North into national prominence, spur development of the Beaufort Sea deposits, provide a cash flow to the government of the Northwest Territories and the government of Canada (subject to revenue-sharing agreements), and provide evidence of the Arctic's potential. The timely and properly managed implementation of the Mackenzie Valley Pipeline could help transform the country's view of Arctic resources and the value of holding on to the Far North.

- **Resource Realism**: The country needs to be realistic about the economic potential of the Far North. The costs and risks associated with exploiting Arctic resources are considerable—and there is more than a little air of desperation about the effort to find the very last drop of gas and oil on the planet. We should realize that the North will produce disappointments as well as happy surprises, and will often fail to meet the expectations placed upon it. Canada could go in a different direction, create the world's largest ecological park and development-free zone and challenge other nations to establish an Antarctic-type zone of protection over the area. Copying and competing with other nations in a "hell-bent for icebergs" approach to Arctic development will produce far less than people expect. Instead of fighting over potential economic crumbs, Canada might take the world lead in tipping the balance away from the exploitation of the final frontier into the creation of a new environmentalism that places preservation over short-term economic gain.

- **Arctic New Economy Strategy**: The new approaches to the economy, based on fly-in, fly-out resource camps, Internet-based commerce, and global competition, have been dramatically changing northern economic options. At present, the

North remains resource dependent, hoping for diamonds, oil, gas, and minerals (and a few tourists) to sustain the economy. The region is vulnerable at all levels. Even Inuit art, the formidable cultural foundation of many Arctic communities, could be displaced by growing global interest in other indigenous cultures and their artistic production. The North urgently needs a creative, forward-looking economic strategy that sees beyond the standard five-year horizon and that determines the real options for the heavily resource- and government-dependent region.

Canada has choices, but they will be difficult ones. The largely symbolic approach to sovereignty and security that Canada pursued through the twentieth century suited the purposes of the Second World War and the Cold War. It is unlikely that they will suffice in the twenty-first century. If we want to truly exercise our sovereignty over the North, rather than simply try to "possess" it through symbols and rhetoric, we need to engage in a national discussion—with northerners at the centre. And we must rethink our national commitment and goals. We are not truly an Arctic nation, but we could become one. Getting there will not be easy, particularly with the media glare that now attends every step and misstep we take on the Arctic stage.

There is another, more simple, way of understanding Canada's dilemma in the North. Throughout much of our history, northern policy has been largely reactive, responding to intrusions, claims, threats, and challenges to Canadian control over the Arctic. Canada has not addressed the opportunities and needs of the North in a sufficiently systematic manner to neutralize foreign claims on the region. The sovereignty issue in the North is not inherently strategic, military, or diplomatic, although it is playing out that way at present. The manner in which the nation occupies and governs its northern regions determines much of the international understanding about a country's interest in its northern region. Incorporation of the North into the country at large—land claims settlements, aboriginal self-government, improvements to regional infrastructure, stabilization of northern communities, long-term economic development, protection of the vulnerable Arctic environment, and scientific research—are acts of sovereignty, demonstrating in tangible and powerful ways that Canada is committed to the North. It is wrong to assume that sovereignty is entirely a matter of national defence and not one of regional development.

Circumpolar co-operation provides a critical second solution, one where Canada is well placed to play a substantial role. The questions of Arctic sovereignty and northern security are not inherently Canadian or national issues. Protecting the integrity of Canada's place in the North does not automatically require the prime minister to stand up for Canada, or for the military to wave the flag over isolated Arctic islands. We could, in league with other circumpolar nations, develop a co-operative response to the contemporary struggles over the Arctic. Co-operation—not unilateral action—might well hold the key to the preservation of national and collective interests in the Far North, for it could transform the debate about the Arctic into a pan-northern dilemma, with broad international support for Canadian interests in the region.

Canada has made critical first steps in this regard, stretching back through both Liberal and Conservative administrations. The Mulroney and Chrétien governments took crucial steps towards empowering the North and improving circumpolar contacts. The current government's "Stand Up for Canada" approach, while as pleasing to Canadians as Newfoundland premier Brian Tobin's famous "Turbot War" with the Spaniards, may not advance the cause anywhere near as fast and as far as improved circumpolar co-operation. In the past, Canadian rhetoric has been considerably stronger than its actions; we made noise about the Arctic Council, the University of the Arctic and other pan-Arctic initiatives, but have not followed through properly. Solidifying ties with Russia, Scandinavia, Alaska, Greenland, and Iceland may not grab as many headlines as icebreakers and Arctic surveillance flights, but may actually be much more effective in defending national interests in the region.

High-profile Canadian steps to reinvigorate and broaden its commitment to circumpolar co-operation are urgently required. It is vital that Canada put more than words behind the country's Arctic strategies and commitments. We need to take a more prominent role in the Arctic Council but, more importantly, we need to deliver on the promises that are made. Canada needs to be assertive, active, and committed to circumpolar affairs, and needs to capitalize on the opportunities that exist for collaborative action. Diplomacy matters, and can be more effective, and re-establishing a strong political presence among the nations of the circumpolar world is an important first step. Placing Canada at the forefront of circumpolar co-operation, this time with political rhetoric matched by resources, would go a long way towards quelling the idea that the country is not committed to the North. A web of collaborative programs, properly supported and sustained, would integrate Canada more fully into the fabric of the circumpolar world and would thereby create a global understanding of the country's commitment to the region. Co-operation and the integration of science, education, economic development, and cultural exchanges tend to mitigate conflict. As Russian assertiveness returns—Putin is no Gorbachev, to be sure—it is critically important that Canada improve its collaborative ties with that country, a process that could well avoid or temper future confrontations.

An Arctic strategy based on current headlines will not work. Today's threats relate to boundaries and resources. Tomorrow, environmental considerations will likely dominate the news, followed by accounts of further difficulties in indigenous communities. Canada and the Canadian government need to step back from the rhetoric of militarization and strategic approaches to the Arctic. The Far North is not going anywhere, the Russians aren't coming, and the real threats to Canadian sovereignty are much less dramatic than current rhetoric would have the country believe. Canada needs a two-pronged approach to the North, a model that this country uses in its approach to fragile states around the world. In Afghanistan, for example, Canada is endeavouring to blend defence and development, military and civil action. The government of Canada should approach the North in a comparable fashion. By all means, bring Arctic defence up to international standards. Improve surveillance, expand scientific research, and develop better response capabilities. Add deep-water ports and expand the military presence. At the same time, Canada needs to continue its efforts to improve the lives of northern residents, complete the land claims and self-government processes, bring Arctic infrastructure up to national standards—even if it costs a lot of money—and through these processes learn how to be a truly northern nation. A colonized, disempowered, and isolated North is vulnerable, difficult to defend, and disconnected from the country at large. An integrated, confident, and properly supported North would be, instead, a well-known and highly regarded part of the country, distinctively aboriginal and clearly Canadian. Sovereignty starts at home. A proper Arctic strategy requires the completion of nation-building within Canada.

A fearless prediction is in order, based not on hope but on the experience of the last century and more, and on the knowledge of what kind of country this is. In the end, Canada will do the smallest amount possible. The Conservative government's commitment to Arctic sovereignty and northern defence will be watered down by the priorities of a minority Parliament and the lack of true passion for the region in the country at large. Any immediate crisis will fade, either because of a short-term turn in the weather or because either other Arctic shipping routes eclipse the need to use the Northwest Passage, or a few ships will sail successfully through the route and Canadians will realize that the world did not end. National concern will abate—it always has in the past—and we will count on the government to make some quiet and peaceful settlements with our partners and rivals. We will continue to pay lip service to circumpolar co-operation and will underestimate the utility of multilateral actions as a means of avoiding conflict.

Canada has long ignored the North. We have gone southern as a country, moving into cities, turning our backs on the North and seeking a future focused on the global economy rather than our backyard. This is a shame. The Arctic is a remarkable place, full of natural wonders, spectacular beauty, and the unique ability to transform the human spirit. But the region has never really penetrated the national consciousness in this country, and we are the lesser for it. Over the generations, visionaries have promoted the idea of a resource-rich northland fuelling Canadian expansion, and we now see elements of this northern dream arising yet again. Yet perhaps the time has come to do something different. Canada should do more with the Arctic regions and for the Arctic people and environment. The current questions about sovereignty, climate change, indigenous peoples, and economic opportunity create a possible foundation for a very different North and a very different Canada. While the weight of history makes it difficult to imagine real change, the opportunity for a dramatically new approach stands before us. Canada has to rediscover its North, with the territories and aboriginal peoples as full partners. It must defend its northern flank from challenges far more significant and real than those of the past. In this process, Canada has a unique opportunity to rise above its history, to remove the mental shackles of the past, and to define a new role for the North in Canada. The next decade promises to be the most important ten years in the evolution of Canada's Arctic. With the right will and with the full realization of the costs and consequences of neglect and apathy, Canadians can redefine the North's place in Confederation and in the process vault this country into a position of global leadership in the circumpolar world.

Sometimes it seems that the number of books on the Canadian Arctic must outnumber the people who live there. For centuries, tales from the northern latitudes have fascinated armchair explorers in southern Canada and around the world. Many of the published works focus on the search for the Northwest Passage—the famous lost expedition of John Franklin has been chronicled in many books—and events such as the Klondike gold rush and the construction of the Alaska Highway have attracted writers as diverse as Robert Service, Jack London, and Pierre Berton. First-person accounts abound, with volumes produced by missionaries, police officers, scientists, government officials, prospectors, and adventurers. More recently, aboriginal writers have joined the ranks of Arctic authors, their descriptions of changing northern life finding audiences inside and outside the region. Academics have done their share to bring the northern regions to the nation's attention. The foundational work of Morris Zaslow provided an outline of the history of the region and a base for much subsequent writing. Shelagh Grant's detailed studies of sovereignty issues, books by political scientists Gurston Dacks, Franklyn Griffiths, and Mark Dickerson, and contributions by scholars such as Sherrill Grace, I.S. McLaren, William Wonders, Robert Bone, and others have added immeasurably to our understanding of the post-Confederation North. Two academics, Michael Byers and Rob Huebert, have been particularly active and provocative in their contributions to the contemporary debates about Arctic sovereignty. The national attention to books on the Arctic, and about Arctic sovereignty, illustrates the nature of Canadian concern about the region and an ongoing effort to come to grips with Canada's northern responsibilities. The list of books below will provide the reader with an introduction to the main currents in academic and public debate about the Canadian North.

Abel, K.M., and K. Coates. *Northern Visions: New Perspectives on the North in Canadian History*. Peterborough: Broadview Press, 2001.

Abele, Frances. "Canadian Contradictions: Forty Years of Northern Political Development," *Arctic* 40/4 (December 1987): 310-20.

Abele, Frances, and Thierry Rodon. "Inuit Diplomacy in the Global Era: The Strengths of Multilateral Internationalism," *Canadian Foreign Policy* 13/3 (2007): 45-64.

Amundsen, Roald. *The North West Passage*. London: Constable, 1908.

Arctic Institute of North America. *Information North*. Fall 1986. Special issue on militarization of the North.

Arctic Monitoring and Assessment Programme (AMAP), *Arctic Pollution Issues: A State of the Arctic Environment Report*. Oslo: AMAP, 1997.

Aronsen, Lawrence R. "American National Security and the Defense of the Northern Frontier, 1945-51," *Canadian Review of American Studies* 14/3 (Fall 1983). 259-77.

Bankes, Nigel D. "Forty Years of Canadian Sovereignty Assertion in the Arctic, 1947-87," *Arctic* 40/4 (December 1987): 292-99.

Bastedo, Jamie. *Shield Country: Life and Times of the Oldest Piece of the Planet*. Calgary: Arctic Institute of North America, 1994.

Bercuson, David J. "Continental Defense and Arctic Security, 1945-50: Solving the Canadian Dilemma," in *The Cold War and Defense*, eds. K. Neilson and R.G. Haycock (New York: Praeger, 1990): 153-70.

———. *True Patriot: The Life of Brooke Claxton, 1898-1960*. Toronto: University of Toronto Press, 1993.

Berger, Thomas R. *Northern Frontier/Northern Homeland: The Report of the Mackenzie Valley Pipeline Inquiry, vol. 1*. Ottawa: Department of Supply and Services, 1977.

———, ed. *The Arctic: Choices for Peace and Security*. Vancouver: Gordon Soules, 1989.

Berton, Pierre. *Klondike: The Last Great Gold Rush*. Toronto: McClelland & Stewart, 1972.

———. *The Arctic Grail: The Quest for the Northwest Passage and the North Pole, 1818-1909*. Toronto: McClelland & Stewart, 1988.

Bockstoce, J.R. *Steam Whaling in the Western Arctic*. New Bedford: Old Dartmouth Historical Society, 1977.

Bone, Robert. *The Geography of the Canadian North: Issues and Challenges*. Toronto: Oxford, 1992.

Bray, E.F. *A Frenchman in Search of Franklin*. Toronto: University of Toronto Press, 1992.

Briggs, Philip J. "The *Polar Sea* Voyage and the Northwest Passage Dispute," *Armed Forces & Society* 16/3 (1990): 437-52.

Brody, Hugh, *Maps and Dreams*. Vancouver: Douglas & McIntyre, 1981.

———. *The Living Arctic*. Vancouver: Douglas & McIntyre, 1987.

Byers, Michael. *Intent for a Nation: What Is Canada For?* Vancouver: Douglas & McIntyre, 2007.

Caldwell, Nathanial F. *Arctic Leverage: Canadian Sovereignty and Security*. New York: Praeger, 1990.

Canada. Department of Foreign Affairs and International Trade. *The Northern Dimension of Canada's Foreign Policy*. 1998.

Canada. House of Commons Standing Committee on Foreign Affairs and International Trade. *Canada and the Circumpolar World: Meeting the Challenges of Cooperation into the Twenty-First Century*. April 1997.

Canada. *Government Response to Standing Committee on Foreign Affairs and International Trade Report "Canada and the Circumpolar World: Meeting the Challenges of Cooperation Into the Twenty-First Century."* 1998.

Coates, K.S. *The Alaska Highway: Papers of the 40th Anniversary Symposium*. Vancouver: University of British Columbia Press, 1985.

———. *Canada's Colonies: A History of the Yukon and Northwest Territories*. Toronto: James Lorimer, 1985.

Coates, K.S., and Judith Powell. *Canada's Colonies: A History of the Yukon and Northwest Territories*. Toronto: James Lorimer, 1985.

Coates, K.S., and W.R. Morrison, eds. *For Purposes of Dominion: Essays in Honour of Morris Zaslow*. Toronto: Captus University Press, 1989.

———. *Interpreting Canada's North: Selected Readings*. Toronto: Copp Clark, 1989.

————. *The Alaska Highway in World War II: The American Army of Occupation in Canada's Northwest*. Norman, OK: University of Oklahoma Press; Toronto: University of Toronto Press, 1992.

————. *The Forgotten North*. Toronto: James Lorimer, 1992.

————. *Land of the Midnight Sun: A History of the Yukon*. Montreal: McGill-Queen's University Press, 2005.

Cody, H.A. *An Apostle of the North: Memoirs of the Right Reverend William Carpenter Bompas, DD*. Toronto: Musson, 1908.

Cohen, Maxwell. "The Arctic and the National Interest," *International Journal* 26/1 (1970-71): 52-81.

Conant, Melvin. *The Long Polar Watch: Canada and the Defence of North America*. New York: Harper, 1962.

Dacks, Gurston. *A Choice of Futures*. Toronto: Methuen, 1981.

Daniels, Roy. *Alexander Mackenzie and the North West*. London: Faber and Faber, 1969.

Dawson, G.M. *Report on an Exploration in the Yukon District, N.W.T. and Adjacent Northern Portion of British Columbia, 1887*. Ottawa: King's Printer, 1888.

Dickerson, Mark. *Whose North? Political Change, Political Development, and Self-Government in the Northwest Territories*. Vancouver: University of British Columbia Press, 1992.

Diubaldo, R.J. *Stefansson and the Canadian Arctic*. Montreal: McGill-Queen's University Press, 1978.

Dosman, Edgar. *The National Interest*. Toronto: McClelland and Stewart, 1975.

————. *Sovereignty and Security in the Arctic*. London: Routledge, 1989.

————, ed. *The Arctic in Question*. Toronto: Oxford University Press, 1976.

Downie, David L., and Terry Fenge. *Northern Lights Against POPs: Combatting Toxic Threats in the Arctic*. Montreal: McGill-Queen's University Press, 2003.

Duffy, R. Quinn. *The Road to Nunavut: The Progress of Eastern Arctic Inuit since the Second World War*. Montreal: McGill-Queen's University Press, 1988.

Dziuban, Stanley W. *Military Relations Between the United States and Canada 1939-1945*. Washington: Office of the Chief of Military History, Department of the Army, 1959.

Elliot-Meisel, Elizabeth B. *Arctic Diplomacy: Canada and the United States in the Northwest Passage*. New York: Peter Lang, 1998.

———. "Still unresolved after fifty years: the Northwest Passage in Canadian-American relations, 1946-1998," *The American Review of Canadian Studies* 29/3 (Fall 1999): 407-30.

Eyre, Kenneth C. "Custos Borealis: The Military in the Canadian North." Ph.D. thesis, University of London-King's College, 1981.

———. "Forty Years of Military Activity in the Canadian North, 1947-87," *Arctic* 40:4 (December 1987): 292-99.

Fagan, Brian M. *The Great Journey: The Peopling of North America*. New York: Thames and Hudson, 1987.

Fairley, T.C. *Sverdrup's Arctic Adventures*. London: Longmans, 1959.

Finnie, O.S. *Canada Moves North*. Toronto: Macmillan, 1942.

Francis, Daniel. *Discovery of the North: The Exploration of Canada*. Edmonton: Hurtig, 1986.

Freuchen, Peter. *Book of the Eskimos*. Greenwich, CT: Fawcett Crest, 1961.

Fumoleau, René. *As Long as This Land Shall Last: A History of Treaties 8 and 11*. Toronto: McClelland and Stewart, 1973.

Geiger, John, and Owen Beattie. *Frozen in Time: Unlocking the Secrets of the Franklin Expedition*. Saskatoon: Western Producer, 1988.

———. *Dead Silence: The Greatest Mystery in Arctic Discovery*. Toronto: Viking, 1993.

Grace, Sherrill. *Canada and the Idea of North*. Montreal: McGill-Queen's University Press, 2001.

Grant, Shelagh. *Sovereignty or Security?: Government Policy in the Canadian North, 1936-1950*. Vancouver: University of British Columbia Press, 1988.

———. *Arctic Justice: On Trial for Murder, Pond Inlet, 1923*. Montreal: McGill-Queen's University Press, 2002.

Green, Lewis. *The Gold Hustlers*. Vancouver: J.J. Douglas, 1972.

Griffiths, Franklyn. *Arctic Alternatives: Civility or Militarism in the Circumpolar North?* Toronto: Science for Peace/Samuel Stevens, 1992.

———. *A Northern Foreign Policy*. Toronto: Canadian Institute of International Affairs (CIIA), 1979.

———. "The Shipping News: Canada's Arctic Sovereignty Not on Thinning Ice," *International Journal* 58/2 (Spring 2003): 257-82.

————, ed. *Politics of the Northwest Passage*. Kingston & Montreal: McGill-Queen's University Press, 1987.

Hamelin, L.-E. *Canadian Nordicity: It's Your North Too*. trans. W. Barr. Montreal: Harvest House, 1978.

Hamilton, John D. *Arctic Revolution: Social Change in the Northwest Territories, 1935-1994*. Toronto: Dundurn Press, 1994.

Head, Ivan L. "Canadian Claims to Territorial Sovereignty in the Arctic Regions," *McGill Law Journal* 9 (1963): 200-26.

Henderson, Alicia. *Nunavut: Rethinking Political Culture*. Vancouver: University of British Columbia Press, 2007.

Hesketh, Bob, ed. *Three Northern Wartime Projects*. Edmonton: Canadian Circumpolar Institute, 1996.

Holmes, Douglas. *Northerners: Profiles of People in the Northwest Territories*. Toronto: James Lorimer, 1989.

Honderick, John. *Arctic Imperatives: Is Canada Losing the North?* Toronto: University of Toronto Press, 1987.

Horn, Bernd. "Gateway to Invasion or the Curse of Geography? The Canadian Arctic and the Question of Security, 1939-1999," in *Forging a Nation: Perspectives on the Canadian Military Experience*, ed. Bernd Horn. St. Catharines: Vanwell, 2002: 307-32.

Huebert, Rob. "Steel, Ice and Decision-Making: The Voyage of the *Polar Sea* and Its Aftermath." Unpublished Ph.D. dissertation, Dalhousie University, 1994.

————. "Polar Vision or Tunnel Vision: The Making of Canadian Arctic Waters Policy," *Marine Policy* 19/4 (1995): 343-63.

————. "New Directions in Circumpolar Cooperation: Canada, the Arctic Environmental Protection Strategy, and the Arctic Council," *Canadian Foreign Policy* 5/2 (1998): 37-58.

————. "Canadian Arctic Security Issues: Transformation in the Post–Cold War Era," *International Journal* 54/2 (1999): 203-29.

————. "Climate Change and Canadian Sovereignty in the Northwest Passage," *Isuma* (Winter 2001): 86-94.

————. "A Northern Foreign Policy: The Politics of Ad Hocery," in *Diplomatic Departures: The Conservative Era in Canadian Foreign Policy, 1984-93*, eds. N. Michaud and K.R. Nossal. Vancouver: University of British Columbia Press, 2001: 84-112.

———. "The Shipping News Part II: How Canada's Arctic Sovereignty is on thinning ice," *International Journal* (Summer 2003): 295-308.

Inuit Tapiriit Kanatami (ITK), *An Integrated Arctic Strategy*. January 2008.

Inuit Tapiriit Kanatami (ITK) and Inuit Circumpolar Council (Canada), *Building Inuit Nunaat: The Inuit Action Plan*. 2006.

Jenness, Diamond. *Eskimo Administration II: Canada*. Montreal: Arctic Institute of North America, 1964.

Jenness, Stuart, ed. *Arctic Odyssey: The Diary of Diamond Jenness*. Ottawa: Canadian Museum of Civilization, 1991.

Jockel, Joseph. *No Boundaries Upstairs: Canada, the United States, and the Origins of North American Air Defence, 1945-1958*. Vancouver: University of British Columbia Press, 1987.

Johnston, V. Kenneth. "Canada's Title to the Arctic Island," *Canadian Historical Review*, 14 (1933): 24-41.

Jull, Peter. "Canada, Arctic Peoples, and International Affairs." *Behind the Headlines* 45/6 (July/August 1988): 1-14.

Karamanski, Theodore. *Fur Trade and Exploration: Opening the Far Northwest, 1821-1852*. Vancouver: University of British Columbia Press, 1978.

Kirkey, Christopher. "The Arctic Waters Pollution Prevention Initiatives: Canada's Response to an American Challenge," *International Journal of Canadian Studies* 13 (Spring 1996), 41-59.

———. "Smoothing Troubled Waters: The 1988 Canada–United States Arctic Co-operation Agreement," *International Journal* 50 (1995): 401-26.

Kirton, John, and Don Munton. "Protecting the Canadian Arctic: The Manhattan Voyages, 1969-1970," in *Canadian Foreign Policy: Selected Cases*, eds. Kirton and Munton. Toronto: Prentice-Hall, 1992: 206-21.

Lackenbauer, P. Whitney. "The Canadian Rangers: A Postmodern Militia That Works." *Canadian Military Journal* 6/4 (Winter 2005-6): 49-60.

———. "Right and Honourable: Mackenzie King, Canadian-American Bilateral Relations, and Canadian Sovereignty in the Northwest, 1943-1948," in *Mackenzie King: Citizenship and Community*, eds. John English, Kenneth McLaughlin, and P.W. Lackenbauer. Toronto: Robin Brass Studios, 2002: 151-68.

———. "Canada's Northern Defenders: Aboriginal Peoples in the Canadian Rangers, 1947-2005," in *Aboriginal Peoples and the Canadian*

Military: Historical Perspectives, eds. P.W. Lackenbauer and Craig Mantle. Kingston: CDA Press, 2007: 171-208.

Larsen, Henry. *The Big Ship*. Toronto: McClelland and Stewart, 1967.

Larson, David L. "United States Interests in the Arctic Region," *Ocean Development and International Law* 20 (1989): 167-91.

Lee, H.P. *Policing the Top of the World*. London: John Lane, 1928.

Lloyd, Trevor. "New Perspective on the North," *Foreign Affairs* 42/2 (1964), 293-308.

Lopez, Barry. *Arctic Dreams: Imagination and Desire in a Northern Landscape*. New York: Charles Scribner's Sons, 1986.

Lotz, Jim. *Northern Realities: The Future of Northern Development in Canada*. Toronto: New Press, 1972.

Loukacheva, Natalia. *The Arctic Promise: Legal and Political Autonomy of Greenland and Nunavut*. Toronto: University of Toronto Press, 2007.

Lysyk, K. et al. *Alaska Highway Pipeline Inquiry*. Ottawa: Supply and Services Canada, 1977.

MacDonald, Brian, ed. *Defence Requirements for Canada's Arctic*. Vimy Paper 2007. Ottawa: Conference of Defence Associates, 2007.

MacDonald, R. St. J., ed. *The Arctic Frontier*. Toronto: University of Toronto Press, 1966.

McClellan, Catherine. *Part of the Land, Part of the Water: A History of the Yukon Indians*. Vancouver: Douglas & McIntyre, 1987.

McCullum, Hugh. *This Land is Not for Sale*. Toronto: Anglican Book Centre, 1975.

McGhee, Robert. *The Last Imaginary Place: A Human History of the Arctic World*. Chicago: University of Chicago Press, 2005.

McMahon, Kevin. *Arctic Twilight: Reflections on the Destiny of Canada's Northern Land and People*. Toronto: James Lorimer, 1988.

McRae, Donald M. "Arctic waters and Canadian sovereignty," *International Journal* 38/3 (1983): 476-92.

―――. "Arctic Sovereignty: Loss by Dereliction?," *Northern Perspectives* [Canadian Arctic Resources Committee] 22/4 (1994-95).

―――. "Arctic Sovereignty: What Is at Stake?," *Behind the Headlines* 64/1 (2007).

Metayer, Maurice, trans. *I, Nuligak*. New York: Pocket Books, 1971.

Mitchell, Marybelle. *From Talking Chiefs to a Native Corporate Elite: The Birth of Class and Nationalism Among Canadian Inuit*. Montreal: McGill-Queen's University Press, 1996.

Morenus, Richard. *DEW Line: Distant Early Warning, The Miracle of America's First Line of Defense*. New York, Rand McNally, 1957.

Morison, S.E. *The European Discovery of America: The Northern Voyages*. New York: Oxford University Press, 1971.

Morrison, William R. *Showing the Flag: the Mounted Police and Canadian Sovereignty in the North, 1894-1925*. Vancouver: University of British Columbia Press, 1985.

———. "Eagle Over the Arctic: Americans in the Canadian North, 1867-1985," *Canadian Review of American Studies* (Spring 1987): 61-85.

———. *True North: The Yukon and Northwest Territories*. Toronto: Oxford University Press, 1998.

Morrison, W.R., and K.S. Coates. *Working the North: Labor and the Northwest Defense Projects, 1942-1945*. Fairbanks: University of Alaska Press, 1994.

Moss, John. *Enduring Dreams: An Exploration of Arctic Landscape*. Don Mills: Anansi, 1994.

Mowat, F. *The Desperate People*. Boston: Little, Brown, 1959.

Moyles, R.G. *British Law and Arctic Men*. Saskatoon: Western Producer Prairie Books, 1979.

Neatby, Leslie. *The Search for Franklin*. Edmonton: Hurtig, 1970.

North, Dick. *The Mad Trapper of Rat River*. Toronto: Macmillan, 1972.

———. *The Lost Patrol*. Anchorage, Alaska: Northwest Publishing, 1978.

Nuttal, Mark. *Protecting the Arctic: Indigenous Peoples and Cultural Survival*. Amsterdam: Harwood, 1998.

Page, Robert. *Northern Development: The Canadian Dilemma*. Toronto: McClelland & Stewart, 1986.

Peake, F.A. *The Bishop Who Ate His Boots: A Biography of Isaac O. Stringer*. Don Mills, ON: Anglican Church of Canada, 1966.

Pharand, Donat. *Canada's Arctic Waters in International Law*. Cambridge: Cambridge University Press, 1988.

———. "Arctic Waters and the Northwest Passage: A Final Revisit," *Ocean Development and International Law* 38/1&2 (January 2007): 3-69.

Phillips, R.A.J. *Canada's North*. Toronto: Macmillan, 1967.

Pullen, Thomas C. "What Price Canadian Sovereignty?," *U.S. Naval Institute Proceedings* 113/9 (1987): 66-72.

Purver, Ron. "The Arctic in Canadian Security Policy, 1945 to the Present," in *Canada's International Security Policy*, eds. David B. Dewitt and David Leyton-Brown. Scarborough, ON: Prentice-Hall, 1995: 81-110.

Rea, K.J. *The Political Economy of the Canadian North*. Toronto: University of Toronto Press, 1968.

Robertson, Gordon. *Northern Provinces: A Mistaken Goal?* Ottawa: Institute of Public Policy Research, 1986.

———. *Memoirs of a Very Civil Servant: Mackenzie King to Pierre Trudeau*. Toronto: University of Toronto Press, 2000.

Rohmer, Richard. *The Arctic Imperative*. Toronto: McClelland & Stewart, 1973.

Ross, W.G. ed. *An Arctic Whaling Diary: The Journal of Captain George Comer in Hudson Bay, 1903-1905*. Toronto: University of Toronto Press, 1984.

Rothwell, Donald R. "The Northwest Passage Dispute: A Reassessment," *Cornell International Law Journal* 26 (1993): 331-72.

———. *The Polar Regions and the Development of International Law*. Cambridge: Cambridge University Press, 1996.

Rowley, Graham. *Cold Comfort: My Love Affair with the Arctic*, 2nd ed. Montreal: McGill-Queen's University Press, 2007.

Steele, S.B. *Forty Years in Canada*. London: Jenkins, 1915.

Stefansson, V. *My Life With the Eskimo*. New York: Macmillan, 1913.

———. *The Friendly Arctic*. New York: Macmillan, 1921.

———. *Discovery*. New York: McGraw-Hill, 1964.

Sverdrup, O. *New Land: Four Years in the Arctic Regions*. 2 vols. London: Longmans Green, 1904.

Tester, Frank J., and Peter Kulchyski. *Tammarniit (Mistakes): Inuit Relocation in the Eastern Arctic, 1939-63*. Vancouver: University of British Columbia Press, 1994.

Tynan, Thomas M. "Canadian-American Relations in the Arctic: The Effect of Environmental Influences upon Territorial Claims," *The Review of Politics* 41/3 (July 1979): 402-27.

VanStone, James. *Athapaskan Adaptations: Hunters and Fishermen of the Subarctic Forests*. Chicago: Aldine, 1975.

Wallace, H.N. *The Navy, the Company, and Richard King: British exploration in the Canadian Arctic, 1829-1860*. Montreal: McGill-Queen's University Press, 1980.

Webb, Melody. *The Last Frontier: A History of the Yukon Basin of Canada and Alaska*. Albuquerque: University of New Mexico Press, 1985.

Whittington, Michael. *The North*. Toronto: University of Toronto Press, 1985.

Wonders, William C., ed. *Canada's Changing North*. Toronto: McClelland & Stewart, 1971.

———. *Canada's Changing North*, rev. ed. Toronto: McClelland & Stewart, 2003.

Woodman, David. *Unravelling the Franklin Mystery: Inuit Testimony*. Montreal: McGill-Queen's University Press, 1991.

Wright, A.A. *Prelude to Bonanza: The Discovery and Exploration of the Yukon*. Whitehorse: Arctic Star Printing, 1980.

Young, Oran R. *Arctic Politics: Conflict and Cooperation in the Circumpolar North*. Hanover: University Press of New England, 1992.

———. "Governing the Arctic: From Cold War Theatre to Mosaic of Cooperation," *Global Governance* 11 (2005): 9-15.

Young, Steven B. *To The Arctic: An Introduction to the Far Northern World*. New York: John Wiley, 1989.

Yukon Native Brotherhood. *Together Today for Our Children Tomorrow*. Whitehorse: Yukon Native Brotherhood, 1973.

Zaslow, Morris. *The Opening of the Canadian North, 1870-1914*. Toronto: McClelland & Stewart, 1971.

———. *The Northward Expansion of Canada, 1914-1967*. Toronto: McClelland & Stewart, 1988.

———, ed. *A Century of Canada's Arctic Islands 1880-1890*. Ottawa: The Royal Society of Canada, 1981.

CHAPTER I

1 There was a bit of unnecessary bullying during the Alaska Boundary Dispute (see below), unnecessary because the Americans had the better case and would have won anyway.

2 The Kingdom of Great Britain came into being with the Act of Union of 1707 that joined Britain and Scotland. The United Kingdom dates from the Act of Union that brought in Ireland in 1800. The Hudson's Bay Charter was an English document, but events after 1707 are properly British rather than English.

3 There were other, all-Canadian routes, but they were impractical.

4 A jurist is not necessarily a judge nor a juror, but a person with thorough knowledge and experience of law.

5 Sir Louis-Amable Jetté (1836-1920).

6 Sir Allen Aylesworth (1854-1952).

7 This is by no means an unimportant issue, for it has implications for fisheries and oil drilling on the continental shelf. There are agreements in place between Canada and the United States covering the region, but they are only temporary. See Tony Forgarassy, *The Alaska Dispute: History and International Law*. Vancouver: Clark, Wilson [a law firm], accessible at http://www.cwilson.com/pubs/energy/alaska.pdf (September 2007).

8 The miners' meeting is analyzed by Thomas Stone in *Miner's Justice: Migration, Law and Order on the Alaska-Yukon Frontier, 1873-1892* (New York: Peter Lang, 1989).

9   By way of comparison, one of us lived a number of years ago in a community of 40,000 that had a police force of fifty, including civilian employees.

10 In *Canada North* (Toronto, 1968).

11 Baleen is the tough cartilage arranged like great combs, attached to the upper jaws of whales, and used for filtering their food. Before plastics were developed, it was in great demand for corset stays, buggy whips, and other uses where a tough, flexible material was required.

12 I.O. Stringer, later famous as the "bishop who ate his boots."

13 M. Metayer, trans., *I Nuligak*. New York: Pocket Books, 1971.

14 Library and Archives Canada (LAC), RCMP Papers, Record Group (RG) 18, Comptroller's Correspondence, vol. 293, J.A. Smart, memo, n.d. (probably summer 1903).

15 See W.R. Morrison, *Showing the Flag: The Mounted Police and Canadian Sovereignty in the North, 1894-1925* (Vancouver: University of British Columbia Press, 1985).

16 Murray Lundberg, "Joseph-Elzéar Bernier Arctic Mariner," in *Explore North* (http://explorenorth.com/library/weekly/aa102000a.htm), September 2007.

17 Gordon W. Smith, "Sovereignty in the North: The Canadian Aspect of an International Problem," in *The Arctic Frontier*, ed. R. St. J. MacDonald (Toronto: University of Toronto Press, 1966), 214-16; Season L. Osborne, "Closing the Front Door of the Arctic: Capt. Joseph E. Bernier's Role in Canadian Arctic Sovereignty" (unpublished master of journalism thesis, Carleton University, 2003), 67-72; and J.L. Granatstein, "A Fit of Absence of Mind: Canada's National Interest in the North to 1968," in *The Arctic in Question*, ed. E.J. Dosman (Toronto: Oxford University Press, 1976), 16. In 1925, the minister of the interior, Charles Stewart, claimed this territory for Canada making it, in Smith's assessment, "official in every respect, except that it had not been incorporated in a statute." Smith, "Sovereignty in the North," 216.

18 Murray Lundberg, "Joseph-Elzéar Bernier Arctic Mariner," in *Explore North* (http://explorenorth.com/library/weekly/aa102000a.htm), September 2007.

19 Captain J.E. Bernier, "The Arctic Regions of Canada," in *The Empire Club of Canada Speeches 1909-1910*, ed. J. Castell Hopkins (Toronto, Canada: The Empire Club of Canada, 1910), 67-76.

20 This point is made in W.R. Morrison, *Showing the Flag* (Vancouver: University of British Columbia Press, 1985), chapter 11, "The Police and the Native Peoples of the Northern Frontier."

21 From the RNWMP *Report* 1916, quoted in Morrison, *Showing the Flag*, 139.

22 Quoted in K.S. Coates and W.R. Morrison, *Strange Things Done: Murder in Yukon History* (Montreal: McGill-Queen's University Press, 2004), 115-16.

23 The chronology of events relating to this episode has been taken from Gordon W. Smith, "The Transfer of Arctic Territories from Great Britain to Canada, and Some Related Matters, as Seen in Official Correspondence." The text is available at the website of the Arctic Institute of North America, http://pubs.aina.ucalgary.ca/Arctic/Arctic14-1-53.pdf. Smith's 1952 master's thesis for Columbia University was "The Historical and Legal Background of Canada's Arctic Claims."

24 Completely unknown to anyone, not just to Europeans. Some of the islands of the High Arctic had never been occupied.

25 Mintzer eventually did go north, and returned, according to newspaper reports, with a load of mica worth more than $150,000, on which no royalty was paid.

26 April 25, 1874, Signature illegible, quoted in Gordon Smith, 54.

27 In this period relations of this sort between the British and Canadian governments were conducted through the Governor General's office.

28 Smith, 57.

29 Smith, 63.

30 H.R. Holmden, *Memo re the Arctic Islands* (Ottawa, 1921), quoted in Smith, 69.

31 The best biography of him is Richard Diubaldo, *Stefansson and the Canadian Arctic* (Montreal: McGill-Queen's University Press, 1978).

32 The Yukon's population shrank from nearly 40,000 at the height of the rush in 1898 (no census was taken until 1901) to only 4,100 in 1921, of whom 1,500 were First Nations, a fall of 90 percent.

33 Cited in a copy of a letter from Rasmussen to V. Stefansson, quoted in Morrison, *Showing the Flag*, 164.

34 Memo, n.a., n.d., quoted in Morrison, 164.

35 The idea that "effective possession" of inhospitable areas requires physical inhabitation akin to other regions was challenged in the Permanent

Council of International Justice decision in the *Eastern Greenland* case (1933) between Norway and Denmark. The court found that Denmark's legislation and other administrative acts applicable to all of Greenland were sufficient to oust Norway's claim in eastern Greenland, even though Norwegians had inhabited the area concerned. Thanks to Rodney Neufeld, a lawyer with the Oceans Law Section at the Department of Foreign Affairs and International Trade Canada for this clarification. See also Oscar Svarlien, *The Eastern Greenland Case in Historical Perspective* (Gainesville: University of Florida Press, 1964).

36 Memo prepared for W.W. Cory, deputy minister of the interior, quoted in Morrison, 165.

37 Harkin to W.W. Cory, 26 May 1921, NAC, Harkin Papers, vol. 1.

38 They were always called Eskimos in this era, but the modern term is used here.

39 Shelagh Grant, *Arctic Justice: On Trial for Murder, Pond Inlet, 1923* (Montreal: McGill-Queen's University Press, 2002) is a fascinating and sensitive account of this case.

40 October 17, 1922.

41 V.K. Johnston, "Canada's Title to the Arctic Islands," *Canadian Historical Review*, vol. 14, no. 1, March 1933, 40.

42 There is some question whether Norway (which was in Royal and political union with Sweden until 1905 and loaned him the steamer *Fram* to support his voyage, which was privately sponsored by the consul Axel Heiberg and the Ringes Brothers brewery) gave Sverdrup authority to claim land. Neither King Oscar of Sweden and Norway nor the Norwegian Foreign Ministry officially pursued the claim. See Per Egil Hegge, *Otto Sverdrup Aldri Radlos* (Oslo: Stenersens Forlag A/G, 1996), and Gordon W. Smith, "The Historical and Legal Background of Canada's Arctic Claims" (Ph.D. thesis, Columbia University, 1952), 251-55.

43 This account relies on a recent graduate thesis: Thorlief T. Thorliefsson, "Norway 'Must Really Drop Their Absurd Claims Such as That to the Otto Sverdrup Islands.' Bi-Polar International Diplomacy: the Sverdrup Islands Question, 1902-1930," master's thesis, Simon Fraser University, 2006.

44 Thorliefsson, 3.

45 Jan Mayen Island lies very roughly equidistant from Iceland, Norway, and Greenland in the Arctic Ocean. It was a Dutch whaling station in

the early seventeenth century. Norway built a meterological station there in 1921 and the island formally became a part of Norway in 1930. There was no economic activity on the island at the time.

46 Thorliefsson, 3.

47 When he was hired to lead External Affairs in 1921, the department had a total of two other employees.

48 His autobiography is *The Big Ship* (Toronto: McClelland & Stewart, 1967).

CHAPTER 2

1 Vincent Massey, *What's Past Is Prologue* (Toronto: Macmillan, 1963), 371; Clyde Sanger, *Malcolm MacDonald: Bringing an End to Empire* (Montreal and Kingston: McGill-Queen's University Press, 1995), 237-39; William Lyon Mackenzie King Diary, March 29, 1943, available online at http://king.collectionscanada.ca/. The full text of MacDonald's memorandum is reprinted in *The Alaska Highway*, ed. Coates, 95-101.

2 J.L. Granatstein, *Canada's War: The Politics of the Mackenzie King Government, 1939-1945* (Toronto: Oxford University Press, 1975), 323.

3 *Ibid.* William Lyon Mackenzie King Diary, March 21, 1942.

4 Elizabeth Brebner, "Sovereignty and the North: Canadian-American Cooperation, 1939-45," in *Three Northern Wartime Projects*, ed. Bob Hesketh (Edmonton: Canadian Circumpolar Institute, 1996), 55; Clyde Sanger, *Malcolm MacDonald: Bringing an End to Empire* (Montreal and Kingston: McGill-Queen's University Press, 1995), 241; Granatstein, *Canada's War*, 322; Stanley Dziuban, *Military Relations Between the United States and Canada, 1939-1945* (Washington: Office of the Chief of Military History, Department of the Army, 1959), 210-11; John W. Holmes, *The Shaping of Peace: Canada and the Search for World Order* (Toronto: University of Toronto Press, 1979), 174-77. On the prolonged negotiations over the disposal of the Canol project, see Richard Diubaldo, "The Canol Project," and Dziuban, *Military Relations*, 331-34.

5 C.P. Stacey, *Arms, Men and Governments: The War Policies of Canada, 1939-1945* (Ottawa: Queen's Printer, 1970), 386-87; Dziuban, *Military Relations*, 137-41.

6 Margaret A. Campbell, "Defence Forces Operations in Hudson Bay," in *Science, History & Hudson Bay*, vol. 2, eds. C.S. Beals and D.A. Shenstone (Ottawa: Department of Energy, Mines and Resources, 1968), 899-900.

7 R.J. Sutherland, "The Strategic Significance of the Canadian Arctic," in *The Arctic Frontier*, ed. R. St. J. MacDonald (Toronto: University of Toronto Press, 1966), 262.

8 L.B. Pearson, "Canada Looks 'Down North,'" *Foreign Affairs* 24/4 (July 1946), 638.

9 MGen H.F.G. Letson, "Memorandum on Continued Collaboration between U.S.-Canada," 14 December 1945, National Archives and Records Administration, RG 59, Permanent Joint Board on Defence (PJBD), Box #2, file Basic Security Plan II.

10 D.J. Bercuson, "Continental Defense and Arctic Sovereignty, 1945-1950: Solving the Canadian Dilemma," in *The Cold War and Defense*, eds. K. Neilson and R.G. Haycock (New York: Praeger, 1990), 154.

11 Final Report of the Advisory Committee on Post-Hostility Problems, January/February 1945, and Extract of Minutes of Cabinet War Committee, *Documents on Canadian External Relations*, vol. XI (1944-45), Part II, 1567-74; D.J. Bercuson, *True Patriot: The Life of Brooke Claxton, 1898-1960* (Toronto: University of Toronto Press, 1993), 154-55.

12 K. Eyre, "Forty Years of Military Activity in the Canadian North, 1947-87," *Arctic* 40/4 (December 1987), 294.

13 L.B. Pearson, "Canada's Northern Horizons," *Foreign Affairs*, 31/4 (July 1953), 583. These observations are based upon Sutherland, "Strategic Significance of the Canadian Arctic," 256, 264.

14 J.L. Granatstein, "A Fit of Absence of Mind: Canada's National Interest in the North to 1968," in *The Arctic in Question*, ed. E.J. Dosman (Toronto: Oxford University Press, 1976), 22.

15 See, for example, Memorandum of Conversation, "Integration of Canadian and American Armed Forces," July 26, 1945, National Archives and Records Administration (Washington), RG 59 (State Department Records), Decimal File 1945-49.

16 See Robert A. Spencer, *Canada in World Affairs: From UN to NATO 1946-1949* (Toronto: Oxford University Press, 1959), 284-324.

17 Joseph Jockel, *No Boundaries Upstairs: Canada, the United States, and the Origins of North American Air Defence, 1945-1958* (Vancouver: University of British Columbia Press, 1987), 9, 11.

18 Ron Purver, "The Arctic in Canadian Security Policy, 1945 to Present," in *Canada's International Security Policy*, eds. D.B. Dewitt and D. Leyton-Brown (Scarborough: Prentice Hall, 1995), 82-84; James Eayrs, *In Defence of Canada*, vol. III: Peacemaking and Deterrence (Toronto: University of Toronto Press), 343-44; Bercuson, "Continental Defense and Arctic Sovereignty," 161.

19 Top-secret memorandum, J. Graham Parsons, State Department Member, PJBD, to Secretary of State, January 24, 1947, National Archives and Records Administration (Washington), RG 59, PJBD, File: 36th Recommendation: General Principles.

20 C.D. Howe, March 4, 1947, House of Commons, *Debates*, 990; N.D. Bankes, "Forty Years of Canadian Sovereignty Assertion in the Arctic, 1947-87," *Arctic* 40/4 (December 1987), 287; Elizabeth Elliot-Meisel, *Arctic Diplomacy: Canada and the United States in the Northwest Passage* (New York: Peter Lang, 1998), 79-89. In practical terms, however, Canada did not have the naval resources to conduct annual JAWS resupply missions. See Elliot-Meisel, *Arctic Diplomacy*, 82-91.

21 Sutherland, "Strategic Significance of the Canadian Arctic," 267.

22 John T. Correll, *The Air Force and the Cold War* (Air Forces Association Special Report, September 2005), 10.

23 On the radar chains, see Jockel, *No Boundaries Upstairs*; Matthew Farish, "Strategic Environments: Militarism and the Contours of Cold War America" (unpublished Ph.D. dissertation, University of British Columbia, 2003); and Jeffrey David Noakes, "Under the Radar: Defence Construction (1951) Limited and the Military Infrastructure in Canada, 1950-1965" (unpublished Ph.D. dissertation, University of British Columbia, 2005).

24 Adam Lajeunesse, "The Distant Early Warning Line and the Canadian Battle for Public Perception," *Canadian Military Journal* (Summer 2007), 55, 57.

25 Sutherland, "Strategic Significance of the Canadian Arctic," 271.

26 James Eayrs, "Problems of Canadian-American Relations" in *Canada in World Affairs October 1955 to June 1957* (Toronto: Oxford University Press, 1959), 151.

27 Eayrs, "Problems of Canadian-American Relations," 151.

28 Ralph Allen, "Will DEWline Cost Canada its Northland?," *Maclean's*, 26 May 1956, 16-17, 68-72. Contrast also Leslie Roberts's two articles:

"The Great Assault on the Arctic," *Harper's Magazine* (July 1955) spoke glowingly about Canadian-American co-operation, while "Should We Bring Our NATO Troops Home?," *Saturday Night*, October 29, 1955, accused the Canadian government of failing to safeguard Canadian interests.

29 Canada, House of Commons, *Debates*, August 3, 1956, 6967.

30 Blair Fraser, "Could Canada Stay Out of a U.S. War?," *Maclean's*, December 6, 1958, 72.

31 John Nicholas Harris, "National Defence and Northern Development: The Establishment of the DEWLine in the Canadian North" (unpublished master's thesis, Simon Fraser University, 1980), 160.

32 Colin Gray, *Canadian Defence Priorities: A Question of Relevance* (Toronto: Clarke, Irwin, 1972), 185.

33 Eyre, "Forty Years of Military Activity," 296.

34 "The Canadian Forces and the Maintenance of Canadian Sovereignty," paper drafted by Arthur Kroeger, c. August 1968, Library and Archives Canada (LAC), Record Group (RG) 25, file no. 27-10-2-2 pt. 1, acquired under Access to Information.

35 Thomas M. Tynan, "Canadian-American Relations in the Arctic: The Effect of Environmental Influences upon Territorial Claims," *The Review of Politics* 41/3 (1979), 424.

CHAPTER 3

1 T.C. Pullen, "What Price Canadian Sovereignty?," *U.S. Naval Institute Proceedings* 113 (September 1987), 70.

2 On these themes, see Elizabeth Elliot-Meisel, "Still Unresolved After Fifty Years: The Northwest Passage in Canadian-American Relations, 1946-1998," *American Review of Canadian Studies* 29/3 (1999), 407-30; Donat Pharand, *Canada's Arctic Waters in International Law* (Cambridge: Cambridge University Press, 1988); and Donald R. Rothwell, "The Northwest Passage Dispute: A Reassessment," *Cornell International Law Journal* 26 (1993), 331-72.

3 W.G. Lamarque to G. Sicotte, March 5, 1958, LAC, RG 25, f. 9057-40, pt. 9-2, acquired under ATIP. Donat Pharand calculates that, in Canada's case, the close link between land and sea necessary to draw

straight baselines is very strong. The sea to land ratio is 0.822 to 1, much better than the 3.5 to 1 ratio for the Norwegian Archipelago upon which the original legal decision was based. Furthermore, he notes that "the quasi-permanency of the ice over the enclosed waters bolsters the physical unity between land and sea." Pharand, "The Arctic Waters and the Northwest Passage," 18.

4 G. Sicotte to W.G. Lamarque, April 14, 1958, LAC, RG 25, f. 9057-40, pt. 9-2, acquired under Access to Information.

5 G.W. Rowley, Memorandum for the Advisory Committee on Northern Development, "Canadian Sovereignty in the Arctic Basin and the Channels Lying Between the Islands of the Arctic Archipelago," September 16, 1958, LAC, RG 25, f. 9057-40, pt. 9-2, acquired under Access to Information.

6 Pharand, "The Arctic Waters and the Northwest Passage," 10.

7 Elizabeth Elliot-Meisel, "Arctic Focus: The Royal Canadian Navy in Arctic Waters, 1946-1949," *The Northern Mariner* 9/2 (1999), 23-39.

8 Pullen, "What Price Canadian Sovereignty?," 67.

9 J.M. Leeming, "HMCS *Labrador* and the Canadian Arctic" in *RCN in Retrospect*, ed. James A. Boutilier (Vancouver: University of British Columbia Press, 1982), 286-307; and Louis St. Laurent, House of Commons *Debates*, April 6, 1957, excerpted in "Public Statements regarding Arctic Sovereignty," c. June 1960, copy on LAC, RG 25, f. 9057-40, acquired under Access to Information.

10 Pullen, "What Price Canadian Sovereignty?," 68.

11 Leslie Wilson, "Canada Supplying Arctic: Big Gain for Sovereignty," *Financial Post*, September 27, 1958.

12 R.G. Robertson to Jules Leger, March 8, 1955; and M.H. Wershof to R.G. Robertson, March 3, 1955, f. 9057-40, pt. 5.

13 R.G. Robertson, draft letter, c. fall 1958, LAC, RG 25, f. 9057-40, pt. 5, acquired under ATIP.

14 "Arctic Sovereignty: Canada Ownership of Polar Islands Tacitly Recognized," *Montreal Star*, August 8, 1958.

15 Memorandum for file 500-370-40, "U.S. Request for Permission to Make Submarine Installations off Cape Dyer, Baffin Island in connection with the BMEWS Cable to Thule," July 29, 1958, LAC, RG 25, f. 9057-40, acquired under ATIP.

16 For a brief overview, see Morris Zaslow, *Northward Expansion of Canada, 1914-1967* (Toronto: McClelland & Stewart, 1988), 331-40.

17 Norman Robertson to External Affairs, Ottawa, August 1, 1958, and reply, August 8, 1958, LAC, RG 25, f. 9057-40, acquired under Access to Information.

18 Leeming, "HMCS *Labrador* and the Canadian Arctic," 306-7.

19 Maxwell Cohen, "Polar Ice and Arctic Sovereignty," *Saturday Night*, August 30, 1958, 12-13.

20 Diplomatic telegram Washington, D.C., to External Affairs, Ottawa, October 10, 1958, LAC, RG 25, f. 9057-40, pt. 7, acquired under Access to Information.

21 David L. Larson, "United States Interests in the Arctic Region," *Ocean Development and International Law* 20 (1989), 170, 177. Although the archival record containing diplomatic correspondence on these transits is largely exempted from public release, excerpts acquired through Access to Information suggest that there was a working agreement between Canada and the U.S. regarding submarine transits, with service-to-service notification procedures in place without prejudice to either country's legal claim. See, for example, E.B. Armstrong to Under-Secretary of State for External Affairs, July 18, 1962, LAC, RG 25, f. 9057-40.

22 Ivan L. Head, "Canadian Claims to Territorial Sovereignty in the Arctic Regions," *McGill Law Journal* 9 (1963), 200-26.

23 Margaret W. Morris, "Boundary Problems Relating to the Sovereignty of the Canadian Arctic," in *Canada's Changing North*, ed. William C. Wonders (Toronto: McClelland & Stewart, 1971), 311, 334.

24 These definitions are based upon Donald M. McRae, "Arctic Sovereignty: Loss by Dereliction?," *Northern Perspectives* [Canadian Arctic Resources Committee] 22/4 (1994-95); Evan Browne, "Canada and the seas: Sovereignty questions remain after century in the Arctic," *International Perspectives* (July/August 1980), 7-8; Morris, "Boundary Problems"; Pharand, "Arctic Waters and the Northwest Passage"; and the UN Convention on the Law of the Sea, available online at http://www.un.org/Depts/los/convention_agreements/convention_ov erview_convention.htm.

25 Browne, "Canada and the seas," 8; Pharand, *Canada's Arctic Waters in International Law*; Gordon W. Smith, "Sovereignty in the North: The

Canadian Aspect of an International Problem," in *The Arctic Frontier*, ed. MacDonald, 228.

26 Territorial Sea and Fishing Zones Act, 22, 1964-65 S.C. 153 (1964); Morris, "Boundary Problems," 322; Smith, "Sovereignty in the North," 236-37; and Elliot-Meisel, *Arctic Diplomacy*, 140.

27 Trevor Lloyd, "New Perspective on the North," *Foreign Affairs* 42/2 (1964), 293-308.

28 Christopher Kirkey, "The Arctic Waters Pollution Prevention Initiatives: Canada's Response to an American Challenge," *International Journal of Canadian Studies* 13 (Spring 1996), 41-42.

29 Maxwell Cohen, "The Arctic and the National Interest," *International Journal* 26/1 (1970-71), 72.

30 Thomas M. Tynan, "Canadian-American Relations in the Arctic: The Effect of Environmental Influences Upon Territorial Claims," *The Review of Politics* 41/3 (1979), 426-27.

31 Pullen, "What Price Canadian Sovereignty?," 71.

32 Trudeau quoted in Kirkey, "Arctic Waters Pollution Prevention Initiatives," 42.

33 Elliot-Meisel, *Arctic Diplomacy*, 141. On Humble's position, see Canadian Embassy in Washington, D.C., to External Affairs, June 3, 1969, Raymont Collection, Department of National Defence, Directorate of History and Heritage, f. 73/1223/987, box 52.

34 Quoted in Tynan, "Canadian-American Relations in the Arctic," 415-16.

35 Cohen, "Arctic and National Interest," 72. See also L.C. Green, "Canada and Arctic Sovereignty," *The Canadian Bar Review* 68/4 (1970), 740-75; *Globe & Mail*, March 12, 1970; and E.J. Dosman, "The Northern Sovereignty Crisis, 1968-70," in *The Arctic in Question*, ed. Dosman, 34-57.

36 See the chapters in *The Arctic in Question*, ed. Dosman. On the American response, see Theodore T. Eliot Jr., "Information Memorandum for Mr. Kissinger, the White House—Subject: Imminent Canadian Legislation on the Arctic," July 12, 1970, declassified and amended July 12, 2005, United States Department of State, Foreign Relations, 1969-1976, vol. E-1, Documents on Global Issues, 1969-1972, available online at http://www.state.gov/r/pa/ho/frus/nixon/e1/53180.htm.

37 House of Commons *Debates*, October 24, 1969, 39.

38 Trevor Lloyd's *Foreign Affairs* article, published in 1969/70, was tellingly entitled "Canada's Arctic in the Age of Ecology." See also P.W. Lackenbauer and Matthew Farish, "The Cold War on Canadian Soil: Militarizing a Northern Environment," *Environmental History* 12/3 (October 2007), 932-33.

39 D.M. McRae, "Arctic waters and Canadian sovereignty," *International Journal* 38/3 (1983), 478.

40 Larson, "United States Interests," 178. Pharand explains that even foreign warships still had the right to innocent passage through these "gateways" because they were territorial and not internal waters. Pharand, "Arctic Waters and the Northwest Passage," 11.

41 Trudeau, House of Commons, *Debates*, May 15, 1969, 8720.

42 Tynan, "Canadian-American Relations in the Arctic," 419.

43 Quoted in Evan Browne, "Sovereignty questions remain after century in the Arctic," *International Perspectives* (July/August 1980), 8.

44 See documents on LAC, RG 25, f. 27-10-2-2, pt. 1, acquired through Access to Information.

45 McRae, "Arctic Sovereignty: Loss by Dereliction?" available online at www.carc.org/pubs/v22no4/loss.htm.

46 Larson, "United States Interests," 179.

47 Milton Viorst, "Arctic waters must be free," *Toronto Star*, September 20, 1969, 16.

48 A good survey of bilateral discussions is found in Kirkey, "The Arctic Waters Pollution Prevention Initiatives."

49 Eliot Jr., "Information Memorandum for Mr. Kissinger."

50 Tynan, "Canadian-American Relations in the Arctic," 418-19.

51 William Morrison, "Eagle Over the Arctic: Americans in the Canadian North, 1867-1985," *Canadian Review of American Studies* (Spring 1987): 61-85.

52 "The 'compulsory jurisdiction' of the International Court of Justice is not truly compulsory," lawyer Stanimir Alexandrov explains. "The Court's jurisdiction is based on the consent of the parties. States have the option to accept or not to accept the Court's jurisdiction and can do so under terms and conditions they determine themselves. However, once a State has granted its consent, and when a dispute that falls within

the scope of that consent is submitted to the Court, the State must subject itself to the Court's jurisdiction." See "The Compulsory Jurisdiction of the International Court of Justice: How Compulsory Is It?," *Chinese Journal of International Law* 5/1 (2006), 15-28. In 1971, the Soviet Union passed similar protective legislation over the Northeast Passage, and two other Arctic states (Denmark and Norway) did not protest the AWPPA. Philip J. Briggs, "The *Polar Sea* Voyage and the Northwest Passage Dispute," *Armed Forces & Society* 16/3 (1990), 439.

53 Pharand, "Arctic Waters and the Northwest Passage," 11.

54 Don Munton and John Kirton, "The Manhattan Voyages and Their Aftermath," in *Politics of the Northwest Passage*, ed. Franklyn Griffiths (Toronto: University of Toronto Press, 1987). On this theme, see also Maxwell Cohen, "Arctic and the National Interest," 77.

55 K. Eyre, "Forty Years of Military Activity in the Canadian North," 296.

56 E.B. Wang, "Role of Canadian Armed Forces in Defending Sovereignty," April 30, 1969, LAC, RG 25, f. 27-10-2-2, pt. 1, acquired under Access to Information.

57 M. Shenstone, "Joint Intelligence Committee 1970-71 Work Programme: the Canadian Arctic," June 10, 1970, LAC, RG 25, f. 27-10-2-2, pt. 1, acquired under Access to Information.

58 Eyre, "Forty Years of Military Activity in the Canadian North," 297.

59 "A Draft Study of the Future International Scene," April 5, 1968, 4 & 8. Directorate of History and Heritage f. 112.11.003 (D3), box 3.

60 K. Eyre, "Custos Borealis: The Military in the Canadian North" (unpublished Ph.D. thesis, King's College, University of London, 1981), 273-75.

61 Interdepartmental Committee on the Law of the Sea, Meeting of the Working Group on the Enforcement of Fisheries Anti-Pollution and Territorial Seas Legislation, March 18, 1971, LAC, RG 25, f. 27-10-2-2, pt. 2, acquired under Access to Information.

62 Draft Memorandum to Cabinet, "Northern Development 1971-81," May 5, 1971, LAC, RG 25, f. 27-10-2-2, pt. 2, acquired under Access to Information. See also Department of Indian Affairs and Northern Development, *Canada's North, 1970-1980* (Ottawa: Queen's Printer, 1969).

63 Wain King, "New Look for Arctic Patrols: To See and Be Seen," *Ottawa Journal*, April 3, 1971.

64 Ron Purver, "The Arctic in Canadian Security Policy, 1945 to the Present," in *Canada's International Security Policy*, eds. D.B. DeWitt and D. Leyton-Brown (Scarborough: Prentice-Hall, 1995), 87-89; Eyre, "Forty Years of Military Activity in the Canadian North," 297.

65 Eyre, "Forty Years of Military Activity in the Canadian North," 297.

66 J.J. Greene, Minister of Energy, Mines and Resources, "National Resource Growth: By Plan or By Chance? Oil and Gas Pipeline Development," speech before the Vancouver Men's Canadian Club, February 12, 1971, reprinted in United States, Congressional Record 117 Part 32 (1971), and quoted in Christopher Kirkey, "Moving Alaskan Oil to Market: Canadian National Interests and the Trans-Alaskan Pipeline, 1968-1973," *American Review of Canadian Studies* 27/4 (1997), 495-522.

67 Kirkey, "Moving Alaskan Oil to Market."

CHAPTER 4

1 Frances Abele, "Canadian Contradictions: Forty Years of Northern Political Development," *Arctic* 41/4 (1987), 314-15. For background on northern development projects and environmental thinking, see David Ivor Williams, "Environmentalism, Development, and the Last Frontier: The Rise of Environmental Thought and the Canadian North, 1958-1974" (unpublished master's thesis, University of Alberta, 1995).

2 Thomas R. Berger, *Northern Frontier—Northern Homeland: The Report of the Mackenzie Valley Pipeline Inquiry*, vol. 1 (Ottawa: Minister of Supply and Services Canada, 1977), 1. See also CBC archives, "The Berger Pipeline Inquiry," http://archives.cbc.ca/IDD-1-73-295/politics_economy/pipeline/.

3 On bilateral relations in the early 1980s, see Robert Bothwell and J.L. Granatstein, *Pirouette: Pierre Trudeau and Foreign Policy* (Toronto: University of Toronto Press, 1990); Stephen Clarkson and Christina McCall, *Trudeau and Our Times*, vol. 2 (Toronto: McClelland & Stewart, 1994); and Mark MacGuigan, *An Inside Look at External Affairs during the Trudeau Years* (Calgary: University of Calgary Press, 2002).

4 D.M. McRae, "The Negotiation of Arctic 234," in *Politics of the Northwest Passage*, ed. Franklyn Griffiths (Kingston and Montreal: McGill-

Queen's University Press, 1987), 98-114; Larson, "United States Interests," 180; and Rob Huebert, "Canadian Arctic Security Issues: Transformation in the Post–Cold War Era," *International Journal* 54/2 (1999), 220.

5 Ironically, the *Northwind* had originally been selected to accompany the *Manhattan* in 1969 but had to withdraw due to machinery break-downs. Sixteen years later, machinery problems prevented it from carrying out the assigned task that precipitated the *Polar Sea* debate. Pullen, "What Price Canadian Sovereignty?," 71.

6 Pullen, "What Price Canadian Sovereignty?," 71.

7 Rob Huebert, "Steel, Ice and Decision-Making: The Voyage of the *Polar Sea* and Its Aftermath" (unpublished Ph.D. dissertation, Dalhousie University, 1994), 213-14, 217, 225; P.G. Kirkey, and Pharand, 39.

8 Huebert, "Steel, Ice and Decision-Making," 232, 243-67, 292. See also "The New Race for the North," *Maclean's*, August 19, 1985; Briggs, "*Polar Sea* Voyage and the Northwest Passage Dispute," 440-41.

9 George Lindsey, *Strategic Stability in the Arctic*, Adelphi Paper 241 (London: International Institute for Strategic Studies, 1989); Oran R. Young, "Arctic Shipping: An American Perspective," in *Politics of the Northwest Passage*, 119; and G. Leonard Johnson, David Bradley, and Robert S. Winokur, "United States Security Interests in the Arctic," in *United States Arctic Interests: The 1980s and 1990s*, eds. W.M. Westermeyer and K.M. Shusterich (New York: Springer-Verlag, 1984), 268-94. On American legal considerations, see William L. Schachte, "International Straits and Navigational Freedoms," *Ocean Development and International Law* 24 (1993), 179-95.

10 Rob Huebert questioned the assumption that there was a large "public outcry" based upon a Gallup poll conducted by the *Ottawa Citizen* in September 1885 in which only 54 percent of those polled were even aware of the voyage. "Steel, Ice and Decision-Making," 257-63.

11 Joe Clark, House of Commons *Debates*, September 10, 1985, 6463.

12 Fulton quoted in Elliot-Meisel, *Arctic Diplomacy*, 148.

13 The most comprehensive study of these initiatives is Rob Huebert, "Steel, Ice and Decision-Making."

14 Rothwell, "Canadian-U.S. Northwest Passage Dispute," 345; Pharand, "Arctic Waters and the Northwest Passage," 12. On limitations

to Canada's claim of internal waters based on historic title but the strength of its straight baseline claim, see Pharand's article.

15 Rob Huebert, "Polar Vision or Tunnel Vision: The making of Canadian Arctic waters policy," *Marine Policy* 19/4 (1995), 343-63; Pharand, "Arctic Waters and the Northwest Passage," 26.

16 Elliot-Meisel, *Arctic Diplomacy*, 152.

17 McRae, "Arctic Sovereignty."

18 Pullen, "What Price Canadian Sovereignty?," 71-72.

19 Huebert, "Polar vision or tunnel vision," 354. This article also describes earlier icebreaker proposals during the 1970s and 80s.

20 Paul George, "Arctic defence too hard to handle?" *Globe and Mail*, March 12, 1987, A7.

21 Briggs, "*Polar Sea* Voyage and the Northwest Passage Dispute," 447.

22 Eyre, "Forty Years of Military Activity in the Canadian North," 298.

23 House of Commons, *Debates*, March 13, 1985.

24 Huebert, "Polar vision or tunnel vision," 350-52; and Eyre, "Forty Years of Military Activity in the Canadian North," 299.

25 On negotiations and the Mulroney-Reagan relationship, see Christopher Kirkey, "Smoothing Troubled Waters: The 1988 Canada-United States Arctic Co-operation Agreement," *International Journal* 50 (1995), 408-16, 422-26.

26 Quoted in Larson, "United States Interests," 183.

27 Larson, "United States Interests," 183-84.

28 Rob Huebert, "A Northern Foreign Policy: The Politics of Ad Hocery," in *Diplomatic Departures: The Conservative Era in Canadian Foreign Policy, 1984-93*, eds. N. Michaud and K.R. Nossal (Vancouver: University of British Columbia Press, 2001), 84-112.

29 Eyre, "Forty Years of Military Activity in the Canadian North," 299.

30 Eliot Jr., "Information Memorandum for Mr. Kissinger."

31 J.T. Jockel, *Security to the North. Canada-U.S. Defence Relationships in the 1990s* (East Lansing: Michigan State University Press, 1991), 193.

32 Dan Hayward, "Gorbachev's Murmansk Initiative: New Prospects for Arms Control in the Arctic?," *Northern Perspectives* 16/4 (1988).

33 Memorandum, "DND Paper on 'Canadian Defence Policy in the 1970's'," Legal Division, External Affairs, August 5, 1970, LAC, RG 25, f. 27-10-2-2, pt. 1, acquired under Access to Information.

34 Elliot-Meisel, "Still Unresolved," 407.

35 Pullen, "What Price Canadian Sovereignty?," 66.

36 Kirkey, "The Arctic Waters Pollution Prevention Initiatives," 56.

37 Briggs, "*Polar Sea* Voyage and the Northwest Passage Dispute," 449.

38 On the Goose Bay low-level flying controversy, see Peter Armitage and John C. Kennedy, "Redbaiting and Racism on Our Frontier: Military Expansion in Labrador and Quebec," *Canadian Review of Sociology and Anthropology* 26 (1989): 798-817; and P. Whitney Lackenbauer, *Battle Grounds: The Canadian Military and Aboriginal Lands* (Vancouver: University of British Columbia Press, 2007), 221-27.

39 Georges Erasmus, "Militarization of the North: Cultural Survival Threatened," *Information North* (Fall 1986): 1; Mary Simon, "Security, Peace and the Native Peoples of the Arctic," in *The Arctic: Choices for Peace and Security*, ed. Thomas R. Berger (West Vancouver: Gordon Soules, 1989), 36, 67.

40 Mary Simon, 1988, 265.

41 Frances Abele and Thierry Rodon, "Inuit Diplomacy in the Global Era: The Strengths of Multilateral Internationalism," *Canadian Foreign Policy* 13/3 (2007), 55-57. The Inuit Circumpolar Conference (ICC) emerged in 1977 under the leadership of Eben Hopson, an Alaskan Inuit. It developed an international organization, as well as four national organizations (Greenland, Alaska, Canada, and Russia). Originally, the Inuit from the Soviet Union, like the Sami in Scandinavia, were excluded because of the Cold War; in the early meetings, the conference organizers kept an empty chair on display, symbolizing the absence of Soviet representatives. Buoyed by changes occurring in the Soviet Union under Gorbachev, ICC President Aqqaluk Lynge successfully lobbied Soviet authorities in 1985 to include Russian Inuit in the ICC. Other organizations such as the Arctic Athabaskan Council, Gwich'in Council International, Aleut International Association, and the Russian Association of the Indigenous Peoples of the North called for international attention to their struggles.

42 Rob Huebert, "Canadian Arctic Security Issues: Transformation in the Post–Cold War Era," *International Journal* (Spring 1999), 207.

43 "Ailing Arctic Ocean focus of Inuit talks," *Globe and Mail*, July 20, 1992.

44 Rob Huebert, "New Directions in Circumpolar Cooperation: Canada, the Arctic Environmental Protection Strategy, and the Arctic Council,"

Canadian Foreign Policy 5/2 (1998), 37-58; Huebert, "The Arctic Council and Northern Aboriginal Peoples," in *Issues in the North*, vol.3, eds. Jill Oakes and Rick Riewe (Edmonton: Canadian Circumpolar Institute, 1998), 144; and Mark Nuttal, *Protecting the Arctic: Indigenous Peoples and Cultural Survival* (Amsterdam: Harwood, 1998), 40.

45 "Canada to join eight-nation Arctic protection body," *Globe and Mail*, June 10, 1991.

46 Huebert, "Canadian Arctic Security Issues," 224, and Donat Pharand, "The Case for an Arctic Region Council and a Treaty Proposal," *Revue générale de droit* 23 (1992), 163-95. Maxwell Cohen, for example, proposed in 1970 that Canada should promote an "Arctic basin treaty" to develop policies on maritime- and environmental-protection issues. Cohen, "The Arctic and the National Interest," 79-81. Donat Pharand and a working group of the Canadian Institute for International Affairs revived his idea in 1988. See Donald R. Rothwell, *The Polar Regions and the Development of International Law* (Cambridge: Cambridge University Press, 1996), 242.

47 "Making the Arctic a Zone of Civility," *Toronto Star*, January 20, 1992.

48 Lackenbauer and Cooper, "The Achilles Heel of Canadian Good International Citizenship"; Marshall Beier, *International Relations in Uncommon Places: Indigeneity, Cosmology, and the Limits of International Theory* (New York: Palgrave Macmillan, 2005); and Franke Wilmer, *The Indigenous Voice in World Politics Since Time Immemorial* (London: Sage, 1993).

49 "Let's invite Yeltsin to join our club," *Toronto Star*, November 6, 1991.

50 "Rallying around the North Pole," *Globe and Mail*, November 13, 1992.

51 "New Arctic Council to police environment," *Globe and Mail*, March 22, 1996.

52 Huebert, "Canadian Arctic Security Issues," 210, 223; Gary N. Wilson, "Inuit Diplomacy in the Circumpolar North," *Canadian Foreign Policy* 13/3 (2007), 70. The council adopted the indigenous organizations' commitment to consensus decision-making for its formal deliberations. In addition, the Arctic Council included official observers from major Arctic organizations, including the Northern Forum, the University of the Arctic, IASSA and IASC. The council oversees such working groups as the Arctic Monitoring and Assessment Program (AMAP), Protection of the Arctic Marine Environment (PAME), Con-

vention of Arctic Flora and Fauna (CAFF), and Emergency Prevention, Preparedness and Response (EPPR). The Sustainable Development Working Group (SDWG) emerged later with responsibility for addressing the human dimensions of Arctic policy and research. The list of Arctic observers includes representatives from the Arctic circumpolar route, the Association of World Reindeer Herders, the Circumpolar Conservation Union, the International Union for Circumpolar Health, the World Conservation Union (IUCN), the International Work Group for Indigenous Affairs, the North Atlantic Marine Mammal Commission, the Nordic Council of Ministers, the Nordic Environmental Finance Corporation, the Northern Forum, the Standing Committee of Parliamentarians of the Arctic Region, the United Nations Development Programme and the United Nations Environmental Program (Ardenal).

53 "Canada to steer new body on protecting the Arctic," *Toronto Star*, January 20, 1996. A parallel organization, the Conference of Parliamentarians of the Arctic Region, provided a forum for elected officials to meet biannually, with indigenous representatives participating in deliberations. Conference of the Parliamentarians of the Arctic Region, http://www.Arcticparl.org/.

54 Report of the House of Commons Standing Committee on Foreign Affairs and International Trade, *Canada and the Circumpolar World: Meeting the Challenges of Cooperation into the Twenty-First Century* (April 1997), ix, 100.

55 Huebert, "Security and the Environment in the Post–Cold War Arctic," *Environment & Security* 4 (2000), 107; Arctic Monitoring and Assessment Programme (AMAP), *Arctic Pollution Issues: A State of the Arctic Environment Report* (Oslo: AMAP, 1997), 113, 117-18, available online at http://www.amap.no/documents/index.cfm?dirsub=/Arctic%20Pollution%20Issues%20%20A%20State%20of%20the%20Arctic%20Environment%20Report.

56 *Government Response to Standing Committee on Foreign Affairs and International Trade Report "Canada and the Circumpolar World: Meeting the Challenges of Cooperation Into the Twenty-First Century"* (1998), available online at http://www.dfait-maeci.gc.ca/circumpolar/response-en.asp.

57 Department of Foreign Affairs and International Trade (DFAIT), *The Northern Dimension of Canada's Foreign Policy* (1998), available online at http://www.international.gc.ca/circumpolar/pdf/ndcfp-en.pdf.

58 DFAIT, *Northern Dimension of Canada's Foreign Policy*. The Canadian government defined "human security" as "freedom from pervasive threats to people's rights, safety and lives." For an overview, see Walter Dorn, "Human Security: An Overview" (Pearson Peacekeeping Centre, 2001), http://www.rmc.ca/academic/gradrech/dorn24_e.html#e2. On facets of "sustainable development" in the North, see DFAIT, *Toward a Northern Foreign Policy for Canada: A Consultation Paper* (September 1998), http://www.dfait-maeci.gc.ca/circumpolar/final4-en.asp.

59 *Arctic Capabilities Study*, June 2000, 9-10, DND f. 1948-3-CC4C (DGSP). Acquired through Access to Information. On the Rangers, see Lackenbauer, "The Canadian Rangers: A Postmodern Militia That Works," *Canadian Military Journal* 6/4 (Winter 2005-6), 49-60.

60 *Arctic Capabilities Study*, 2, 9-11.

61 Huebert, "Climate Change and Canadian Sovereignty in the Northwest Passage," *Isuma* 2/4 (2001), 92.

62 Lloyd Axworthy's address to the inaugural meeting of the Arctic Council, Iqaluit, September 17, 1998. (http://w01.international.gc.ca/minpub/PublicationContentOnly.asp?publication_id=375749&Language=E&MODE=CONTENTONLY&Local=False).

63 McRae, "Arctic Sovereignty."

CHAPTER 5

1 "Navigable Arctic passage draws claims on seabed," *Washington Times*, September 4, 2007.

2 "Anxiously watching a different world," *The Economist*, May 26, 2007.

3 "Heat's on in the Arctic," *Toronto Sun*, March 10, 2007.

4 "Fight for the Top of the World," *Time*, October 1, 2007.

5 http://www.ndp.ca/page/5646.

6 Although the United States refuses to sign the UNCLOS, it accepts the application of Canada's strict pollution controls consistent with article 234. See U.S. "Limits in the Seas" No. 192 (1991). As mentioned earlier, the U.S., Canada, and Russia were the three states that reached a negotiated solution that led to article 234.

7 "Northern Exposure," *South China Morning Post*, August 23, 2007.

8 "Arctic Opportunities," *Lloyd's List*, February 10, 2006.

9 "Navigable Arctic passage draws claims on seabed," *Washington Times*, September 4, 2007.

10 "Canada Warns US OFF Claims to Arctic," *Irish Times*, January 28, 2006.

11 "Ex-US Envoy backs Canada's Arctic claim," *Toronto Star*, August 20, 2007.

12 "Arctic defence," *Toronto Star*, August 19, 2006.

13 "Breaking fresh ground in New Arctic Ocean," *Lloyd's List*, May 24, 2007.

14 "Arctic Riches Coming Out of the Cold," *New York Times*, October 10, 2005.

15 "Melting ice starts rush for Arctic resources," *The Times* (London), January 28, 2006.

16 "Treading on thin ice," *Globe and Mail*, October 20, 2007.

17 "Battle for final frontier," *The Times* (London), July 6, 2007.

18 "Danes flag up claim to the rock of gold," *Birmingham Post*, March 27, 2007.

19 "Northern Exposure," *Natural Gas Week*, May 1, 2006.

20 "Fire and Ice," *Financial Times* (London), August 23, 2006.

21 "Russia leads race for North Pole oil," *The Observer* (London), July 29, 2007.

22 "Anxiously watching a different world," *The Economist*, May 26, 2007.

23 "Scramble for the Arctic," *Financial Times*, August 20, 2007.

24 "Taming the unfrozen North," *Toronto Star*, August 31, 2006.

25 Donald R. Rothwell, *The Polar Regions and the Development of International Law* (Cambridge: Cambridge University Press, 1996), 182. Kenn Harper explains that: "Both parties agreed to stop the median line referred to in that agreement at the low-water mark on the south coast of the island and start it again at the low-water mark on the north shore. Because these lines reach the island, the agreement noted that 'the island has no territorial sea.'" *Canadian Geographic* website, "Hans' history," http://www.canadiangeographic.ca/hansIsland/background.asp.

26 "Danes flag up claim to the rock of gold," *Birmingham Post*, March 27, 2007.

27 "Northern Exposure," *Natural Gas Week*, May 1, 2006.

28 "Gas and Glory Fuel Race for Pole," *Moscow Times*, July 27, 2007.

29 "Russia to make claim in fight for Arctic," *National Post*, June 29, 2007.

30 "Gas and Glory Fuel Race for Pole," *Moscow Times*, July 27, 2007.

31 "Russia stakes its North Pole claim," *The Times* (London), July 28, 2007.

32 "The North Pole, A New Imperial Battleground," *The Independent* (London), July 31, 2007.

33 "Drawing lines in melting ice," *The Economist*, August 18, 2007.

34 "Canada's Arctic Race with Russia," *Globe and Mail*, July 29, 2007.

35 "Russian mini-subs lay claim to North Pole," *Globe and Mail*, August 2, 2007.

36 "A Russian or Canadian flag shouldn't matter," *Globe and Mail*, August 2, 2007.

37 "Mineral war begins after Russia plants flag 2 miles under pole," *The Times* (London), August 3, 2007.

38 "Ottawa assails Moscow's Arctic ambitions," *Globe and Mail*, August 3, 2007.

39 "US rises to Kremlin bait," *Daily Telegraph*, August 4, 2007.

40 Hans Corell, "Arctic Meltdown?," *Globe and Mail*, April 28, 2008.

41 "An Ice-Cold War," *New York Times*, August 8, 2007.

42 *National Post*, February 13, 2008.

43 "Treading on thin ice," *Globe and Mail*, October 20, 2007.

44 UNCLOS articles 76 and 77.

45 "Cold war brewing under the icy Arctic," *New Zealand Herald*, July 31, 2007.

46 "Russia's Seabed Flag Heralds Ocean Carve-Up," Chinadaily.com.cn, August 16, 2007. Those who have carefully followed the process will point out that the last final and binding deadline for many parties was 2004, and this was extended to 2009!

47 Borgerson, "Arctic Meltdown."

48 Corell, "Arctic Meltdown?"

49 "Treading on thin ice," *Globe and Mail*, October 20, 2007.

50 "The North Pole a New Imperial Battleground," July 31, 2007.

51 "This claim is our claim," *Toronto Sun*, February 24, 2007.

52 "Heat's on in Arctic," *Toronto Sun*, March 10, 2007.

53 "Harper's Arctic Stand Makes for Grand Politics," *Toronto Star*, January 28, 2006.

54 "Tiff Over Northwest Passage Heats Up As Ice Melts," *USA Today*, April 4, 2006.

55 "Arctic defence," *Toronto Star*, August 19, 2006.

56 "Arctic solution already in place," *Toronto Star*, February 8, 2006.

57 "Arctic defence," *Toronto Star*, August 19, 2006.

58 "North is our land," *Toronto Sun*, February 24, 2007.

59 Bob Weber, "Budget's icebreaker welcomed," CNews, February 27, 2008, http://cnews.canoe.ca/CNEWS/Canada/2008/02/27/4880696-cp.html.

60 "Assert Arctic rights," *Toronto Sun*, January 6, 2007.

61 "Our true north strong and free," *Toronto Sun*, February 23, 2007.

62 "Tighten northern grip," *Toronto Sun*, February 23, 2007.

63 "Our true north strong and free," *Toronto Sun*, February 23, 2007.

64 "$3B for Arctic Ships," *National Post*, July 10, 2007.

65 "Harper's prudent Arctic spending," *Toronto Star*, July 10, 2007.

66 "Stand up for the North," *Toronto Sun*, August 20, 2007.

67 "The true north may be strong, but the plan to protect it is feeble," *Globe and Mail*, July 17, 2007.

68 "Inuit: The Bedrock of Arctic sovereignty," *Globe and Mail*, July 26, 2007.

69 "Layton joins Arctic fray," *Toronto Sun*, August 30, 2007.

70 "The Russians are coming," *Globe and Mail*, July 30, 2007.

71 "Arctic Sprawl," *National Post*, August 8, 2007.

72 "Exerting 'hard power' in the Arctic," *National Post*, August 9, 2007.

73 "PM on northern sovereignty mission," *Toronto Star*, August 8, 2007.

74 "PM expands northern presence," *National Post*, August 11, 2007.

75 "Two new sites back claim Arctic is ours," *Winnipeg Free Press*, August 11, 2007.

76 The text of the throne speech from October 16, 2007, can be found at http://www.sft-ddt.gc.ca/eng/media.asp?id=1364.

77 "Passage's thaw a recipe for chilly foreign relations," *Globe and Mail*, July 10, 2007.

78 "Arctic issues make for good politics," *Toronto Star*, July 10, 2007.

79 "Ice May Thwart Mission to Claims Arctic Territory," *National Post*, August 9, 2007.

80 "Base the debate over the North on fact, not politics, scientists say," *Globe and Mail*, August 23, 2007.

81 "A simple act, but complex questions," *Toronto Star*, August 12, 2007.

82 "Russia's Arctic claims need to be backed by military power," BBC Worldwide Monitoring, August 12, 2007.

83 "Battle for North Pole Oil," *Sunday Express*, August 19, 2007.

84 "Worried about Putin," *International Herald Tribune*, August 21, 2007.

85 "There is no new chill in the Arctic," *Financial Times* (London), August 21, 2007.

86 "Relations thaw after flag 'stunt,'" *Toronto Star*, September 26, 2007.

87 "Fight for the Top of the World," *Time*, October 1, 2007.

88 "Arctic military bases signal new Cold War," *The Times* (London), August 11, 2007.

89 "Canada flexes its muscles in scramble for the Arctic," *The Guardian* (London), July 11, 2007.

90 "Arctic sprawl," *National Post*, August 8, 2007.

91 Katherine O'Neill, "Arctic ice shelf now split in three, mission finds," *Globe and Mail*, April 14, 2008.

CONCLUSION

1 Franklyn Griffiths, "The Shipping News: Canada's Arctic Sovereignty Not on Thinning Ice," *International Journal* 52/2 (Spring 2003), 257-82.

2 Major Paul Dittman, "In Defence of Defence: Canadian Arctic Sovereignty and Security" (Master of Defence Studies research project, Canadian Forces College, 2008), 100. Major Dittman has given his permission to quote from this work.